Administration

ADMINISTRATION

Vernon Dennis

The Law Society

The forms reproduced on pp. 46–8, 64, 65, 68, 69, 76–8, 83, 84, 86 and 87 are Crown copyright material and are reproduced here with the permission of the Controller of Her Majesty's Stationery Office

ISBN–13: 978–1–85328–878–4

Published in 2010 by the Law Society
113 Chancery Lane, London WC2A 1PL

Typeset by Columns Design Ltd, Reading, Berks
Printed by Hobbs the Printers Ltd, Totton, Hants

FSC
Mixed Sources
Product group from well-managed forests and other controlled sources
Cert no. SA-COC-001530
www.fsc.org
© 1996 Forest Stewardship Council

The paper used for the text pages of this book is FSC certified. FSC (the Forest Stewardship Council) is an international network to promote responsible management of the world's forests.

Contents

About the author   viii

Preface   ix

Acknowledgements   xi

Table of cases   xii

Table of statutes   xvii

Table of statutory instruments   xxii

Table of European legislation   xxvi

List of abbreviations   xxvii

1 An introduction to administration   1

    1.1   Corporate insolvency and the use of administration   1

    1.2   What is administration?   5

    1.3   When is administration available?   7

    1.4   Why use administration?   12

2 Who may initiate the administration process and why?   25

    2.1   Company and/or its directors   25

    2.2   Qualifying floating charge holder   34

    2.3   A creditor   39

    2.4   An insolvency office holder   40

    2.5   Magistrates' court/Financial Services Authority   40

3 Commencement of administration process   41

    3.1   Court appointment   41

    3.2   Out-of-court appointment by holder of floating charge   56

    3.3   Out-of-court appointment by company/directors   73

4   The effect of administration   **93**

4.1   Introduction of a statutory moratorium   93
4.2   The effect of administration upon any winding-up petition   94
4.3   The effect of administration on receivers/secured creditors   95
4.4   Moratorium on insolvency proceedings   97
4.5   Moratorium on other legal processes   98
4.6   Court's permission to take legal proceedings   100
4.7   Powers of directors   103
4.8   Interim moratorium   104

5   The administration process   **106**

5.1   Initial steps following appointment   106
5.2   Statement of company's affairs   108
5.3   Administrator's proposals   110
5.4   Meeting to consider the administrator's proposals   113
5.5   Business and result of creditors' meeting   114
5.6   Revision of administrator's proposals, further meetings
       and creditors' committee   117
5.7   Progress report   118

6   The role, functions and powers of an administrator   **120**

6.1   The role of the administrator   120
6.2   Administrator's power to deal with charged property   124
6.3   Administrator's power to deal with property subject to a
       hire purchase agreement   125
6.4   Protection for secured or preferential creditors   126
6.5   Challenge to administrator's conduct of the company   126
6.6   Administrator's liability for contracts   129
6.7   Administrator's liability for expenses incurred
       post-administration   130

7   Ending administration   **132**

7.1   Automatic end of administration   133
7.2   Extension by creditors' consent   134
7.3   Extension by court order   135
7.4   Determination of administration on application to court
       by an administrator   135
7.5   Termination of administration where objective achieved   137

7.6	Court ending administration on application of creditor	138
7.7	Cessation of appointment on public interest winding-up petition	139
7.8	Moving from administration to creditors' voluntary liquidation	139
7.9	Moving from administration to dissolution	141
7.10	Resignation of an administrator	143
7.11	Replacement of an administrator	144
7.12	The effect of vacation of office	145
7.13	Administrator's remuneration	146
8	**The future for administration**	**148**
8.1	Infinity and beyond	148
8.2	It's rescue Jim ... but not as we know it	149
8.3	How do you solve a problem like ... administration?	153
8.4	Foreign affairs	157
8.5	The need for certainty	158
8.6	Back to the future	159
Table: Comparative analysis of corporate insolvency procedures		**163**
Appendix 1	**The use of receivership vs. administration**	**165**
Appendix 2	**The procedure for appointment of an administrator**	**169**
Appendix 3	**The administration process and procedure post-appointment**	**172**
Appendix 4	**The effect of administration and distribution to creditors**	**176**
Glossary		**179**
Index		183

About the author

Vernon S. Dennis is a Partner and Head of the Corporate Recovery and Reconstruction Group at Howard Kennedy Solicitors.

Vernon's career in insolvency began in the early 1990s. Since that time he has acted for insolvency practitioners, creditors and debtors on a wide range of corporate recovery, reconstruction and rescue issues.

He is a member of R3, the Association of Business Recovery Professionals and the Turnaround Management Association. He lectures regularly in the UK and abroad on a wide variety of topics including issues arising from corporate rescue and reconstruction on a domestic and cross-border level, mirroring the developments of his own practice.

His first work was as co-author of *The New Law of Insolvency* (Law Society, February 2003). He has since authored two editions of *Insolvency Law Handbook* (Law Society, 2005 and 2007). This book is the first of three planned works on specific insolvency processes; others on liquidation and bankruptcy will follow shortly.

Preface

This book has been written against the backdrop of the 'credit crunch' and the consequent global recession, a recession from which the UK is only slowly emerging. Following corporate insolvency law reforms introduced in the Enterprise Act 2002, from 15 September 2003 administration became the principal method of corporate rescue in the UK. As a result, the administration process has, therefore, been at the forefront of a rapidly developing area of law and practice during turbulent economic times. A book written during such a time, when the process is undergoing testing in extreme and unusual situations may, therefore, lack long-term perspective and an ability to assess empirically the 'success or failure' of the reformed process. However, it is hoped that this is made up for by an ability to refer to the practical problems and considerations that are rapidly driving forward current practice.

It is also interesting to note that some commentators fear that the marked increase in use of administration to date is but a tip of the iceberg and that the use of the process will escalate still further post-recession, when confidence (and credit) begins to return to the economy and greater numbers of companies can be restructured and rescued. As a result it could be some time before the dust settles and we are able to assess how administration practice and procedure has fared.

In the meantime, however, one undoubted development has been the use of the administration process as a means of business rescue, but the failure in all but a small percentage of cases for companies to be 'saved'. This crucial distinction between business and company rescue has huge consequences for the owners of businesses, directors, employees and creditors and leads some to believe that administration is not fulfilling its primary purpose. However, it is the use of one particular practice, namely the pre-pack administration, that has come to dominate much of the continuing debate on the efficiency and fairness of the current insolvency regime. Whether regulation of the regime will come from case law, regulatory or statutory reform is something considered in the final chapter of the book; however, the emergence of administration as a means of business, as opposed to company rescue, and why the practice of pre-pack administration has grown in use are themes consistently returned to throughout this book.

While intended to highlight the issues at the forefront of the current debate on the use (and alleged abuse) of administration and illustrate why practice seems to have departed from at very least 'the spirit' of the Enterprise Act reforms, this book is primarily intended to be a practical guide to those professionals who are likely to advise companies, directors, creditors, customers and suppliers to businesses who may be initiating and/or considering the initiation of an administration process.

In **Chapters 1** and **2** the situations of when administration may be encountered and the fundamental characteristics and purpose of administration are examined. In **Chapter 3** the reader is guided on how to commence the process and in **Chapters 4** to **6** the process and procedure of administration post-appointment are examined together with the powers, duties and obligations of the administrator. In **Chapter 7** analysis as to how the administration process may end is provided before the final chapter in this guide concludes with an analysis of the strengths and weaknesses of the current regime as well as outlining possible reforms.

Flowcharts, guides to procedures and summaries of the law and/or of certain processes encountered during administration are drawn together in the **Appendices**. This section is intended to provide 'at a glance' advice.

The book is written with the law as applicable as at January 2010. A problem facing authors of legal publications is the constant march of change. In this book, reference is made to changes proposed by the Insolvency (Amendment) Rules 2010 (SI 2010/686), which came into effect on 6 April 2010. While I have hopefully anticipated and made reference to the most significant changes brought about by these amending rules, one issue that I cannot deal with is the future use of prescribed forms as set out in the Insolvency Rules. The policy of the Insolvency Service is to move away from the prescription of forms in the Insolvency Rules and instead specify the information which must be provided. This move will be welcomed as it will allow the use of precedents that contain the same information as the forms but also allow for bespoke additions. At present, however, there is a state of flux, with no new forms being prescribed in the amending rules but no timetable for the replacement or phasing out of the forms. As a result, when a prescribed form is discussed the reader may need to refer to **www.insolvency.gov.uk/forms/englandwalesforms.htm**, **www. companieshouse.gov.uk/forms/insolvencyForms.shtml** or a commercial provider of legal forms.

Vernon S. Dennis
April 2010
Partner, Howard Kennedy Solicitors
Email: v.dennis@howardkennedy.com

Acknowledgements

I would like to thank my colleague Terry Ashby for her invaluable assistance in drawing together my notes, jotting and diagrams. I would express my huge appreciation to my wife Sarah-Jane and children Tom and Emma for their patience and understanding when I have been distracted by the demands of writing about administration law and practice. I am acutely conscious that during the course of 2009 free time has been at a premium, due not least to the understandable demands of my professional practice during a recession. My ability to use much of that precious free time to write this book would not have been possible without S.-J.'s love and support and it is to her that I dedicate this book.

Table of cases

A Straume (UK) Ltd *v.* Bradlor Developments Ltd [2000] BCC 333, ChD . . 100
AA Mutual International Insurance Co Ltd, *Re* [2004] EWHC 2430
    (Ch); [2005] 2 BCLC 8, ChD 8, 9, 42
Ah Toy, *Re* (1986) 4 ACLC 480 6
Air Ecosse Ltd *v.* Civil Aviation Authority 1987 SC 285; (1987) 3 BCC
    492 100
Airbase (UK) Ltd, Re; *sub nom.* Airbase Services International Ltd, *Re*
    [2008] BCC 213 . . . . 122, 182
Aldersley Battery Chairs Ltd, *Re* (Case No.9003/2008) unreported,
    14 January 2008 23
ARV Aviation Ltd, *Re* (1988) 4 BCC 708, ChD 125
Atlantic Computer Systems plc, *Re* [1992] Ch 505; [1992] 2 WLR 367;
    [1990] BCC 859, CA 13, 20, 21, 101, 126, 130, 131
Ballast plc (In Administration), *Re* [2004] EWHC 2356 (Ch); [2005]
    1 WLR 1928; [2005] BCC 96. . . . . 136, 141, 142
BCPMS (Europe) Ltd *v.* GMAC Commercial Finance plc [2006] EWHC
    3744 (Ch); [2006] All ER 285 59
Bibby Trade Finance Ltd *v.* McKay [2006] EWHC 2836 (Ch); [2006]
    All ER (D) 266 19
Biosource Technologies Inc *v.* Axis Genetics plc [2000] 1 BCLC 286, ChD . 100
Blights Builders Ltd, *Re* [2006] EWHC 3549 (Ch); [2007] 3 All ER 776;
    [2007] BCC 712 . . . . 45, 75
BRAC Rent-a-Car International Inc, *Re* [2003] EWHC 128 (Ch); [2003]
    1 WLR 1421; [2003] BCC 248. 8
Bristol Airport plc *v.* Powdrill [1990] Ch 744, CA 96
British American Racing (Holdings) Ltd, *Re* [2004] EWHC 2947 (Ch);
    [2005] BCC 110 . . . . 40, 44, 138
Brownbridge Plastics Ltd, Re, unreported, Birmingham District Registry 7
Brumark Investments Ltd; *sub nom.* Agnew *v.* IRC [2001] UKPC 28;
    [2001] 2 AC 710; [2001] 2 BCLC 188 57
Business Properties Ltd, *Re* (1988) 4 BCC 684, ChD 42
Byblos Bank SAL *v.* Al-Khudhairy [1987] BCLC 232, CA 42

Cabletel Installations Ltd, *Re* [2005] BPIR 28, ChD. 146, 147

Cabvision Ltd *v.* Feetum [2005] EWCA Civ 1601; [2006] Ch 585; [2006]
BPIR 379 171

Centre Reinsurance International Co *v.* Freakley [2005] EWCA Civ 115;
[2006] 1 WLR 2863 . . . . 19, 129

Charalambous *v.* B & C Associates [2009] EWHC 2601 (Ch) 7, 37

Charnley Davies Ltd, *Re* (No.2) [1990] BCC 605, ChD. 127

Chelmsford City Football Club (1980) Ltd, *Re* [1991] BCC 133, ChD 44

Chesterton International Group plc *v.* Deka Immobilien Inv GmbH [2005]
EWHC 656 (Ch); [2005] BPIR 1103 74

Ci4net.com Inc, *Re* [2005] BCC 277. 55

Clarence Café Ltd *v.* Comchester Properties Ltd [1999] L & TR 303, ChD . . . 96

Clydesdale Financial Services *v.* Smailes [2009] EWHC 1745 (Ch) 17, 53

Collins & Aikman Europe SA, *Re* [2006] EWHC 1343 (Ch); [2006]
BCC 861 123

Colt Telecom Group plc, *Re* (No.2) [2002] EWHC 2815 (Ch); [2003]
BPIR 324 . . . . 9, 40, 42, 43, 45, 71

Company, *Re* a (No.001992 of 1988) [1989] BCLC 9 100

Condon, Re, *ex p.* James (1873–74) LR 9 Ch App 609. 6

Consumer and Industrial Press Ltd, *Re* (No.2) (1988) 4 BCC 72, ChD 125

Corbett *v.* Nysir UK Ltd [2008] EWHC 2670 (Ch). 40

Cosslett (Contractors) Ltd, *Re* [1998] Ch 495, CA 13

Cosslett (Contractors) Ltd, *Re* [2004] EWHC 658 (Ch) 94

Courts plc, *Re* [2008] BCC 917. 182

Croftbell Ltd, *Re* [1990] BCLC 844, ChD. 58

Crompton's Leisure Machines Ltd, *Re* [2006] EWHC 3583 (Ch). 122

Cuckmere Brick Co *v.* Mutual Finance [1971] 2 All ER 633, CA. 36

David Meek Plant Ltd, *Re* [1993] BCC 175, ChD 98

Designer Room Ltd, *Re* [2004] EWHC 720 (Ch); [2005] 1 WLR 1581. 122

Dianoor Jewels Ltd, *Re* [2001] 1 BCLC 450, ChD. 42

Divine Solutions (UK) Ltd, *Re* [2003] EWHC 1931 (Ch); [2004]
BCC 325 100

DKLL Solicitors *v.* Revenue and Customs Commissioners [2007]
EWHC 2067 (Ch); [2007] BCC 908 . . . . 42, 43, 53, 94, 115, 136

Doltable Ltd *v.* Lexi Holdings plc [2005] EWHC 1804 (Ch); [2006]
1 BCLC 384 . . . . 42, 56, 138

Donaldson *v.* O'Sullivan [2008] EWHC 387 (Ch); [2009] BCC 99 144

Downsview Nominees Ltd *v.* First City Corp [1993] AC 295, PC 36

Duomatic Ltd, *Re* [1969] 2 Ch 365, ChD 26, 73

Equity Nominees Ltd, *Re* [2000] BCC 84, ChD 144

E-Squared Ltd, *Re* [2006] EWHC 532 (Ch); [2006] 1 WLR 3414; [2006]
BCC 379. 141

Euro Commercial Leasing Ltd *v.* Cartwright & Lewis [1995] BCC 830;
[1995] 2 BCLC 618, ChD. 13, 96

Exeter City Council v. Bairstow; *sub nom. Re* Trident Fashions Ltd [2007]
    EWHC 400 (Ch); [2007] 4 All ER 437; [2007] BCC 236 . . . 20, 21, 37, 130
Fliptex Ltd v. Hogg [2004] EWHC 1280 (Ch); [2004] BCC 870 59
GHE Realisations Ltd, *Re* [2005] EWHC 2400 (Ch); [2006] 1 WLR 287;
    [2006] BCC 139 . . . . 123, 133, 136, 140, 142
Goldacre (Office) Ltd v. Nortel Networks UK Ltd (In Administration)
    [2009] EWHC 3389 (Ch) 21, 131
Gomba Holdings (UK) Ltd v. Homan [1986] 1 WLR 1301, ChD. 36
G-Tech Construction Ltd, *Re* [2007] BPIR 1275, ChD. 51, 134
Harris Simons Construction Ltd, *Re* [1989] 1 WLR 368; (1989) 5 BCC 11,
    ChD. 42
Horsham Properties Group Ltd v. Clark [2008] EWHC 2327 (Ch). 35
Innovate Logistics Ltd (In Administration) v. Sunberry Properties [2008]
    EWCA Civ 1321; [2009] BCC 164 . . . . 17, 21, 99, 131
Intercontinental Properties Pty Ltd, *Re* (1977) 2 ACLC 488. 6
International Sections Ltd, *Re* [2009] BCC 574 182
J Smiths Haulage Ltd, *Re* [2007] BCC 135, ChD 136
Kaupthing Singer & Friedlander Ltd (In Administration), *Re* [2009] EWHC
    2308 (Ch) 123
Kayley Vending Ltd, *Re* [2009] EWHC 904 (Ch). 16, 23, 43
Land and Property Trust Co plc, *Re* (No.2) [1991] BCLC 849. 43
Lathia v. Dronsfield Bros [1987] BCLC 321, QBD. 37
Lehman Brothers International (Europe) Ltd, Re; *sub nom.* Four Private
    Investment Funds v. Lomas [2009] BCC 632; [2009] 1 BCLC 161. . . 6, 127
Lomax Leisure Ltd, *Re* [2000] Ch 502; [2000] BCC 352, ChD 9
London Flight Centre (Stansted) Ltd v. Osprey Aviation Ltd [2002] BPIR
    1115, ChD. 96
Lune Metal Products Ltd, *Re* [2006] EWCA Civ 1720; [2007] BCC 217 . . . 122
March Estates plc v. Gunmark Ltd [1996] 2 BCLC 1, ChD 96
Meadrealm Ltd v. Transcontinental Golf Construction, unreported,
    29 November 1991, ChD 58
Medforth v. Blake [2000] Ch 86; [1999] 3 All ER 97, CA 37
Midland Bank Ltd v. Joliman Finance Ltd (1967) 203 EG 1039, ChD. 37
National Westminster Bank plc v. Spectrum Plus Ltd [2005] UKHL 41;
    [2005] 2 AC 680. 57
Newscreen Media Group plc, *Re* [2009] 2 BCLC 353 145
Newtherapeutics Ltd v. Katz [1991] Ch 226, ChD 103
Northern Development (Holding) Ltd v. UDT Securities [1976] 1 WLR
    1230; [1977] 1 All ER 747 37
Oakley Smith v. Greenberg [2002] EWCA Civ 1217; [2003] BPIR 709 136
Oldham v. Kyrris [2003] EWCA Civ 1506; [2004] BCC 111; [2004]
    BPIR 165 . . . . 6, 120, 129
Olympia & York Canary Wharf Ltd, *Re* (No.1) [1993] BCLC 453, ChD. 97
P & C and R & T (Stockport) Ltd, *Re* [1991] BCLC 366, ChD 22, 103

Paramount Airways Ltd, *Re* [1990] Ch 744; [1990] BCC 130, ChD 6

Permacell Finesse Ltd, *Re* [2007] EWHC 3233 (Ch); [2008] BCC 208 182

Powdrill *v.* Watson; *sub nom. Re* Paramount Airways Ltd (No.3) [1994]
2 All ER 513, CA 129

Practice Statement (Ch D: Fixing and Approval of Remuneration of
Appointees) [2004] BPIR 953 147

Professional Computer Group Ltd, *Re* [2008] EWHC 1541 (Ch); [2009]
BCC 323 40

RA Cripps (Pharmaceutical) and Son Ltd *v.* Wickenden [1973] 1 WLR 944;
[1973] 2 All ER 606, ChD 169

Razzaq *v.* Pala [1997] 1 WLR 1336, QBD 96

Redman Construction Ltd, *Re* [2004] EWHC 3468 (Ch); [2004] All ER
(D) 146 42

Rhondda Waste Disposal Ltd, *Re* [2001] Ch 57, CA. 100

Rover Espana SA, *Re* [2006] EWHC 3426 (Ch); [2006] BCC 599 122

Royal Trust Bank *v.* Buchler [1989] BCLC 130 . . . . 101, 102

Sabre International Products Ltd [1991] BCC 694, ChD 6

Salmet International Ltd, *Re* [2001] BCC 796, ChD. 129

Scottish Exhibition Centre Ltd *v.* Mirestop Ltd 1993 SLT 1034; [1993]
BCC 529 102

SE Services Ltd, Re, unreported, 9 August 2006. 23

Sendo Ltd, *Re* [2005] EWHC 1604 (Ch); [2006] 1 BCLC 395. 8

Sheppard & Cooper Ltd *v.* TSB Bank plc (No.2) [1996] 2 All ER 654;
[1996] BCC 965, ChD 169

Sibec Developments Ltd, *Re* [1992] 1 WLR 1253; [1993] BCC 148,
ChD. 145

Sisu Capital Fund Ltd *v.* Tucker [2005] EWHC 2170 (Ch); [2006] BPIR
154 . . . . 128, 145

Somerfield Stores Ltd *v.* Spring (Sutton Coldfield) Ltd [2009] EWHC 2384 (Ch)
100

Sporting Options plc, *Re* [2004] EWHC 3128 (Ch); [2005]
BCC 88 . . . . 81, 107, 111

Standard Chartered Bank Ltd *v.* Walker [1982] 1 WLR 1410, CA 37

T & D Industries plc, *Re* [2000] 1 WLR 646; [2000] 1 BCLC 471, ChD. . 6, 124

TBL Realisations plc, *Re* [2002] EWCA Civ 1217; [2004] BCC 81. 102

The Oracle (North West) Ltd *v.* Pinnacle Financial Services (UK) Ltd
[2008] EWHC 1920 (Ch); [2009] BCC 159. 43, 54

TM Kingdom Ltd, *Re* [2007] EWHC 3272 (Ch); [2007] BCC 480 136

Toshoku Finance UK plc, *Re* [2002] UKHL 6; [2002] 1 WLR 671;
[2002] 3 All ER 961 . . . . 20, 24, 37, 130

Transbus International Ltd, *Re* [2004] EWHC 932 (Ch); [2004] 2 All
ER 911; [2004] 1 WLR 2654 . . . . 6, 124, 136

Trident Fashions plc, *Re see* Exeter City Council *v.* Bairstow

TT Industries Ltd, *Re* [2006] BCC 372, ChD 134

Unidare plc *v.* Cohen [2005] EWHC 1410 (Ch); [2006] Ch 489; [2006]
  2 WLR 974; [2005] BPIR 1472 . . . . 12, 127, 140
West Mercia Safetywear Ltd (In Liquidation) *v.* Dodd [1988] BCLC 250,
  CA. 28
World Class Homes Ltd, *Re* [2004] EWHC 2906 (Ch); [2005] 2 BCLC 1. . . . 53
Yorkshire Woolcombers Association Ltd, *Re* [1903] 2 Ch 284, CA 57
Zegra III Holdings Inc, Re; *sub nom.* BLV Realty Organization Ltd *v.*
  Batten [2009] EWHC 2994 (Ch) 7

Table of statutes

Banking Act 2009 . . . . 8, 157
Building Societies Act 1986
  s.119 8
Companies Act 1985 . . 7, 46, 140, 161
Companies Act 1989
  s.173 172
Companies Act 2006 . . . . 28, 81
  s.172 . . . . 27, 28
    (1) 91
  s.177 91
  s.288 73
  s.860 60
  s.871 169
  ss.895–901 32
  s.1029 143
Company Directors Disqualification
  Act 1986. 165
Criminal Justice Act 1982
  s.74 106
Criminal Justice Act 1991
  s.17 106
Criminal Procedure (Scotland) Act
  1995
  s.225(8). 106
Energy Act 2004
  s.159 8
Enterprise Act 2002 . . . . ix, x,
      4, 10, 11, 15, 16, 18, 19, 20,
    22, 23, 25, 33, 36, 37, 38, 41,
    42, 45, 56, 58, 61, 73, 107, 113,
     122, 124, 130, 132, 133,
     138, 140, 149, 153, 155, 157
  s.249 8

Finance Act 2001
  s.92 171
Financial Services and Markets Act
  2000 8
  s.359 . . . . 40, 44
  s.367 . . . . 95, 97, 105, 132,
                 139, 179
Friendly Societies Act 1974. 9
Friendly Societies Act 1992. 9
Housing Act 1996
  Part I 172
Industrial and Provident Societies
  Act 1965. 9
Insolvency Act 1986 . . . . 1, 2, 149
  s.7(4)(b) 40, 44, 46
  s.7B. 76, 86
  Part II 8
  s.8(3). 2, 11
  s.14(3). 122
  s.18(3). 122
  s.19 130
    (4), (5) 129
  s.27 127
  s.29(2). 58, 170
  ss.72A–72G 4, 170, 172
  s.72A 52, 61
    (1) 56, 170
  s.72B. 170
  ss.72C, 72D, 72DA, 72E 171
  ss.72F, 72G, 72GA 172
  s.84(2A) 61
  s.98 . . . . 12, 139, 141, 156
  s.117(6). . . . 49, 66, 67, 78, 82, 85

Insolvency Act 1986 *continued*
s.123 .42
(1) .9
s.124A 95, 97, 105, 132,
139, 179
s.124B 95, 97, 132, 139
s.175 122
s.176A . . 110, 112, 122, 137, 142,
145, 146, 167, 181, 182
(2)(a) 116, 134
(5) 112
s.178 .21
s.212 .30
s.213 . . . . .30, 166
s.214 . . . . .29, 168
(3) 28
s.234 124
s.235 . . . . .109, 124
s.236 124
ss.238–240 . . . . .52, 53
s.238 . . . . .59, 60, 95, 167
s.239 . . . . .59, 60, 166
s.240 .95
s.244 .60
s.245 . . . . 39, 52, 53, 59, 60,
95, 104
s.248 . . . . .96, 98
s.251 .57
s.339 167
s.340 166
s.422(1) 8
s.423 .60
Sched.A1 . . . . .76, 78, 86, 88
Sched.B1, para.1(1) 5, 22
para.3 120
(1)(a), (b) 10
(c) 10, 38, 61
(2) 7, 17, 37, 120
(c) 133
(4) 7
(b) 10, 38
para.4 . . . . .120, 127, 132
para.5 . . . . .6, 73, 120
para.7 . . . . .39, 61

Insolvency Act 1986 *continued*
Sched.B1 *continued*
para.10 41
para.11 . . . . .42, 44
(a) 10
para.12(1) 44
(a) 46
(b) 44, 46
(c) 39, 44, 46
(d) 40
(2) 52
(3) 56
para.13(1)(e) 55
(f) 23
(3) 55
paras.14–21 56
para.14 . . . . . . 41, 50, 64, 76,
95, 137, 143, 170
(1) 34
(2) 58, 170
(3) 58
para.15 63
(1)(b) 39, 60, 62
(2) 64
para.16 . . . . .10, 39, 61
para.17 61
(a), (b) 39, 61
para.19 71
para.20(b) 72
para.21(2) 59
para.22 . . . . . . 41, 82, 83, 86,
88, 137
(1) 26, 143
(2) 25, 143
paras.23–30 . . . . .82, 88
para.23 134
(2) 74
para.25 74
(a) 25
para.26 . . . . .75, 80
(1) 84
para.27 80
(2), (4) 79
para.28(2) 81
para.29(6), (7) 85, 89

Insolvency Act 1986 *continued*
  Sched.B1 *continued*
    para.31 82
    para.32 90
    para.34 75
    para.35 . . . . . . .46, 47, 49, 50
    para.36(1), (2) 53
    para.37 . . . . 39, 46, 49,
               55, 61, 72
    para.38 . . . . . . .44, 46, 56, 61
      (1) 40
    para.39(1). 52
      (a). 104
    para.40 180
      (1) 94
      (a). 95
      (b) 61
    para.41(1), (2) 95, 180
      (3)(a) 96
      (4)(c) 96
    para.42(2). 97, 180
      (3) 95, 97, 180
      (5) 97
    para.43(2). 96, 98, 180
      (3) 98, 180
      (4) 13, 99, 180
      (6) 100, 180
      (6A) 95, 180
      (7) 98, 100
    para.44 . . . . .75, 104
      (2) 104
        (b) 63
      (6) 104
      (7) 80
    para.45(1). 106
    para.46(3), (4) 107
      (5), (7), (9) 108
    para.47(1). 108
      (2) 109
      (3) 108
    para.48(1). 108, 109
      (2) 109
        (a) 108
      (3), (4) 109

Insolvency Act 1986 *continued*
  Sched.B1 *continued*
    para.49(1). 110
      (2)(b) 111
      (3) 113
      (5) 110
      (6) 112
      (8) 110
    para.51(1). 113
      (4) 114
    para.52 116
      (1) 113
        (b) . . 116, 134, 145
      (2) 114, 116
    para.53 117
      (1) 114
        (b) 114
      (2) 116
    para.54(1). 117
    para.55 . . . . .115, 136
    para.56 118
    para.57 . . . . .115, 118
    para.59(1). 6, 120
      (3) 7, 122
    para.61 . . . . 6, 22,
                103, 122
    para.62 . . . . .6, 118, 122
    para.63 . . . . 95, 97, 118,
                122, 124
    para.64 . . . . .22, 103
      (2)(c) 22
    para.65(1). 122
    para.66 122
    para.67 123
    para.68(1). 115, 123
        (b) 118
      (2) 136
      (3) 123
    para.69 . . . . .6, 120
    para.70(1). 125
      (3). 122
    para.71(1), (5) 125
    para.72(1). 126
    para.73 126

Insolvency Act 1986 *continued*
Sched.B1 *continued*
para.74 . . . . 17, 102,
118, 138
(1) 124, 127
(2) 145
(5) 126
(6) 128
para.75 . . . . 17, 118, 134, 145
(2) 128
(3)(c) 120
(6) 145
para.76(1) 133
(2) 133
(a) 135
para.77(1)(b) 133
para.78 134
(1) 134
(4)(c) 133
(5) 135
para.79 137
(1) 135
(2) 12, 136
(3) 136
para.80 137
(2) 12
para.81(1) 138
(2) 12, 37, 138
(3) 139
para.82 139
para.83 . . . . . . .136, 140, 141
(7) 141
para.84 . . . . . . .136, 141, 142
(4) 142
(6) 141
(7) 142
para.86 . . . . .39, 61, 137
para.87 143
para.88 . . . . .128, 145
para.89 143
paras.91–95 144
para.91(2) 144
para.92 144
para.94 144

Insolvency Act 1986 *continued*
Sched.B1 *continued*
para.96(2) 144
para.97 144
para.98(1) 145
(2)(c) 137, 145
para.99 . . . . .21, 130, 146
(3) 20, 130
(4), (5) 129
para.100(2) 51, 67, 69,
70, 71, 84, 85,
87, 89
para.105 25
para.107 . . . . 111, 114
(2) 111
para.108 111
(5) 111
para.111 134
(1) 42
Sched.1 . . . . .6, 120
Sched.2A 172
paras.1–3 170
paras.7, 9, 10 171
Sched.10 . . . . .106, 108
Sched.16 135
Insolvency Act 1994 129
Insolvency Act 2000 14
Landlord and Tenant Act 1954
Part II 100
Law of Property Act 1925 . . . .36, 166
Limitation Act 1980 . . . . .13, 94
Magistrates' Courts Act 1980
s.32(9) 106
s.87A 40, 44, 46
Perjury Act 1911
s.5 10
Railways Act 1993
s.59 . . . . .8, 172
Statutory Declarations Act 1835 . . 69,
77, 84, 87
Taxes Management Act 1970
s.108(3)(a) 24
Transport Act 2000
s.26 . . . . .8, 172

Value Added Tax Act 1994
    Sched.11 151
Water Industry Act 1991
    Part II, Ch.I 8, 172

France
Business Safeguard Act 2005 158

USA
Bankruptcy Code (USC 11) 22,
                   118, 148, 150,
                     154, 155,
                     157, 159
    s.363(b) 15
    s.364 18

Table of statutory instruments

Banks (Former Authorised Institutions) (Insolvency) Order 2006,
  SI 2006/3107 8
Civil Procedure Rules 1998, SI 1998/3132
  Part 35. 71
Companies (Trading Disclosure) (Insolvency) Regulations 2008,
  SI 2008/1897 106
European Public Limited-Liability Company Regulations 2004,
  SI 2004/2326 . . . . 95, 97, 139
Financial Markets and Insolvency Regulations 1996, SI 1996/1469 172
Financial Markets and Insolvency (Settlement Finality) Regulations 1999,
  SI 1999/2979 172
Financial Services and Markets Act 2000 (Administrative Orders Relating
  to Insurers) (Amendment) Order 2003, SI 2003/2134. 8
Financial Services and Markets Act 2000 (Administrative Orders Relating
  to Insurers) (Amendment) Order 2004, SI 2004/353. 8
Financial Services and Markets Act 2000 (Administrative Orders Relating
  to Insurers) Order 2002, SI 2002/1242. 8
Financial Services and Markets Act 2000 (Regulated Activities) Order 2001,
  SI 2001/544
  art.77. 170
Insolvency Act 1986 (Amendment) (Administrative Receivership and Urban
  Regeneration etc.) Order 2003, SI 2003/1832 172
Insolvency Act 1986 (Prescribed Part) Order 2003, SI 2003/2097 181
Insolvency (Amendment) Rules 2005, SI 2005/527 . . . . 20, 130
Insolvency (Amendment) Rules 2009, SI 2009/642 107
Insolvency Rules 1986, SI 1986/1925. 24
  r.1.17(3). 115
  r.2.2. . . . . 23, 33, 43, 90
    (1) 45
    (2), (3) 50
    (4) 44
  r.2.3. 43
    (2) 44

Insolvency Rules 1986 *continued*
r.2.3(4). 39, 44
(5)(c) 43
r.2.4. . . . . 43, 44, 50
(2) 11
(3) 50
r.2.5. 43
(1) 52
r.2.6(2). 52
(3) 52
(b) 94
r.2.7. 54
r.2.8. . . . . 52, 81
(5) 78
(6) 54
r.2.9(2). 54
r.2.10. 53
r.2.12. 55
(3). 55
r.2.13. 56
r.2.14. 55
rr.2.15–2.18. 56
r.2.15. 63
r.2.16(5). 65, 66
r.2.17(2). 71
r.2.19(3), (7) 72
(8) 71
(10) 72
r.2.20(2). 80
r.2.21. . . . . 79, 85, 89
r.2.22. 73
r,2.27(1). 107
(2) 108
r.2.28(3), (4) 109
r.2.29(1), (2), (4). 109
(7) 110
r.2.30(1)–(4) 110
r.2.31. 109
(1). 108
r.2.32. 110
(3). 110
r.2.33(1). 111
(2) 112
(m). 132

Insolvency Rules 1986 *continued*
r.2.33(4)... 111
    (7) 112
r.2.34(1)–(4) 114
r.2.35(2).. 113
    (3) 114
    (4) 113
r.2.36.. 114
r.2.37.. 117, 118
r.2.38(1), (3), (5) 115
r.2.39.. 116
r.2.40.. 116
    (2) 116
r.2.41.. 116
r.2.42.. 116
r.2.43(1), (2) 115
r.2.45(2), (4) 118
r.2.46.. 117
r.2.47.. 118, 135
    (2) 119
    (5) 118
r.2.48.. 117
    (2), (4), (5) 117
r.2.67.. 20, 23, 130
    (1) 20, 23
      (c) 23
      (j)... 24, 37
    (4) 20, 130, 131
rr.2.85–2.88.. 123
r.2.85.. 115
r.2.106... 112
    (1) 146
r.2.107... 146
r.2.108... 146
r.2.109... 146
r.2.112(1).. 135
r.2.113(1), (3) 137
    (5), (6A).. 138
r.2.114... 137
r.2.117(1).. 140
    (3) 141
r.2.119... 143
r.2.121... 143
r.2.125(1).. 144

Insolvency Rules 1986 *continued*
   r.2.129 145
   r.4.128 130
   r.4.218(1) 20
   r.7.31(5) 119
   r.7.55 133
   r.7.57 173
Insolvent Partnerships (Amendment) Order 2005, SI 2005/1516 8
Insurers (Reorganisation and Winding Up) (Lloyd's) Regulations 2005,
   SI 2005/1998 8
Insurers (Reorganisatiom and Winding Up) Regulations 2003, SI 2003/1102 . . 8
Limited Liability Partnerships (Amendment) Regulations 2005, SI 2005/1989
   art.3 8
   Sched.2 8

Table of European legislation

Regulation 1346/2000 . . . . 7, 113, 158
  Recital 12 51
  Art.1.2 . . . . 47, 49, 65, 66, 68, 70, 76, 79, 82, 83, 86, 88
  Art.3 . . . . 47, 51, 65, 68, 76, 83, 86
  Art.3.1 51
Regulation 2157/2001 139

List of abbreviations

BIS	(Department for) Business, Innovation & Skills
CVA	company voluntary arrangement
FSA	Financial Services Authority
HMRC	Her Majesty's Revenue and Customs
HP	hire purchase
IA 1986	Insolvency Act 1986
IR 1986	Insolvency Rules 1986, SI 1986/1925
PPP	public–private partnership
QFCH	qualifying floating charge holder

CHAPTER 1

An introduction to administration

1.1 CORPORATE INSOLVENCY AND THE USE OF ADMINISTRATION

Insolvency is an inevitable consequence of trading activity within a free market economy. Laws are required to intervene and regulate the affairs between insolvent debtors and their creditors and to define the rights, duties and obligations as between an individual creditor and the creditors as a whole, dealing with the treatment of an insolvent debtor and their assets. Insolvency laws need to provide a just and equitable balance between these competing economic interests.

Administration is the insolvency process most commonly initiated, by an insolvent company and/or its directors, to regulate the affairs of the company with its creditors as it seeks to overcome difficulty and secure financial rehabilitation; administration is also used where *company* rescue is not achievable but it is reasonably believed that a company's business and assets can be saved or 'rescued'. As we shall see, following the statutory reforms that came into force in late 2003, the administration process can also used, subject to certain conditions, by a qualifying floating charge holder as a means of realising their secured interest over a company.

Administration is, however, a comparatively new arrival to UK insolvency law. Despite this, since its introduction, it has come to dominate much of the debate on the requirements and practical application of the laws that regulate the affairs between corporate debtor and creditor.

Tracing the development of administration from its introduction, to its place of primacy in effecting corporate rescue, highlights many of the fundamental tensions that still exist within our current legal framework.

Administration, receivership and statutory reform

Administration was first introduced in the Insolvency Act (IA) 1986 as a corporate rescue process ancillary to the various forms of receivership that have a far longer historical tradition. It should be noted, however, that receivership is a process the aim of which is to effect not corporate rescue, but the realisation of secured assets for a secured creditor.

It is a trite but valid point that a business that is maintained as a going concern is of more value to a purchaser (and therefore to a secured creditor) than one which has ceased trading and whose assets are being sold on a break-up basis (such as on liquidation). As a result, during the 1960s draftsmen acting on behalf of lenders began including in security documentation increasingly innovative and wide powers to be given to a receiver over an ever-increasing class of the borrower company's assets. This enabled the lender to appoint a receiver who could continue to manage and trade the borrower's business pending sale as a going concern. The concept whereby a receiver was appointed over the whole or substantially the whole of the company's undertaking (pursuant to a floating charge) was formally recognised in IA 1986 and termed 'administrative receivership'.

It is noteworthy that when the concept of an administration process was mooted in the Report of the Review Committee on Insolvency Law and Practice (Cmnd 8558, June 1982, commonly referred to as the 'Cork Report' and whose key recommendations led to IA 1986) it was envisaged that administration would be used by companies that did not have the benefit of a lender possessing floating charge security.

As a result, the process of administration introduced in 1986 was one that was designed to complement receivership, not replace it. Not long after its introduction the process was sorely tested by the economic recession of the early 1990s. Despite the availability of the new corporate rescue process the number of appointments made remained small, with around 200 administration appointments a year in the first 10 years following the introduction of the new procedure. The number of receivership appointments continued to dwarf the number of administration appointments.

One of the reasons for this, certainly in the years following the introduction of the administration process, was the greater familiarity with the receivership procedure. Indeed the nature of the recession of the early 1990s (a property bubble that had burst causing a recessionary spiral as lenders sought to act to realise their security, which had the effect of introducing more properties on to an already falling market) was one led by the demands of secured creditors who would opt for the 'tried and tested' method of receivership, which offered them a quick and efficient means of getting assets quickly under control, marketed and sold.

The administration procedure as originally introduced in IA 1986 was in comparison seen by some as being legalistic, cumbersome, inflexible and overly complex. The principal reason for this criticism was that administration was designed as a court-led process. To commence the process a court order was required following a petition supported by evidence. As a result the insolvent company's directors (or in some rare cases its creditors) were required to produce very significant evidence to satisfy the court that at least one of the four statutory purposes of the administration, previously found in IA 1986, s.8(3) (as amended) would be achieved. A report from an insolvency

Table 1.1 Number of receiverships compared to administrations 1987 to 2003

	Receiverships	Administration
1987	1265	131
1988	1094	198
1989	1706	135
1990	4318	211
1991	7515	206
1992	8324	179
1993	5362	112
1994	3877	159
1995	3226	163
1996	2701	210
1997	1837	196
1998	1713	338
1999	1618	440
2000	1595	438
2001	1914	698
2002	1541	643
2003	1261	497

Source: Insolvency Service Statistical Directorate

practitioner (a so-called 'Rule 2.2 Report') providing the court with a comparative assessment of the various alternatives available to the company was mandatory.

Not only that, administration was also seen as costly. An expensive court application was required to initiate the process and, during that process, the company in administration would need to trade profitably, or the administrator would need to be funded or at least indemnified by a solvent party. These factors together made administration an unattractive option, particularly for many small companies.

The failure to make greater use of the administration process introduced in 1986 was seen as a major weakness in the UK legal framework for rescuing companies, the business operated by the companies and ultimately jobs. As a result, the incoming Labour Government of 1997 made it clear that it was committed to reforming insolvency law (both corporate and personal) and in 1999 a joint Department of Trade and Industry/Treasury Review Group was set up to look at how best to develop a 'rescue culture'.

After undertaking three major consultation processes, the Review Group reported in May 2000. This was followed by the White Paper 'Productivity and Enterprise: Insolvency – A Second Chance' (Cm 5234, published in July 2001). However, the White Paper and resulting Enterprise Bill were criticised in some quarters for providing a number of innovations (such as the out-of-court process for appointing an administrator) which had not been subject to consultation, while at the same time failing to introduce some of the more radical measures discussed in the consultation process, including those which would have more limited the power and role of secured creditors in the insolvency process.

The eventual reforms contained in the Enterprise Act 2002, however, represent a highly significant development in insolvency law, the centrepiece of the corporate insolvency reforms being the 'abolition' of administrative receivership and the introduction of a completely new administration process. Save in a number of special exempted circumstances, a floating charge creditor can no longer appoint an administrative receiver as a means of realising their security (see **Appendix 1** – Summary 2; IA 1986, ss.72A–72G).

The reformed administration procedure, which came into force on 15 September 2003, was designed to offer an efficient, less costly and more streamlined process. The objectives of the reformed process outlined by Lord Sainsbury, Parliamentary Under Secretary of State for Trade and Industry (House of Lords on the second reading of the Enterprise Bill, 2 July 2002) were to:

- provide a clearer focus on company rescue;
- secure a better return to creditors as a whole where company rescue is not practical;
- provide a clearer timescale to ensure that the administration is not drawn out at the expense of creditors;
- ensure that an administrator owes wider duties to creditors as a whole.

The use of administration in place of administrative receivership as the primary method of corporate rescue since 2003 was clearly designed and anticipated. As can be seen below there has been an explosion in the use of administration as an insolvency process and this is before taking into account the rise in insolvency numbers that will undoubtedly occur in 2009/10 as the recession starting in late 2008 takes wider effect.

Table 1.2 Number of administrative receiverships compared to administrations 2003 to 2009

	Receiverships	Administration
2004	864	1,601
2005	590	2,257
2006	588	3,560
2007	337	2,509
2008	867	4,820
2009*	1,468	4,161

Source: Insolvency Service Statistical Directorate
*N.B. 2009 figures provisional

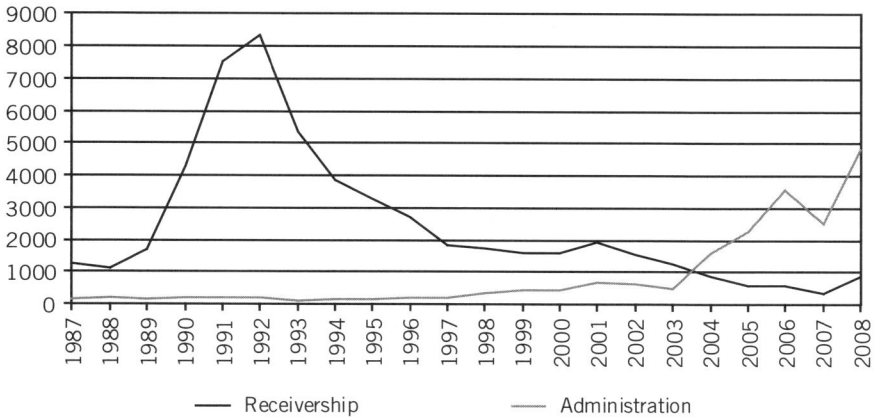

Figure 1.1 Receiverships vs. administrations 1987–2008

Perhaps what was less anticipated was the use of the new administration process in place of voluntary liquidation (certainly this occurred in the first 12–18 months after the introduction of the reformed process) and the growing use of the process to effect the sale of the insolvent company's business and assets on or soon after appointment (the pre-pack administration). Whether these are unwelcome consequences of the reformed process is a question that will be returned to throughout this book.

Before exploring in depth the process and procedure of administration, the remainder of this chapter will deal with some fundamental questions and features of the administration process.

1.2   WHAT IS ADMINISTRATION?

Administration is a legal process used to facilitate the 'rescue' of an insolvent company, which involves the appointment of an administrator.

The process is initiated by:

- court order; or
- the filing of a requisite notice at the court (the out-of-court route) by a qualifying floating charge holder; or
- the filing of a requisite notice at the court (the out-of-court route) by the company or its directors.

The administrator is appointed to manage the company's affairs, business and property (IA 1986, Sched.B1, para.1(1)) and a company is deemed to be 'in administration' while the appointment of the administrator has effect.

The administrator is an officer of the court, whether appointed by the court, a qualifying floating charge holder or the company or its directors (IA 1986, Sched.B1, para.5). This has a number of important consequences:

1. A third party may be guilty of contempt of court if that party seeks to unjustifiably interfere with the performance of the administrator's duties (see *Re Paramount Airways Ltd* [1990] BCC 130 and *Re Sabre International Products Ltd* [1991] BCC 694), although it must be noted that this remains a rarely used remedy.
2. The administrator can seek direction of the court if thought necessary to assist in the discharge of his duties. Conversely the court retains an inherent jurisdiction to direct an administrator to take a particular course of action.
3. The administrator must act fairly and reasonably, in accordance with the so-called 'rule in *Ex parte James*' (see *Re Condon, ex p. James* (1873–74) LR 9 Ch App 609). Although somewhat ill-defined in scope this 'rule' has been taken to mean that an administrator should be candid with the court (see *Re Ah Toy* (1986) 4 ACLC 480), providing evidence of all relevant circumstances, whether that assists the administrator or otherwise (see *Re Colt Telecom Group Plc (No.2)* [2003] BPIR 324). The administrator should also not rely on the strict letter of the law, if it produces 'dishonourable', unfair or obtuse results and must act independently and impartially and be seen to do so (see *Re Intercontinental Properties Pty Ltd* (1977) 2 ACLC 488).

The administrator acts as agent of the company (IA 1986, Sched.B1, para.69) and may do anything necessary or expedient for the management of the affairs, business and property of the company (IA 1986, Sched.B1, para.59(1)).

The administrator has by virtue of these general provisions and specifically by virtue of the powers listed in IA 1986, Sched.1 very wide discretionary powers. The court is unlikely to intervene on any question of commercial judgment exercised by the administrator, save in cases of manifest bad faith, irrationality or unreasonableness/negligence (see *T&D Industries Plc* [2000] 1 BLC 471; *Re Transbus International Ltd* [2004] 2 All ER 911; *Re Lehman Brothers International Ltd* [2009] BCC 632).

The powers of an administrator over the company are wider than those conferred on a director of the company and extend to the management of the 'affairs' of the company, including the power to remove/appoint directors (IA 1986, Sched.B1, para.61) and the ability to call a meeting of members or creditors (IA 1986, Sched.B1, para.62).

Like a director, the administrator owes fiduciary duties to the company (see *Oldham* v. *Kyrris* [2004] BPIR 165), although unless specifically provided the administrator will not incur personal liability for contracts entered into by him on behalf of the company. Importantly the administrator can claim an indemnity from the company's assets for any liabilities incurred.

Under common law rules of agency a party dealing/contracting with the administrator in good faith and for value need not enquire into whether the administrator is acting within his powers (this is also expressly provided in IA 1986, Sched.B1, para.59(3)).

Most importantly the administrator (unlike a receiver, whose duties are primarily referable to the secured creditor who has appointed him) has a responsibility to manage the company for the benefit of all creditors and all those interested in the estate (IA 1986, Sched.B1, para.3(2)).

The administration process is collective in nature. This is only modified in cases where the administrator is appointed by a qualifying floating charge holder, and the only likely return is that to the secured creditor who has appointed the administrator; even then the administrator must not act in a way which unnecessarily harms the interests of the creditors as a whole (IA 1986, Sched.B1, para.3(4)).

See *Zegra III Holdings Inc.*; sub nom. *BLV Realty Organization Ltd* v. *Batten* [2009] EWHC 2994 (Ch) where it was held that the duty to act in the interests of the creditors as a whole did not mean that treatment needed to be in an identical fashion; 'unequal treatment' was not necessarily unfair where it was for sound commercial reasons. It should however be noted that an administrator owes no general common law duty to a specific unsecured creditor absent the creation of some form of special relationship (*Charalambous* v. *B&C Associates* [2009] EWHC 2601 (Ch)).

A key feature of the administration process is the moratorium that comes into effect, which prevents a creditor during the administration period from enforcing the payment of debt, or from exercising certain rights (proprietary or otherwise) whether by an insolvency or other legal processes. In theory this allows the company breathing space in which to calmly evaluate its prospects, free from creditor pressure, with the hope of achieving financial rehabilitation via proposals formulated by the administrator and approved by the creditors. In practice the rescue and survival of the debtor company is rare, the company exiting administration and being returned to its directors and members occurring in less than five per cent of cases.

1.3 WHEN IS ADMINISTRATION AVAILABLE?

The process of administration is available to:

- a company registered under the Companies Act in England and Wales;
- a company registered in Scotland; although it must enter into administration in the jurisdiction of incorporation, i.e. Scotland (see *Dear IP* No.25 December 2005 and *Re Brownridge Plastics Ltd* (unreported, Birmingham District Registry, Hart J));
- a foreign registered company that has its centre of main interests in England and Wales (see Council Regulation (EC) No.1346/2000 of 29 May 2000 on insolvency proceedings);

- a foreign registered company that has its centre of main interests in another EU Member State (apart from Denmark) and an 'establishment' in England and Wales (see *BRAC Rent-a-Car International Inc* [2003] BCC 248 and *Re Sendo Ltd* [2006] 1 BCLC 395);
- a partnership (by virtue of the Insolvent Partnerships (Amendment) Order 2005, SI 2005/1516 post-1 July 2005); and
- a limited liability partnership (by virtue of the Limited Liability Partnerships (Amendment) Regulations 2005, SI 2005/1989, art.3, Sched.2 as from 1 October 2005).

The extension of the administration regime (with certain modifications) to partnerships means that save where specifically mentioned it is possible to treat this guide on company administration as having equal application to partnerships.

The administration process is not available however to certain specific types of company. A modified administration process is also available for certain companies which are subject to separate distinct legislation. This book intentionally focuses on the most common forms of administration and thus specialist works should be referred to when tackling issues relating to such entities. Undertakings excluded from the provisions of IA 1986, Part II or subject to separate distinct legislation such as where a 'special administration regime' (see Enterprise Act 2002, s.249) applies, include:

- water and sewerage undertakers (Water Industry Act 1991, Part II, Chapter I);
- protected railway companies (Railways Act 1993, s.59);
- air traffic control companies (Transport Act 2000, s.26);
- building societies (Building Societies Act 1986, s.119);
- insurers within Financial Services and Markets Act 2000 (see Financial Services and Markets Act 2000 (Administration Orders Relating to Insurers) Order 2002, SI 2002/1242 as from 31 May 2002 as amended by SI 2003/2134 and SI 2004/353 as from 18 February 2004) and Insurers (Reorganisation and Winding Up) Regulations 2003, SI 2003/1102 and 2004, SI 2004/353 and Insurers (Reorganisation and Winding Up) (Lloyd's) Regulations 2005, SI 2005/1998; the cumulative effects of which mean that a modified administration process is now available to insurance companies: *Re AA Mutual International Insurance Co Ltd* [2005] 2 BCLC 8);
- banks and analogous institutions referred to in IA 1986, s.422(1) (Banks (Former Authorised Institutions) (Insolvency) Order 2006, SI 2006/3107 as from 15 December 2006; the effect of which is that a modified administration process is available to banks and other such financial institutions with certain Financial Services Authority participation, see also the Banking Act 2009);
- companies licensed to supply energy (Energy Act 2004, s.159);

- societies registered under the Industrial and Provident Societies Act 1965; and
- societies registered under the Friendly Societies Acts 1974 and 1992 and unregistered friendly societies.

Administration should be considered as an option when financial rehabilitation of a company needs to be undertaken but creditor pressure is such that any plan of reconstruction (whether through a formal process or informal negotiation and arrangement) will be hampered. It is available to companies (and their directors) where they are insolvent and in circumstances where the purpose of administration is reasonably likely to be achieved.

Where the company is insolvent

A company may be insolvent on either a cash flow or a balance sheet test.

The *cash flow test* is a measure of whether a debtor is insolvent and is based on whether the debtor can pay its debts as they fall due.

The *balance sheet test* is a measure of whether a debtor is insolvent and is based upon whether the debtor's total liabilities exceed assets.

The insolvency of the company is therefore something that is capable of both objective and subjective assessment. Indeed in certain circumstances a company (and, in particular, group companies with complex cross-claims, obligations and indemnities) may feel that it requires an insolvency practitioner and/or accountant in order to assist it in its determination of whether or not it is insolvent. The advice that the company is insolvent following this independent expert assessment may therefore lead the company (through its directors) to conclude that an administration process should be commenced.

In some instances insolvency is more easily assessed, perhaps through an inability to meet a due demand. As we shall see insolvency is deemed to arise where a company is unable to pay its debts:

- after service and failure to meet the terms of a statutory demand; or
- where execution or other legal process issued on a judgment is returned unsatisfied in whole or in part (see IA 1986, s.123(1)).

It is also quite possible that a company could be solvent on one basis and not the other; and while it may therefore on one form of test be seen as solvent as at the date of assessment, after taking into account prospective, future and even contingent liabilities it may not be deemed solvent (see *Re Lomax Leisure Ltd* [2000] BCC 352; *Re Colt Telecom Group Plc (No.2)* [2003] BPIR 324; *Re AA Mutual International Insurance Co Ltd* [2005] 2 BCLC 8). As a result, while a company needs to be insolvent to enjoy the privileges and advantages of the administration process, in many cases this is an easy test to pass and in practice is almost 'taken as read'.

Despite this it should be noted that in the notice of intention to appoint an administrator (Form 2.8B) and in the notice of appointment of an administrator by the company or directors (Forms 2.9B and 2.10B) a duly authorised individual acting on behalf of the appointor is required to make a statutory declaration that includes the statement 'the company is or is likely to become unable to pay its debts'. An individual who knowingly and wilfully makes a false declaration commits a criminal offence under Perjury Act 1911, s.5 and may be imprisoned for up to two years or fined or both. In reality, professional standards of integrity, regulatory control and ultimately creditor challenge through due court process will all act as moderating factors preventing abuse.

Furthermore if an administration order is sought, the court needs to be satisfied that 'the company is or is likely to become unable to pay its debts' (IA 1986, Sched.B1, para.11(a)), which in practice will mean the need to adduce some persuasive evidence of insolvency.

It should, however, be noted that because of the restrictions on a secured creditor's right to appoint an administrative receiver post-15 September 2003 (i.e. after commencement of the corporate insolvency law reforms contained in the Enterprise Act 2002), a concession granted to secured creditors and contained in the post-Enterprise Act administration regime is that a company does need not be insolvent if the appointment is made by the out-of-court route by a qualifying floating charge holder. While it is a requirement that the floating charge security has become enforceable (IA 1986, Sched.B1, para.16) and in practice this may arise through some failure to meet financial liabilities defined within the facilities, it is possible that some other form of breach of facility has arisen (e.g. a breach of the loan to value covenant) which entitles the floating charge holder to realise its security. As we shall see however, where the administrator is appointed to realise property in order to make a distribution to a secured creditor (IA 1986, Sched.B1, para.3(1)(c)), the administrator must not unnecessarily harm the interests of the creditors as a whole (IA 1986, Sched.B1, para.3(4)(b)).

Where it is reasonably likely that the purpose of administration will be achieved

However and by whomever appointed, the administrator of the company must perform his functions with the objective of achieving the overriding purpose for administration as contained in IA 1986, Sched.B1, para.3(1), namely:

    (a)   rescuing the company as a going concern, or

    (b)   achieving a better result for the company's creditors as a whole than would be likely if the company were wound up (without first being in administration), or

    (c)   realising property in order to make a distribution to one or more secured or preferential creditors.

It therefore follows that the administration should not be commenced unless the purpose of administration is reasonably likely to be achieved.

The old (pre-Enterprise Act) administration regime had four differing purposes for administration (formerly IA 1986, s.8(3) (as amended)); in the post-reform regime it should be noted that there is now one single purpose of administration with a hierarchy of objectives.

The new regime provides that the administrator is required to seek to fulfil the first objective, namely company rescue, and it is only if the achievement of this objective is not reasonably practicable, or a better result can be obtained for the creditors as a whole, that the administrator may proceed to the second objective. The administrator should then seek to fulfil the second objective, namely achieving a better result for the company's creditors as a whole than would be likely if the company were wound up (without first being in administration) and it is only if this objective is not reasonably practicable that the administrator may proceed to the third objective. The administrator may only proceed with the third objective on condition that in doing so the administrator does not unnecessarily harm the interests of the creditors of the company as a whole.

It should be noted that the administrator is required in an out-of-court appointment to file Form 2.2B, which includes a statement that 'I am of the opinion that the purpose of administration is reasonably likely to be achieved'.

This simple statement is a radical departure from the pre-Enterprise Act administration process where in order to obtain a court order an independent report on the likely benefit of administration, showing how at least one of the purposes of administration was reasonably likely to be achieved, was required. The need to produce a detailed report (a so-called Rule 2.2 Report) was a significant cost and deterrent in the use of the administration process. As a result, its replacement in the case of an out-of-court appointment with a single statement is a major innovation of the reformed administration regime, significantly reducing complexity and cost. It should also be noted that where an appointment is sought by court order, while the court stills needs to be persuaded on evidence that the purpose of administration is reasonably likely to be achieved, there is no longer a need for an independent report containing the same detail as under the old regime (Insolvency Rules 1986, SI 1986/1925 (IR 1986), r.2.4(2)).

As we shall see, however, the relaxation in the requirement as to evidence/justification has led to concern that the proposed administrator has not adequately considered whether the purpose of administration can be achieved and/or whether an alternative process may be in the better interests of the creditors as a whole. In regard to pre-pack administration sales, the Statement of Insolvency Practice 16 (SIP16) issued in January 2009 has encouraged administrators to disclose to creditors the thinking and justification as to why the pre-pack administration sale is in the best interests of the creditors, so ensuring that the purpose of administration will be achieved.

Save for the requirement imposed by SIP16, it should however be noted that the administrator is not required to state which of the objectives will be fulfilled; he is simply required to state that 'the purpose' of administration is reasonably likely to be achieved. In deciding which objective is to be pursued, the administrator retains a wide discretion based on his subjective opinion as to likely results. This will only be capable of challenge in instances of bad faith or irrationality (*Unidare Plc* v. *Cohen* [2005] BPIR 1472). A further factor to consider is the width of the definition of 'the purpose' of administration; in most circumstances of insolvency and financial difficulty for an active/trading company it would be seem justifiable for the proposed administrator to state that the purpose of administration is reasonably likely to be achieved.

While therefore administration may be 'justifiable' (i.e. it can be said that the purpose is reasonably likely to be achieved) secondary questions still arise. Was it the most appropriate insolvency process to use? Did it represent best advice to the company? Was it in the best interests of the creditors as a whole?

As we shall see, there is the ability for a creditor to challenge the appointment of an administrator on the basis that the appointment was made for an improper purpose (IA 1986, Sched.B1, para.81(2)), which in theory might be used by a creditor to challenge a decision to appoint an administrator on the basis that an alternative process is arguably in the best interests of the creditors as whole. Certainly in the first 12–18 months after introduction of the new procedures, there was some concern raised that the ease with which the administration process could be commenced was meaning that administration was being used in place of a creditors' voluntary liquidation, as this would avoid the directors having to face the creditors at a 'section 98' meeting and/or to ensure that the company's choice of insolvency practitioner to act as administrator prevailed over the choice that the creditors would have had in appointing a liquidator.

We have yet to be provided with a leading authority on what will be judged to be appropriate grounds to challenge the appointment of an administrator on the basis of improper purpose. Until that time, in reality the administrator's statement as to whether the purpose of administration is reasonably likely to be achieved is most likely to be more a matter of professional regulation and foremost a matter affecting his professional reputation and standing.

The continuation of the administration process remains justifiable as long as the purpose remains reasonably capable of achievement (IA 1986, Sched. B1, para.79(2)) and where it is achieved the administrator must takes steps to bring the administration to an end (IA 1986, Sched.B1, para.80(2)).

1.4 WHY USE ADMINISTRATION?

The advantages of administration

Where a company has an inability to pay its debts and as a result an insolvency procedure is inevitable, and/or creditors are applying pressure/seeking to enforce claims to the company that could jeopardise any rescue/restructuring of the business, any advisers should almost certainly give consideration to administration as an appropriate measure to deal with these dificulties.

Advantage 1: The moratorium and 'breathing space'

A key feature of administration and one of its distinct advantages is that it gives the management and owners of the company, with the assistance of the administrator (who will of course be an insolvency practitioner experienced in corporate rescue and reconstruction), time in which to consider the company's options, as a statutory moratorium on the enforcement of rights and claims by third parties comes into force.

The moratorium provides the company in administration with 'breathing space' (*Atlantic Computer Systems Plc* [1992] 2 WLR 367 per Nicholls LJ) in which to allow the administrator to carry out his functions and make proposals to the creditors. The moratorium thus prevents creditors from taking action or otherwise depriving the company of assets that the administrator may require to fulfil the purpose of administration.

A third party who takes action to enforce claims or rights contrary to the restrictions of the statutory moratorium is in contempt of court. This can give rise to a claim for loss and damage (*Euro Commercial Leasing Ltd* v. *Cartwright & Lewis* [1995] 2 BCLC 618) and the threat of any possible action may be met with injunctive relief.

While the moratorium intervenes and regulates the rights of third parties as against the company in administration it should be noted that it does not destroy those rights (they are simply suspended and can still be enforced, with the consent of the administrator, or leave of the court). Despite this suspension of third party rights, the moratorium does not stop time running for claims subject to the Limitation Act 1980 and as a result potential claimant creditors should be careful to ensure that at very least a protective claim is issued. In turn the administrator should be reasonable and give consent to the issue of a claim in these circumstances (*Re Cosslett (Contractors) Ltd* [1998] Ch 495).

It should also be remembered that contractual rights and obligations as between the company in administration and third parties continue despite the moratorium. For this reason a supplier may be entitled to terminate a contract for supply with the company by reason of its administration (if that is an agreed contractual term); it is the enforcement of claims and exercise of rights as against the property of the company that is affected. Contrast the position of a supplier having a contractual right to terminate with that of a landlord who may well have a right contained within the lease to forfeit on a tenant's administration but cannot enforce that right without consent of the administrator or leave of the court (IA 1986, Sched.B1, para.43(4)).

A moratorium on creditor actions in this form is only otherwise found in UK insolvency legislation in the case of a company voluntary arrangement (CVA) for an eligible 'small' company where a moratorium pending the creditors' meeting to consider the CVA proposal can be obtained. This procedure introduced in Insolvency Act 2000 (which came into force on 1 April 2003) has however been little used. Following the 2009 Budget, the Government has consulted upon the intention to extend these provisions to all companies and make the CVA more attractive to all insolvent companies.

Advantage 2: Cheap and easy process

The new procedures are also speedy and cost effective as it is possible for the company and/or its directors to appoint the administrator by an out-of-court route. While reforms have also been made to the procedure for appointments by court order, this method still remains relatively time consuming and costly. The introduction of the out-of-court route of appointment has revolutionised the administration procedure and makes it much more attractive to smaller companies, as shown by the rapid expansion in the number of administrations.

As we shall see in more detail in **Chapter 3**, the out-of-court process requires the filing of requisite forms at court. The forms are short and simple to complete, although this should not detract from the serious consequences that arise from the initiation of the process. In the case of a company appointment, or appointment by the directors, a meeting resolving to place the company in administration is required and evidence of that decision needs to be filed. A statutory declaration contained within the notice of appointment (and notice of intention to appoint) is required to be made by someone authorised by the appointor (which will require attendance before a solicitor who is independent and not engaged by the appointor and/or the insolvent company) and the notice of appointment needs to be accompanied by a form completed by the proposed administrators, consenting to the appointment and most importantly stating that 'I am of the opinion that the purpose of administration is reasonably likely to be achieved'.

On filing the requisite notice, the appointment comes into effect. The notice of appointment form is endorsed by the court office with a seal, date and time of filing. It is also open to a qualifying floating charge holder to put a company into administration outside court hours.

Advantage 3: Flexibility and gateway

Together with the administrator, on the appointment being commenced, the directors can consider the best option for the company, be that reconstruction, sale of part of the company's assets, a scheme of arrangement, a CVA, or ultimately, liquidation. An advantage of administration is that it gives the company's key stakeholders time, away from creditor pressure, to find a solution that while ultimately needing to be approved by the creditors, can be flexible in terms of scope and duration.

14

Administration was traditionally viewed as an interim insolvency procedure (i.e. a gateway to another procedure). It should be noted that the reforms introduced by the Enterprise Act 2002 have made it possible that the administration can in certain circumstances lead to the company being returned to its existing management and/or distributions being made to all classes of creditors and/or the dissolution of the company. Administration can therefore be the sole insolvency process used.

Advantage 4: The melting ice cube theory

While designed primarily as a means of enabling company rescue, administration has developed into a process and procedure more readily associated with the sale of an insolvent company's business and/or assets. In only approximately four per cent of cases (according to the survey of Dr Sandra Frisby of Nottingham University) will the company be rescued.

It should be remembered that no matter how efficient the administration process is made, it cannot change the underlying basic prospects of the company and a change of ownership, management or fundamental restructuring of the business is likely to be required. This may well be best effected by a sale of the business and assets to new owners, who can acquire the virtuous elements of the business but rid themselves of the difficulties that have beset the insolvent company.

The sale of a business as a trading going concern is likely to be of greater value than one that is sold on a break-up basis, as a trading business hopefully is able to maintain employment of its staff and retain know-how, contacts and goodwill. Taking a phrase found in US jurisprudence emanating from the corporate reconstruction of Polaroid, the going concern value of the company is however like a melting ice cube: it will reduce. As a result in the US Bankruptcy Code (USC 11 s.363(b)) the court is able to sanction the sale of the business and assets of a company in Chapter 11 proceedings, and company reconstructions under Chapter 11 have all but disappeared, with instead the sale of the company's business occurring often in accordance with a pre-arranged sale, a better price being obtained as the buyer can cherry pick the assets of the company and clean the business of its unwanted liabilities (for example TWA, Enron, Budget Cars, Lehman Brothers and Chrysler).

Administration in the UK post-Enterprise Act 2002 has followed a similar developmental arc. To companies in financial difficulty with a need to restructure, perhaps ridding themselves of unwelcome liabilities (e.g. leasehold premises, litigation claims, and divisions of the business) administration offers a highly attractive process. While the proposed administrator will need to assess whether company rescue is possible and whether the offer to buy 'cherry picked' parts of the business is in the best interests of the creditors as a whole, subject to the exercise of this professional judgment, as we shall see the process can be used to quickly transfer the chosen business and assets to a new corporate vehicle free from those liabilities.

Advantage 5: Means to effect efficient transfer of business and assets

While on the commencement of administration the moratorium is important in providing the company with a 'breathing space', we shall see how the use of administration as a process has evolved in practice. As stated above, only in a small percentage of cases is the company itself 'rescued', i.e. administration used as a process to effect corporate reconstruction resulting in the financial rehabilitation of the company and the return of the company to its owner(s)/ shareholders.

As a result, the moratorium is becoming of less importance owing to the fact that instead of being used to effect corporate reconstructions the administration process is predominantly being used to effect the sale of the company's business and assets. Indeed it now appears that, for a variety of reasons that will be explored further, where sales are conducted by an administrator, the majority take place in accordance with an agreement that is negotiated before commencement of the administration process and is completed on or very soon after the commencement of the administration (a pre-pack).

The sale of the company's business and assets free from liabilities, etc. will mean that any creditor seeking to claim and enforce over assets of the company post-administration, by seeking permission from the court, will be deprived of an effective remedy over the assets of the company. The moratorium thus becomes to all intents and purposes redundant, save that it allows the administrator to determine how the empty corporate shell should distribute the realisations obtained, free from creditor pressure.

Post-Enterprise Act the use of the process in this manner was initially seen by some commentators as an abuse of process, as they argued that administration is primarily designed as a process offering the debtor financial rehabilitation by provision of the moratorium. However, the courts have been seen to recognise the value of using the administration process to give effect to a pre-arranged sale, in saving jobs and offering the best option for the creditors as a whole (see *Re Kayley Vending Ltd* [2009] EWHC 904 (Ch)). It therefore appears at present unlikely that the use of the administration process in this manner will be significantly curtailed.

Despite this the debate rages on, as it is argued that businesses using the process to rid themselves of unwanted liabilities gain an uncompetitive advantage in the marketplace. It should be noted that in some administrations, the effect of the pre-pack administration sale is simply to 'lose' unwanted creditors, while all other creditors of the business (such as key suppliers) will be paid. The apparent advantages in using the administration process in this manner is apparent in the world of football; the Football League rules now provide that a club will be deducted points if it enters into administration, this penalty being imposed to ensure that clubs do not gain at the expense of others by using the process. This kind of 'penalty' cannot however be imposed in the general economy and currently there are calls that the administration process should be reformed again and/or that pre-pack administration sales should be more strongly policed. In January 2009 a Statement of Insolvency Practice (SIP16) was introduced and in the Budget speech of April 2009, the Chancellor Alistair Darling announced that the Insolvency Service would continue to monitor practice and report on the developments of the process at six-monthly intervals.

As we shall see the continued 'use' of the moratorium after sale of the company's business and assets has also been met with some criticism in circumstances where the insolvent company has leasehold premises. The pre-pack sale means that in many cases the prior consent of the landlord to the assignment of the lease to the purchaser and even to the purchaser's occupation of the premises has not been obtained. In such circumstances at best the administrator can grant the purchaser an unlawful licence to occupy while the consent of the landlord to the assignment is obtained. The landlord, despite possible arrears of rent, and despite provisions in the lease entitling forfeiture on tenant insolvency/administration and the unlawful occupation of a third party, is not however entitled to exercise any rights of enforcement without consent of the administrator, or leave of the court. Landlords have argued that this is unfair (see *Innovate Logistics Ltd (In Administration)* v. *Sunberry Properties* [2008] EWCA Civ 1321) but there is at present nothing to prevent the process being used in this way.

While any commercial decision taken by an administrator for and on behalf of the company (such as to effect a sale of the business and assets, whether through pre-pack or otherwise) can in retrospect turn out to be a poor one, provided that the administrator has not acted in breach of duty or negligently in reaching any given decision (IA 1986, Sched.B1, para.75), or caused unfair harm (IA 1986, Sched.B1, para.74) his action is unlikely be capable of challenge. See *Clydesdale Financial Services* v. *Smailes* [2009] EWHC 1745 (Ch) which concerned the removal and replacement of an administrator, although it should be noted that this case concerned an attack on the independence of the insolvency practitioner and the ability to investigate the conduct of the directors properly and fairly after the pre-pack sale; it was not an attack on the efficacy of the pre-pack sale itself.

The disadvantages of administration

Disadvantage 1: Funding

In ensuring that the commencement of an administration process is in the interests of the creditors as a whole (IA 1986, Sched.B1, para.3(2)), as a minimum requirement the administrator must make certain that during the course of the administration, the position of the unsecured creditors is not worsened. As a result, if the administrator takes the decision to continue to trade the business, it should not be at a loss and/or such that it could cause unnecessary harm to creditors.

When allied to considerations regarding the costs and expenses incurred during administration, which are considered below, the consequences of possible action challenging the decision/actions of the administrator (breach of duty, negligence and/or unfair harm) and at very least criticism of his professionalism, will mean that often an administrator is understandably risk averse and will not trade the business in administration unless he is assured of funding and/or indemnified by a third party against possible losses.

In addition to concerns as to possible trading loss, the administrator must also have regard to the company's cash flow position. In effecting a rescue of the business it is a truism that 'cash is king' and obtaining healthy reserves of cash is often a vital first step for any administrator. This is a matter that requires careful planning and discussion with the proposed administrator. If, however, a company pre-administration was in difficulty and trading at a loss/had cash flow difficulties, the administrator will be extremely wary of trading the business post-administration. Indeed the administrator may find that post-administration trading becomes even more difficult with suppliers restricting terms of credit and/or insisting on 'cash on delivery'. With cash flow restricted one of the key difficulties will be for the administrator to ensure that the business has sufficient funding to allow it to continue to trade at all.

The problem in the UK is that often, and particularly for owner-managed businesses, there is no party willing or able to provide funding to the distressed company and particularly one that is in administration. The absence of funding means that if administration is an option, it is better for the administrator to minimise the risk of trading loss/lack of cash flow by selling the business and assets as early as possible. This is, therefore, a significant contributory factor in the rise of pre-pack administrations.

In the US the Bankruptcy Code deals with the problem of funding by providing for 'debtor in possession financing'. This means that with court approval (USC 11 s.364) the company can obtain further credit and the court may order:

(a) the creditor will be granted 'super-priority' over all administrative expenses in respect of additional credit provided;
(b) the creditor will be granted a lien on unencumbered property, or a junior lien on encumbered property; or
(c) in special circumstances, the creditor can be granted a lien in priority over any existing lien.

These provisions provide additional protection for any party willing to risk funding the company in administration, effectively rewarding risk capital.

The absence of any equivalent statutory provision in the UK administration procedure has been criticised and remains a significant weakness of the current system. The question of funding during administration was much debated during the reform process leading up to the Enterprise Act and more recently following the 2009 Budget and subsequent consultation process 'Encouraging

Company Rescue'. The Government, however, has rejected calls for some form of super-priority funding on the basis that, for the time being, it was for banks and other lenders to assess the commercial viability of administration and/or that it might push up the cost of lending generally. The Government felt if the banks were satisfied that there was a need for administration they would be willing to provide additional funding. It has therefore been left to lenders to vet administration proposals and support only those with a sufficient chance of success, in doing so taking a large commercial risk in providing further funding to an insolvent company.

In practice, the provision of funding by a lender to a distressed company will remain unlikely unless the circumstances of the case dictate that the only return to an existing secured creditor of the company will be if the business continues to trade as a going concern. The lender may in those circumstances be prepared to (continue to) fund the company in administration in the hope of finding a buyer for the business. In this type of scenario however, it is often the case that the only likely recipient of any return on the sale of the business will be the secured creditor, who will by this stage be very closely involved in the direction the company is taking and may themselves ultimately be the party that commences the administration process.

The courts have provided some relief for those seeking to fund the administration in such circumstances. In *Bibby Trade Finance Ltd* v. *McKay* [2006] All ER (D) 266 it was held on appeal that an administrator was entitled to deduct as an expense of the administration additional monies that had been advanced by a financer post-administration, which had enabled the company in administration to complete a valuable contract. This the court felt accorded with the flexible approach to administration expenses as set out in *Centre Reinsurance International Co* v. *Freakley* [2005] EWCA Civ 115, namely an expense was recoverable if it was incurred in furtherance of the purpose of the administration.

It should be noted, however, that for many businesses (particularly post-credit crunch) the lack of additional bank support/lending and restrictions on existing facilities are the cause of their difficulties. The bank may consider that its debts are fully secured, irrespective of whether the business is sold on a break-up basis or on a going concern basis. It would not be in the bank's interests in such circumstances to inject risk capital. Meanwhile the other creditors, be they employees, suppliers or customers (i.e. the creditors as a whole), may be greatly affected if the business were to continue through the use of the administration process but have little ability to provide the necessary funding.

Disadvantage 2: Uncertainty as to the costs and expenses of administration

A significant drawback of the reformed, post-Enterprise Act regime has been the continuing uncertainty as to what does and what does not constitute an administration expense, i.e. a cost that will be payable from the floating charge realisations. This issue is of significant practical importance to the administrator, as these costs and expenses are payable in priority to the remuneration that the administrator would receive for taking the appointment. Obviously for all parties the greater the expenses and associated costs of the process, the less attractive it will seem and if administration is used, a pre-pack administration (with no risk of trading costs and expenses) may offer a better, less risky alternative.

Pre-Enterprise Act treatment of costs and expenses was more flexible. Following the leading authority of *Re Atlantic Computer Systems* [1992] Ch 505 the administrator would look to see whether the expense that had been incurred by the company in administration was in furtherance of the administration. If a creditor was dissatisfied with any decision of the administrator as to what did or did not constitute an expense they had the right to apply to court for direction. In opining on whether the cost was one that should be treated as an expense of the administration, the court would look at all circumstances of the case and seek to balance the rights and interests of the individual creditor against the interests of the creditors as a whole.

This practice was called into question following the introduction of IR 1986, r.2.67 (which had been introduced post-Enterprise Act as a necessary addendum required to deal with the unusual situation where an administrator was seeking to distribute to unsecured creditors). The new rule intentionally mirrored the liquidation counterpart (IR 1986, r.4.218(1)). Furthermore IR 1986, r.2.67(4) (introduced by Insolvency (Amendment) Rules 2005, SI 2005/527 as from 1 April 2005) clarified that the costs and expenses of administration, for the purposes of IA 1986, Sched.B1, para.99(3) were as set out in IR 1986, r.2.67(1).

In *Re Trident Fashions Plc* [2007] EWHC 400 (Ch) the court determined that this latter amendment imparted into the administration regime an equivalent treatment of expenses as that which occurred in liquidation (see *Re Toshoku Finance UK Plc* [2002] 1 WLR 671). *Re Toshoku* had firmly established that an expense/necessary disbursement (which in that case was a post-liquidation tax liability assessed on interest that had not in fact been received by the company) was one that was incurred in the liquidation, it was not a matter of discretion on the part of the liquidator; its payment as an expense was an inflexible determination as to whether the expense was incurred or not. In *Trident Fashions*, the court determined that in the case of business rates and other taxes whether or not the administrator 'incurred' these expenses voluntarily and of their own volition was irrelevant. This was taken to mean by many commentators that the courts were not allowed to exercise the flexible balance allowed for by the decision in *Re Atlantic Computer Systems* [1992] Ch 505.

This posed significant problems in the context of an administration; it should be remembered that the administrator has no choice as to whether to perform the contracts and obligations incurred by the company since, unlike a liquidator, the administrator has no power of disclaimer (IA 1986, s.178). As a result the administrator could find that the company in administration continued to incur expenses, which given the opportunity, the administrator would not have incurred. The best example of this is the company's ongoing liability to pay rent in respect of empty premises; as the administrator has no power to disclaim the lease it is argued that the rent continues to be a properly incurred cost and expense of the administration.

This inflexible approach erodes the principle outlined in IA 1986, Sched. B1, para.99, namely that it is only those debts and liabilities arising out of contracts entered into by the administrator (not the company) for which the administrator will be responsible. It also makes administration unattractively expensive and risky (remembering the not unreasonable commercial motivation of an administrator to receive payment for his services).

We shall see later how the issue of payment of business rates by an administrator was resolved by statutory amendment (like a liquidator an administrator is now no longer liable to pay business rates on empty premises). However, the *Trident Fashion* decision has still left open a question of whether expenses such as rent, whether the property was occupied or unoccupied by the administrator, are payable as an expense if incurred by the company, irrespective of the administrator's actions/inaction in incurring that liability.

This issue appeared to have been partly clarified by the decision of the Court of Appeal in the case of *Innovate Logistics* v. *Sunberry* [2009] BCC 164, where it was held obiter that rent arising in respect of an empty property was not necessarily a cost and expense of the administration. The court determined that one would need to look at all the circumstances of the case to do justice to the parties. This marked a possible return to the more flexible treatment afforded in *Re Atlantic Computer Systems* of what does and does not constitute a cost and expense of an administration. However, the case of *Goldacre (Office) Ltd* v. *Nortel Networks UK Ltd (In Administration)* [2009] EWHC 3389 (Ch) in December 2009 made it clear that where a leasehold property is being retained by the company for the purposes of the administration, the rent falling due (including where rent falls due quarterly in advance) is payable as an expense of the administration, the court having no discretion in the matter. It is of note that while the court in *Goldacre* was clearly following the 'salvage approach' as seen in cases of liquidation, an administrator cannot disclaim the company's interest in leasehold property and markedly there was no guidance on what in those circumstances would constitute being retained for the purposes of administration.

As a result of these contrasting decisions there remains considerable uncertainty as to what constitutes an administration expense. This has a knock-on effect regarding the funding of the administration process, owing to the fact that it is unclear what are the costs and implications of the procedure. However, as a result of this uncertainty trading administrations remain unattractive.

Disadvantage 3: Loss of management control

It should be the case that the management of the company is most likely to be able to spot the warning signs of financial distress and acting in the best interests of the creditors it should be the management that initiates an insolvency process. As we have seen, the company and its directors can commence the process easily and at minimum cost. However, when advising the directors of the insolvent company it must be borne in mind that administration will lead to a loss of management control. The administrator is appointed to manage the company's affairs, business and property (IA 1986, Sched.B1, para.1(1)) and can remove or appoint directors of the company (IA 1986, Sched.B1, para.61). Even if they remain in office the directors may not exercise a management power without the consent of the administrator (IA 1986, Sched.B1, para.64).

In contrast in the US, Chapter 11 procedures provide for 'debtor in possession', which means continuing control and management by the directors during the reconstruction process. It is therefore seen as a 'debtor friendly' remedy and one that is perhaps relied upon too readily by management, to provide themselves (as opposed to the company) the 'breathing space' described previously.

Although in the UK the administrator may well delegate back some powers to existing management (IA 1986, Sched.B1, para.64(2)(c) and see also *Re P&C and R&T (Stockport) Ltd* [1991] BCLC 366) management may fear removal from office or in practice exclusion from the administration process. Whether this is a justifiable fear is almost certainly dependent upon the nature of the business, whether the director has a unique skill set or offering to the company (e.g. he is essential to the business for technical business know-how, his contacts, etc.) and what is likely to be the result of the administration in practice. For example, the existing management is most likely to remain closely involved in the process if there is a possibility that the business might be saved, either by trading through its difficulties or more likely if it were to sell to a third party/or to a management buy-out team.

The reluctance of management to hand over control and management to a third-party administrator remains one of the most significant stumbling blocks to the greater use of the administration procedure. It also explains why, when the process is initiated, pre-packs are attractive to an owner-manager/a buy-out team, who will initiate the process if a pre-pack sale (to themselves) can be negotiated and agreed before the process commences. For management in these circumstances this is ideal, as they have the use and advantages of the procedure but never lose control of the management of the business.

Disadvantage 4: Pre-administration costs

One issue that has caused difficulty post-Enterprise Act is the question of whether an administrator is entitled to recover as an expense of the administration the costs incurred in advising and assisting the company prior to the commencement of the administration. Pre-Enterprise Act when a company sought to obtain an administration order it was common practice to ask the court for an order that the costs of preparing the Rule 2.2 Report and the costs of applying to the court for the order should be treated as an expense of the administration.

The position unfortunately became less clear post-Enterprise Act. The Insolvency Service issued guidance (*Dear IP* No.24 September 2005) suggesting that pre-administration costs could either be paid by the company prior to entering into administration or be recovered as an expense post-administration where they had been incurred in completing the Form 2.2B statement (i.e. the statement of the administrator that in his belief the purpose of administration can be achieved). This latter guidance accords with IR 1986, r.2.67(1)(c) which provides for the recovery of 'costs and expenses of the appointor in connection with the making of the appointment'.

This guidance was, however, unclear as to whether pre-appointment advice in its wider sense, such as the costs of investigations that may have been needed by the insolvency practitioner to assess whether the company was suitable for administration, could be recoverable.

In *Re SE Services Ltd* (unreported, 9 August 2006), Norris J held that the costs of assessing whether it was appropriate to commence administration, and thereby those incurred by an administrator in completing Form 2.2B, should be treated as an expense of the administration. This approach was followed by Purle J in *Aldersley Battery Chairs Ltd*, Case No.9003/2008 (unreported, 14 January 2008) and in *Re Kayley Vending Ltd* [2009] EWHC 904 (Ch) by David Cooke J where he went further and made an order that the administrator's pre-appointment costs incurred in negotiating a pre-pack sale could be treated as an expense of the administration.

The approach in all these cases was the same, namely that the recovery of the pre-appointment fees was not as of right (i.e. an expense as per IR 1986, r.2.67(1)) but rather could be obtained following an order (pursuant to IA 1986, Sched.B1, para.13(1)(f)). This order could be made by exercise of the court's discretion after weighing up the advantages to the creditors as whole. In the *Kayley* case this included an assessment of whether the 'balance of benefit arising from the incurring of pre-appointment costs is in favour of the creditors rather than the management as potential purchasers'. In the *Kayley* case, the pre-pack sale had been to a third party and the return to creditors as a whole was improved as a result. Presumably a pre-pack sale to existing management which saves the business but provides no return to unsecured creditors would not find favour with the court.

It should be noted therefore that at the present time for an out-of-court appointment (the majority of administrations) the ability to recover pre-administration costs is limited to costs incurred in completing Form 2.2B and the work associated with that. Without a court order IR 1986, r.2.67 does not provide for the recovery of costs incurred in providing general strategic advice, planning and reconstruction which may lead to a pre-pack. In such cases most work will be carried out by the proposed administrator pre-appointment. As a result, the administrator will still need to ensure he is paid by the company for this pre-appointment work or obtain an agreement from the purchaser that it will pay pre-administration costs in addition to the purchase price for the company's business and assets. In practice, in low value company transactions this is not always possible, particularly if the only purchaser is the existing owner-manager who has no available funds (evidenced by the inability to continue to support the company).

Even where a pre-pack is not proposed the inability to recover the majority of pre-appointment costs may mean that strategic planning of the company's reconstruction will occur following administration rather than beforehand, which may not necessarily be advantageous to the company or its creditors.

Changes to the Insolvency Rules are anticipated in 2010 which will see some clarification on this issue and at least some ability to recover pre-administration costs (including negotiating the pre-pack) as an expense, if approved by the creditors post-sale.

Disadvantage 5: Tax consequences of administration

Post-15 September 2003, a company going into administration is subject to a new tax accounting period ending on the day that the company ceases to be in administration (Taxes Management Act 1970, s.108(3)(a)).

The effect of this provision is to make the administrator responsible for making a tax return for his period in office. Tax arising on income during the period of administration is treated as a necessary disbursement (*Re Toshoku Finance Plc* [2002] 3 All ER 961) and as a consequence payable as an expense of the administration. Where a chargeable gain arises on the sale of a property it is treated as a sale by the company and any chargeable gain is also payable as an expense of the administration (IR 1986, r.2.67(1)(j)).

The tax position in administration is to be contrasted with administrative receivership where such tax liabilities remain with the company rather than being treated as an expense of the administrative receivership.

See **Appendix 1** for a summary of advantages and disadvantages of administration as against administrative receivership.

CHAPTER 2

Who may initiate the administration process and why?

In **Chapter 1** we looked at the questions, what is administration, to whom is it available and when may it be appropriate to use, by reference to its advantages and disadvantages as regards the interests of the company and its creditors as a whole. In this chapter we will look at who might take the decision to initiate the process, and the considerations that each party may have as to whether, and then when, to commence the process.

In brief, the parties who may initiate the administration process are:

- the company and/or its directors;
- a qualifying floating charge holder;
- a creditor;
- an insolvency office holder;
- other parties empowered by statute.

2.1   COMPANY AND/OR ITS DIRECTORS

The initial steps and considerations in initiating the process

Following the Enterprise Act 2002 reforms it is now the case that in the majority of cases the administration process will be initiated by the directors of the company using the out-of-court process of appointment (see IA 1986, Sched.B1, para.22(2)). As we shall see, this out-of-court process offers a quick and easy route to commencement, although it is subject to strict procedural conditions.

It is also possible for the directors/company to apply to court for an administration order, and this route may be followed if one or more of the conditions for the out-of-court route cannot be met (e.g. where a petition for the winding up of the company has been presented but not yet disposed of: IA 1986, Sched.B1, para.25(a)).

The directors may act by majority without the need for a formal board resolution (see IA 1986, Sched.B1, para.105) although a 'record' of their decision needs to be attached to the notice of intention to appoint/notice of appointment that will be filed at court. In practice, therefore, a board resolution should be obtained to avoid doubt as to by whom/how the decision was reached.

In the alternative, the company itself may appoint an administrator (see IA 1986, Sched.B1, para.22(1)), although the company is subject to the same restrictions regarding an out-of-court appointment as are the directors. For the company to appoint an administrator, a resolution at a general meeting needs to be passed. While an informal unanimous decision made by all the shareholders following the '*Re Duomatic* principle' (*Re Duomatic Ltd* [1969] 2 Ch 365) may be treated as a resolution (a provision which may assist smaller owner-managed private companies) the need to attach a copy of the written resolution to the intention to appoint/notice of appointment may make it easier and/or more certain for the owner-managers to commence the process in their capacity as directors.

Before looking at how to appoint we shall consider the factors that should be taken into account by the directors in deciding whether to initiate the process and also crucially the timing of that decision. As we shall see below these key decisions are made in circumstances where the directors also need to have regard to both statutory and common law duties that they owe to the company, creditors and employees.

Despite the limited liability status afforded to the company, where a director is in breach of such duties, legal remedies are available to the company and to the administrator (or other insolvency office holder) that can lead to the imposition of personal liability on the individual directors to compensate the company and/or its creditors. Directors can in certain circumstances (which are outside the scope of this work) also face criminal liability and/or a fine.

As we have seen in **Chapter 1**, in order for the directors to commence the process, the company must first be insolvent. It should be remembered that a company may be insolvent on a cash flow basis (the company cannot pay its debts as they fall due) or on a balance sheet basis (the company's liabilities exceed its assets, taking into account contingent, prospective and future debts). The directors need to think carefully about whether the company can continue to trade in the short term, and consider whether, in the longer term, the continuation of trading in the short term could imperil any later reconstruction of the company and/or cause loss to the company's business (i.e. lead to further creditor loss and creditor dissatisfaction/unwillingness to 'support' the reconstructed business). As the financial crisis progresses there may come a point when thought should be given to the initiation of a protective insolvency measure, such as administration. Plans in this regard will need to be discussed and agreed with any creditor holding security.

If, despite financial difficulty and even possible insolvency, the board determines that it is appropriate to continue to trade, the board should have regard to the following:

1. Where the company may be insolvent the position of the company's creditors should be the directors' paramount concern.
2. Obtain accurate, up-to-date financial information, regularly revising forecasts in light of changing circumstances.
3. Seek to identify the causes of cash flow difficulty and if possible seek to resolve those difficulties by specific, identifiable and measureable steps which should be discussed and evaluated at board level. This may include full and frank disclosure of information with creditors, followed by careful negotiation, hopefully leading to agreed payments plans.
4. The board should meet regularly and carefully minute decisions taken. The frequency of meetings should be increased as the situation demands; in times of crisis this may have to be daily.
5. Meet with and discuss the situation with key stakeholders (banks, lenders, employees, customers and suppliers), if possible and if appropriate obtaining their support to any proposed action. Document any meetings held.
6. Review contracts/orders and commitments; be very careful in taking on any additional commitments and in particular incurring any possible further credit.
7. Seek ways whereby current expenditure can be reduced.
8. Consider the contractual liabilities of work undertaken by the company and whether there are dates and milestones where such liabilities increase or decrease.
9. Ultimately the board should keep in mind the possibility of an immediate cessation of business and/or the initiation of an insolvency proceeding if it is deemed necessary to ensure that possible loss to creditors is reduced.

Directors' duties and responsibilities

Where the company is in financial difficulty, the duties and responsibilities of the directors are brought into sharp focus; failure to discharge these duties adequately may well be met with criticism and even possible civil and/ or criminal personal liability. It is therefore of use to put these duties into context before explaining how directors should act when the company may be insolvent and administration is being considered.

The law distinguishes between company directors involved in the management of a company, officers of the company and non-executive directors. Executive directorship entails more serious legal obligations and responsibilities but it should be noted that all those involved in the control, management and conduct of the business bear responsibility and are subject to personal risk if the company becomes insolvent.

The Companies Act 2006 has codified several of the existing statutory duties owed by a director to a company. Central to these duties is the duty to provide for the success of the company (Companies Act 2006, s.172).

27

This section provides that a director must act in good faith and in a way which is likely to promote the success of the company for the benefit of its members as a whole. In fulfilling this duty the director must have regard to:

- the likely consequences of any decision long term;
- the interests of the company employees;
- the company's business relationship with suppliers, customers and others;
- the impact of the company's operation on the community and environment;
- maintaining a reputation for high standards of business conduct; and
- the need to act fairly between members of the company.

This codified duty expands upon the duty to act in the company's best interests and when taking any decisions (irrespective of insolvency) these factors should be borne in mind. In guidance notes issued by the Department for Business, Enterprise and Regulatory Reform on the interpretation of the new Act (which came into effect in October 2007) particular emphasis was placed upon the need to obtain appropriate professional advice in circumstances of financial difficulty.

An executive director will also owe duties to the company, as set out in his contract of employment. A duty of reasonable care and skill is implied into any contract, in addition to any express contractual provisions.

The extent of a director's responsibility, as defined by contract, will be a factor in determining the standard of care which is to be expected from that director. For instance a financial director will have a greater degree of responsibility for the financial affairs of the company than say its marketing director.

The importance of these contractual duties is that any breach of duty may lead to a claim by the company against the director. This may arise irrespective of insolvency. However, it is often the case that the company would not commence proceedings against a director unless or until there is some issue of financial difficulty. Furthermore, once a company has entered into an insolvency procedure, the office holder (liquidator, receiver or administrator) may take action on behalf of the company against the former directors in respect of any such breach. The Companies Act 2006 also makes it somewhat easier for shareholders to bring derivative actions (i.e. claims in the name of the company against its directors) than was previously the case.

Directors' potential liabilities on insolvency

If the directors of the company feel that the company has become insolvent (on either a cash flow or balance sheet test) the directors are obliged to take all reasonable steps to minimise loss to creditors. This arises from both their common law duty (see *West Mercia Safetywear Ltd (In Liquidation)* v. *Dodd* [1988] BCLC 250) and indirectly from IA 1986, s.214(3), which provides such action as a defence to a claim of wrongful trading (see below).

28

The importance of this statutory obligation is to shift the obligation of the directors from acting to promote the success of the company/acting in the best interests of the company (as discussed above) to 'primarily' acting in the best interests of its creditors. This has important implications and may well cause the directors to consider whether the company should cease trading immediately.

However, it should be borne in mind that cessation of trading (and thereby incurring further credit) is not always in the best interests of the company's creditors as a whole. The directors may consider it appropriate to continue trading, possibly to trade through the company's difficulties (if there is a cash flow problem), or alternatively if it is likely that further funding/capital reconstruction of the company is achievable in the not too distant future, to alleviate any balance sheet problems.

The fact that the directors' decision turns out to be wrong, and the company is unsuccessful in trading through its difficulties or further funding is not obtained, does not necessarily lead to criticism of the directors' actions. What is important however is that the directors are fully informed of the company's situation, take professional advice, regularly monitor the position and meet regularly to discuss it. In doing so they must carefully minute their decisions. If they do so it is more likely that they will be seen to have acted reasonably and have taken a course that any reasonable director in the same position would have taken.

In the course of the winding up of the company a liquidator may apply to the court for a declaration that a person who is, or was, a director of the company should make such contribution to the company's assets as the court thinks fit.

An application pursuant to IA 1986, s.214 can be brought if:

- the company has gone into insolvent liquidation;
- sometime before the commencement of the winding up of the company, that person knew or ought to have concluded that there was no reasonable prospect that the company could avoid going into insolvent liquidation; and
- that person was a director of the company at that time.

The court will not make a wrongful trading order if at the time the director concluded that the company had a reasonable prospect of avoiding insolvent liquidation and took every step to minimise the potential loss to the company's creditors. The test to be applied to the director is an objective test but will also take into account the general knowledge, skill and experience of the director. It is therefore both an objective and a subjective test.

Directors cannot rely on the fact that they have been provided with poor financial information, possibly arising out of the nature of their accounting system. Directors should obtain the necessary degree of financial information appropriate to the circumstances. Directors are not entitled to rely on their own lack of skill and inexperience.

It should be noted that the extent of the contribution that a director of the company may be ordered to pay is a matter at the court's discretion. As a starting point the court may look at the depletion of company's net assets occurring between the date that the directors should have concluded that the company could not have avoided insolvent liquidation and the date that it entered into an insolvency process. The award is intended to be not punitive but compensatory and the directors' liability is several and not joint.

If in the course of the winding up of the company it appears that any business of the company has been carried on with an intent to defraud creditors or for any fraudulent purpose, the court may on application of the liquidator declare that any person who has been knowingly a party to this should make such contribution to the company's assets as the court thinks fit.

Fraudulent trading (IA 1986, s.213) is significantly more difficult to prove than wrongful trading as there needs to be proof of actual intent to defraud, actual dishonesty involving moral blame, wilful blindness or reckless indifference.

During the course of the winding up of the company, if it appears that a director of the company or person who has taken part in the promotion, formation and management of the company has misapplied, retained or become accountable for monies or property of the company or been guilty of any misfeasance or breach of fiduciary or other duty in relation to the company, the court may on application of the liquidator order that person to repay, restore or account for money or to contribute to the company's assets as it thinks fit (IA 1986, s.212).

This statutory remedy is not a bar to the general common law remedies for breach of contract or breach of duty of care/breach of fiduciary duty. It is however a speedy and convenient way to proceed in the case of company insolvency, in order to seek a contribution to assets from directors.

The court has the power to disqualify an individual from holding the post of director of a company. Proceedings can only be commenced by the Secretary of State for Business, Innovation & Skills (BIS) (formerly the Department of Trade and Industry).

Proceedings will be taken where the directors disqualification unit of BIS considers that a report made by a liquidator, receiver or administrator as to the conduct of the directors in the case of a corporate insolvency shows that such conduct merits disqualification. A person may be disqualified for a period of 2–15 years; there are a number of grounds for disqualification but most common is where there is a finding by the court of the director's unfitness.

Proceedings by BIS are quite separate from proceedings that may be taken by the administrator, although the reasons for a finding of unfitness may well overlap, e.g. a finding of wrongful trading.

Alternative options available to company in distress

There are many different reasons for a business finding itself in financial difficulty. The most common situation for distressed companies is that they have (or will) run out of cash. This does not necessarily mean the company is insolvent (based on the balance sheet test) and that a formal insolvency procedure is inevitable. Instead steps can be taken to alleviate the problems faced by the business to avoid a formal insolvency process. Informal arrangements can be agreed with creditors, ranging from an individual creditor giving additional time for payment, to an agreed schedule of reduced repayments over time with a number of creditors. Furthermore, restructuring of the business can occur through operational turnaround, cost-cutting measures, refinancing, the provision of additional capital or the sale of certain assets.

Where the company's assets are subject to security, the co-operation of the secured lender is often an essential ingredient to any reconstruction of the business. Ultimately if co-operation is not forthcoming, or agreement cannot be reached, then refinancing and substitution for a new lender may be the company's only option. Options to restructure and potentially refinance a company can be explored in a number of ways, including the offering of equity for debt, consolidation of debt or asset-based finance agreements.

The company can also consider the engagement of a turnaround consultant or employment of a restructuring officer, who can provide hands-on assistance in the restructuring of the business. Such individuals may often instigate a process of identifying and then analysing the problems of the business and planning the reconstruction of it.

Before proceeding on such measures however, the key is to stabilise the business by improving cash flow, which may involve reducing stock levels, improving the debtor profile, reducing staffing costs or other expenditure. It is a trite point but 'cash is king' and with improved cash flow and stability, the company can move forward to plan and implement more significant reconstruction of the business.

If informal reconstruction is not possible formal insolvency measures may need to be considered. In addition to administration the following alternative corporate insolvency processes are available.

(1)   Company voluntary arrangement

In the absence of an informal agreement with creditors it may be appropriate to consider a company voluntary arrangement (CVA). A CVA is a statutory form of binding agreement between the company and its creditors. There is no requirement that the company be insolvent or be unable to pay its debts in order for a CVA to be proposed, although this is likely.

The CVA proposal is made by the directors of the company and put to the company and its creditors. At its simplest, it is a deal between the company and its creditors by nature of a contract. However, it should be remembered that the creditors are bound by the terms of the CVA even if they have not accepted those terms or even voted, hence strictly it is a statutory binding rather than a contract. There is a requirement to obtain the agreement of 75 per cent in value of the unsecured creditors voting at the meeting.

(2) Liquidation

Voluntary liquidation commenced by the members of the company results in the realisation of the company's assets and then distribution of the cash proceeds to creditors in an order of priority as set out in statute.

Compulsory liquidation by a court order may be initiated by the company, or its creditors, following a petition for the winding up of the company.

Liquidation is a collective process carried out for the benefit of all creditors and the winding up of the company is the beginning of its end as, following distribution of the proceeds of sale, the company will be dissolved and struck off the register of companies.

(3) Scheme of arrangement

A scheme of arrangement is a court-approved agreement between a company, its shareholders and creditors.

Provisions dealing with a Companies Act scheme of arrangement are contained in Companies Act 2006, ss.895–901.

The procedure is of great use in large complex reconstructions, offering flexibility and an ability to deal with a wide range of stakeholders. Though the scheme is ultimately approved by the court, meetings are first convened with prior court approval with the creditors/members of the same class and interest, each class being required to approve the proposed scheme by a 75 per cent majority.

Timing of the decision process

If the directors of the company have determined that the company is insolvent and have received suitably qualified professional advice that the purpose of administration is reasonably likely to be achieved then they can move forward to consider when to commence the process.

The timing of the commencement of the process will be dependent on:

(a) finding an insolvency practitioner prepared to act;
(b) a cost/benefit analysis for the company and its creditors as a whole, of administration as against alternative solutions/insolvency processes;
(c) getting 'buy in' from key stakeholders (e.g. secured creditors and key creditors such as landlords, Her Majesty's Revenue and Customs (HMRC) and suppliers);
(d) being ready for administration: namely ensuring funding is available during the administration process and/or possibly finding a buyer.

As we shall see the process cannot be commenced without an insolvency practitioner agreeing to act and providing a statement (in Form 2.2B) to court that he is authorised to act as an insolvency practitioner and that in his opinion the purpose of administration is reasonably likely to be achieved.

Although this is a simple statement, its provision should not be undertaken lightly. In reaching an opinion the insolvency practitioner will need to have satisfied himself, based on the information he has seen and the meetings held with the directors, that the purpose of administration is reasonably likely to be achieved and that this is 'best advice'. Prior to the Enterprise Act reforms the application to court needed to be accompanied by a so-called 'Rule 2.2 Report' from an insolvency practitioner (generally the proposed administrator) evidencing that administration was in the best interests of the creditors as a whole. This report would often provide an estimated financial comparison between administration and other processes, in providing justification for the order being sought. While this formality is no longer required, this type of exercise should still be undertaken by the insolvency practitioner as part of his advice to the directors. In turn the directors can take comfort that they have acted in the proper discharge of their duties to the company and its creditors by pointing to such advice having been sought.

Obtaining such advice will take time and in practice the directors may feel it important to speak to a number of different insolvency practitioners. They may have a different strategy to tackle the company's financial difficulties, possess different depths of resources and cost base proportionate to the debtor company's, all of which are factors that should be borne in mind in reaching a decision as to whom to appoint.

Once an insolvency practitioner is retained by the company to advise, it is often the case that they will outline the plans for the company to key stakeholders. Obtaining support may be vital to achieve the purpose of administration, although one has to be careful to ensure that prior disclosure does not lead to precipitous action by creditors. For example, a supplier may be key to the business and the proposed administrator may feel it appropriate to ensure that the supplier will continue to support the business when it is in administration. The supplier is not compelled to assist and may, on hearing of the plan, withdraw credit terms, refuse to supply and if applicable seek to enforce any retention of title. Actions by landlords and HMRC (such as forfeiture and/ or distraint) may also follow if they learn of the company's difficulties and act before a moratorium comes into effect on the commencement of the process. As a result, it may be the case that the insolvency practitioner considers it is not appropriate to approach certain stakeholders prior to the commencement of the process.

As we shall see, any creditor with a floating charge must be given notice of the company's intention to commence administration. In practice any creditor with fixed charge security over significant company assets is also likely to be approached by the proposed administrator as part of the pre-planning stage, as on appointment the administrator cannot deal with these assets without consent (or leave of the court). Consequently, as a matter of form and practice the major secured creditors holding fixed charges are also likely to be approached, although often the company's principal lenders are likely to have both fixed and floating charge security in any event.

Lastly, the success of the administration will be dependent on ensuring adequate cash flow/funding during the process. If there is a risk that the administration process will deplete available assets then funding/indemnities will need to be obtained to ensure that the process will not worsen the creditor's position. As has been discussed in **Chapter 1**, this risk of worsening the creditors' position has led to the current preponderance of pre-pack administration sales. As a result, an administration often will not be commenced until a buyer is found and negotiations regarding the purchase of the company's business and assets are concluded.

2.2 QUALIFYING FLOATING CHARGE HOLDER

Initial steps and considerations in initiating process

The holder of a qualifying floating charge in respect of the company's property may appoint an administrator by an out-of-court route (IA 1986, Sched.B1, para.14(1)). As we shall see in **Chapter 3** such an appointment is subject to a number of procedural conditions.

It should be noted that a creditor with fixed charge security cannot appoint an administrator other than by application to court. In modern forms of security it is however often the case that the lender obtains both fixed and floating charge security in order to have available a number of options in the event of a borrower's default, or possible financial difficulty of the borrower that may imperil the lender's security.

In deciding whether to appoint an administrator the lender will have regard to the nature of the security possessed and assess what method will be in its best interests.

The choice of the method to be adopted is dependent on the nature of the security, although where a loan is 'fully secured' over both specific property and over the entire undertaking of the corporate borrower, the lender will assess which method is in its best interests – speed, efficiency, control and cost all being factors to be considered. This means that although each of the methods outlined below may be available, with each having its own distinct advantages and disadvantages, the best option to be pursued by the secured creditor will depend on the specific facts arising from the circumstances of the borrower's financial distress.

Alternative options available to secured creditors

The principal methods of realising security are:

(a) the exercise of power of sale, or sale as mortgagee in possession;
(b) receivership (where the lender possesses fixed charge security, or following court appointment);
(c) administrative receivership (where the lender possesses a floating charge created prior to 15 September 2003 or where it falls within one of the limited exemptions. See **Appendix 1** – Summary 2);
(d) administration (where the lender possesses a qualifying floating charge).

(1) Mortgagee in possession

Theoretically a mortgagee is entitled to possession of a mortgaged property irrespective of borrower default. In reality the mortgage deed will however make it clear that the right to possession will only be exercised in specific instances. It should be noted that it is only in respect of residential property that the mortgagee's right to obtain possession is restricted by the occupier's statutory rights to seek a court order to adjourn, stay or suspend possession (note, however, that *Horsham Properties Group Ltd* v. *Clark* [2008] EWHC 2327 (Ch) confirmed that the mortgagee's power of sale may be exercised without court order, which may lead to statutory reform in this area of law).

A secured creditor may also be able to sell under the power of sale contained within any charge. However, this may be subject to the borrower's/company's continuing possession/occupation of property, which may not of course satisfy a purchaser.

As soon as the mortgagee takes possession by court order or by peaceable re-entry, the mortgagee is subject to a wide variety of legal duties, including the following:

(a) a duty to account to the mortgagor, to account for any surplus on the sale/income when in possession. This extends to a duty to account for what the mortgagee ought to have received had it managed the property with due diligence. On sale the mortgagee is under a duty to obtain the best price reasonably available;
(b) a liability for waste/repair: the mortgagee is under a duty not to damage or destroy the property and is under a positive duty to maintain and keep it in good repair;
(c) liabilities under leasehold covenants: if the property is subject to a lease, the mortgagee is liable to the tenant for covenants under any tenancy agreement;
(d) direct responsibility for costs and expenses incurred during possession, e.g. business rates, costs to secure the premises, insurance, etc.

As a result of the above wider duties and obligations, it is generally felt inadvisable to realise security by obtaining possession of the property if it is to be held for any length of time and needs to be carefully managed and/or where the borrower is being unco-operative. Clearly it is not an appropriate remedy where there are wider issues arising from the borrower's corporate status that entail the need to take control of the entire borrower's business as opposed to a property subject to a charge.

(2) Receivership

A receiver may be appointed under the provisions of a fixed charge or a floating charge, or a combination of both (see **Appendix 1** – Guide to Procedure 1: Appointment of a receiver).

A fixed charge is one that applies to ascertained and definite property, which cannot be dealt with except with consent of the chargee. A receiver may be appointed pursuant to the terms of the fixed charge and depending on the nature of the appointment may be termed a 'private', 'extra-judicial', fixed charge or Law of Property Act (LPA) receiver. The receiver's powers are derived from the charge documentation and the individual(s) appointed may be a receiver of the property of a company, or a receiver and manager of the property of a company.

A floating charge is a type of security peculiar to corporate borrowers, being an equitable charge on assets for the time being of a going concern, floating over the property that it is intended to affect, until some event occurs or act is done which causes it to settle and fasten on the property that is the subject of the charge. A receiver appointed pursuant to the terms of a floating charge over the whole or substantially the whole of the company's property will be an administrative receiver. Since the Enterprise Act 2002 the chargee's power to appoint an administrative receiver has been greatly curtailed.

A receiver may also be appointed by the court and the purpose and functions of a court-appointed receiver will very much depend on the particular context in which he is appointed (e.g. generally where assets are in dispute and/or imperilled). It would be extremely rare for a secured creditor to need to use this remedy and hence this form of receivership will not be dealt with in this book.

The principal characteristic of receivership is that the receiver's primary obligation and duty is to the appointor (*Downsview Nominees Ltd* v. *First City Corporation* [1993] AC 295). Receivers are appointed to realise the security of the appointor (*Gomba Holdings (UK) Ltd* v. *Homan* [1986] 1 WLR 1301, Hoffmann J: 'his primary duty is to realise the assets in the interest of the debenture holder, and his powers of management are really ancillary to that duty'). A receiver is therefore under no obligation to continue to trade a business to see if it can be rescued and need only act in good faith in exercising a power of sale; he need not obtain the best possible price (*Cuckmere Brick Co* v. *Mutual Finance* [1971] 2 All ER 633, CA).

A receiver does owe a duty of skill and care to the company (*Medforth* v. *Blake* [1999] 3 All ER 97), to other secured creditors (*Midland Bank Ltd* v. *Joliman Finance Ltd* (1967) 203 EG 1039, ChD, Lane J) and to a guarantor (*Standard Chartered Bank Ltd* v. *Walker* [1982] 1 WLR 1410). Importantly, however, there is no general duty owed to the unsecured creditors of the company (*Northern Development (Holdings) Ltd* v. *UDT Securities* [1977] 1 All ER 747; *Lathia* v. *Dronsfield Bros* [1987] BCLC 321; *Charalambous* v. *B&C Associates* [2009] EWHC 2601 (Ch)) absent some 'special relationship'.

In contrast an administrator, whether appointed by a floating charge holder or otherwise, owes his primary obligation and duty to the creditors as a whole (IA 1986, Sched.B1, para.3(2)). An administrator must carry out his functions to fulfil the statutory purpose of administration. In exercising this function his actions could conflict with the interests of the secured creditor, e.g. rescuing the company may not be in the secured creditor's commercial interests, as it may postpone enforcement of the security – repayment of the secured debt.

On the secured creditor appointing an administrator, the choice and motivation for the appointment may be challenged (IA 1986, Sched.B1, para.81(2) – improper motive). The likelihood of the secured creditor's appointee being removed from office is, however, remote (as yet there has been no reported case).

Expenses of the administration are recoverable from the floating charge realisations; these could include tax on income (*Re Toshoku Finance UK Plc* [2002] UKHL 6) and payment of non-domestic rates (*Exeter City Council* v. *Bairstow* [2007] EWHC 400 (Ch)) (although following this case legislation was enacted which provides that an administrator is not liable to pay business rates as a cost and expense of the administration where the premises are unoccupied).

While a receiver's costs will also be borne from the realisations (generally set as an agreed percentage up to five per cent), the receiver's role is more limited and control of those expenses (including remuneration) rests with the secured creditor. In the case of an administration, the unsecured creditors will set the rates of remuneration, unless no distribution is likely to be made to them, in which case approval is provided by the secured and preferential creditors alone.

Capital gains arising on the sale of company property are also now treated as an expense of the administration and therefore borne from floating charge realisations (IR 1986, r.2.67(1)(j) from 15 September 2003). This contrasts with the pre-Enterprise Act position where sales by either an administrative receiver or an administrator were treated as company gains, which were unsecured claims in any subsequent liquidation.

The role of the creditors and particularly the creditors' committee is central to agreeing the proposals for administration and determining how the administrator exercises his functions in accordance with the proposals. While an administrative receiver may form a creditors' committee, the committee has no power or specific function unless agreed by the administrative receiver.

Despite the above there are in certain circumstances very good reasons for considering the appointment of an administrator.

On appointment, a moratorium comes into effect preventing creditors (including landlords) from exercising certain rights against the borrower company without consent of the administrator or permission of the court.

The administrator enjoys very wide powers of management and control over the borrower company which enables the efficient continuation of the borrower's business during the administration period. The existing management of the borrower company can be retained during the process or replaced. These powers also mean that the administrator can if necessary compel directors to assist in investigations and general enquiries, obtain company documentation from the borrower and, if necessary, from third parties.

Administration is a flexible remedy and can result in the company being rescued, or the sale of the business and/or assets of the company on a 'going concern' basis which generally will realise significantly greater value than a sale on a break-up basis. It can however be used solely as a means to realise the secured creditor's interest. Its flexibility means that the process can develop according to changing circumstances and it is adaptable enough to be used in more innovative methods of dealing with problem assets, such as transfer to a special purpose vehicle (SPV) of the lenders' choosing.

See **Appendix 1** – Summary 1.

Timing of the decision

A qualifying floating charge holder (QFCH) has the ability to appoint an administrator after application to the court, or where the directors/company have given notice of intention to appoint and within five days of this notice the QFCH elects to nominate an alternative insolvency practitioner as administrator, or more likely pursuant to its own right to appoint out of court.

As the Enterprise Act 2002 has removed the right for most qualifying floating charge holders to appoint an administrative receiver in respect of post-15 September 2003 security (see **Appendix 1** – Summary 2), the legislature has amended the provisions regarding the purpose of administration to include 'realising property in order to make a distribution to one or more secured or preferential creditors' (IA 1986, Sched.B1, para.3(1)(c)). If this is the only remaining objective capable of achievement, then the administrator may act in a manner which need not be in the interests of the creditors as a whole, but must not act in a way which unnecessarily harms the interests of the creditors as a whole (IA 1986, Sched.B1, para.3(4)(b)).

A floating charge holder may not appoint an administrator by an out-of-court route:

(a) without first giving two clear days' written notice to the holder of any prior floating charge, where the holder of the prior floating charge has an entitlement to appoint an administrator or administrative receiver. The prior floating charge holder may however give consent, therefore dispensing with the need to give two days' notice (IA 1986, Sched.B1, para.15(1)(b));

(b) where the floating charge is not enforceable (IA 1986, Sched.B1, para.16);

(c) where the company is in voluntary liquidation (IA 1986, Sched.B1, para.86 – note that where voluntary liquidation is proposed notice must now be provided to any qualifying floating charge holder);

(d) where a provisional liquidator has been appointed (IA 1986, Sched.B1, para.17(a));

(e) where an administrative receiver is in office (IA 1986, Sched.B1, para.17(b));

(f) where an administrator is in office (IA 1986, Sched.B1, para.7).

It should also be remembered that the floating charge holder's power to appoint an administrator out of court arises only if there has been a default in the terms of the security and this is an event that entitles the floating charge holder to enforce the charge. However, the circumstances of default in the terms of security documentation are very widely drawn and a charge holder can find an ability to realise their security in most cases. Importantly, the company need not be insolvent in order for the QFCH to appoint. The timing of the decision to appoint can entirely suit the interests of the secured creditor alone. This commercial decision cannot be impeached.

In circumstances where the floating charge holder has not exercised their right to enforce security/appoint an administrator and the company has passed into compulsory or voluntary liquidation, the floating charge holder cannot appoint via an out-of-court route but may seek the appointment of an administrator by application to the court (IA 1986, Sched.B1, para.37). An application for an order should also be made where there is some doubt as to the validity of the floating charge (the provisions of IA 1986, s.245 should be reviewed in this context).

2.3   A CREDITOR

A creditor (including a contingent and future/prospective creditor) may apply to court for an administration order to be made in respect of a company (IA 1986, Sched.B1, para.12(1)(c)). An application can also be made by a number of creditors and if so, these creditors must be identified (IR 1986, r.2.3(4)).

As we have just seen, a creditor may also be a secured creditor and/or a floating charge holder, although this is likely only where there is some doubt as to the validity of the security (e.g. the provisions of IA 1986, s.245 may cause concern).

If there is a genuine and serious dispute to the debt claimed by the creditor an order will not be made (see *Re British American Racing (Holdings) Ltd* [2005] BCC 110 and *Corbett* v. *Nysir UK Ltd* [2008] EWHC 2670 (Ch)). If a judgment has been entered/demand has been made and the sum is payable forthwith and there is no dispute as to the debt then there will be little problem in satisfying the condition that the company is unable to pay its debts. Where a judgment had been obtained the court will view this as an undisputed debt even if it is subject to an appeal. In exercising its discretion however, the court may take into account the appeal in deciding whether to make the administration order, or adjourn/stay the application pending appeal. As administration is a collective insolvency process, it should be noted that if it was felt that, irrespective of the appeal against the judgment, the company was insolvent on some basis (cash flow or balance sheet), and it was in the best interests of the creditors as a whole, an order would be likely to be made.

The court will however view the motive of a creditor very carefully in determining whether or not to make an order. In *Re Professional Computer Group Ltd* [2009] BCC 323 the issue of motive was considered; the court rejected a creditor's application for costs to be borne by the insolvent estate where that creditor had unsuccessfully opposed the making of an administration order and instead ordered costs to be paid by that creditor. See also *Re Colt Telecom Group Plc (No.2)* [2003] BPIR 324 for an example of an unsuccessful application by a creditor with a future/contingent debt (see **3.1** below for further details).

2.4 AN INSOLVENCY OFFICE HOLDER

A liquidator of a company (IA 1986, Sched.B1, para.38(1)) or supervisor of a company voluntary arrangement (IA 1986, s.7(4)(b)) may apply to court for an administration order to be made in respect of the company.

In rare circumstances the liquidator may feel that the company can in fact be rescued, all creditors paid and the company returned to its members (and management). This would require a significant change in circumstances following the commencement of the winding up.

2.5 MAGISTRATES' COURT/FINANCIAL SERVICES AUTHORITY

The justices' chief executive of a magistrates' court in the exercise of the power conferred by Magistrates' Courts Act 1980, s.87A may apply for an administration order in respect of a company where a fine has been imposed (IA 1986, Sched.B1, para.12(1)(d)).

In certain circumstances, the Financial Services Authority (FSA) may apply for an administration order to be made pursuant to its regulatory role in the conduct and management of financial service companies (Financial Services and Markets Act 2000, s.359).

CHAPTER 3

Commencement of administration process

In **Chapter 2** we looked at who may initiate the administration process and examined the reasons and motivations that go into making the decision to appoint. In this chapter we shall look at how the process is commenced.

The methods by which a person may be appointed an administrator of a company are:

- by virtue of an administration order of the court (IA 1986, Sched.B1, para.10);
- by the holder of a qualifying floating charge following an out-of-court route (IA 1986, Sched.B1, para.14);
- by the company or its directors following an out-of-court route (IA 1986, Sched.B1, para.22).

In this chapter we shall look at the practice and procedure for appointments under each method.

3.1 COURT APPOINTMENT

Prior to 15 September 2003 all administrations were commenced following court order. The Enterprise Act 2002 as well as introducing the out-of-court routes of appointment, which will be examined in **3.2** and **3.3**, also relaxed some of the requirements needed to obtain a court order and, in theory, has made this a less cumbersome and less costly process. In practice its use will be limited to the circumstances when the company/directors/floating charge holder cannot appoint, or where other parties who cannot appoint out of court (such as creditors, insolvency office holders or the FSA) wish to apply for an administration order to be made.

Grounds for application to court

The court may make an administration order in relation to a company only if satisfied that:

- the company is or is likely to be unable to pay its debts; and
- the administration order is reasonably likely to achieve the purpose of the administration (IA 1986, Sched.B1, para.11).

The use of the word 'satisfied' was addressed in the case of *Re Colt Telecom Group Plc (No.2)* [2003] BPIR 324. In this pre-Enterprise Act case a creditor was seeking an administration order pointing to the likelihood that, in the future, the company would be unable to pay sums due to the particular applicant/creditor. The creditor's motive for the administration was that a sale of the company's business at that time was in the creditor's own best interest. In dismissing the creditor's petition the court held that 'insolvency' must be established on the 'balance of probabilities'. See also *Re AA Mutual Insurance International Insurance Co Ltd* [2005] 2 BCLC 8 where the position is seen to be unchanged post-Enterprise Act.

The wording 'unable to pay its debts' is also found in IA 1986, s.123. It is specifically provided that the reference in para.11 is to have the same meaning as that in s.123 (IA 1986, Sched.B1, para.111(1)). As a result the court can have regard to either the 'cash flow' test (see *Re Business Properties Ltd* (1988) 4 BCC 684) or the 'balance sheet' test of insolvency (see *Re Dianoor Jewels Ltd* [2001] 1 BCLC 450). Importantly in assessing the balance sheet test, regard is to be had to future, contingent and prospective liabilities (see *Re AA Mutual International Insurance Co Ltd* [2005] 2 BCLC 8) but contingent and prospective assets are not to be considered (see *Byblos Bank SAL* v. *Al-Khudhairy* [1987] BCLC 232). The tests are mutually exclusive and while a company may be solvent on one basis, if it is not solvent on the other, a finding that the company is or is likely to be unable to pay its debts will be made.

In making an administration order, the court needs to be satisfied that it is reasonably likely to achieve the purpose of the administration. In reaching this conclusion the court needs to be satisfied that there is a 'real prospect' that the purpose of administration will be achieved (see *Re Harris Simons Construction Ltd* (1989) 5 BCC 11 and *Re Redman Construction Ltd* [2004] All ER (D) 146 (Jun)). More recent authorities have perhaps watered down the concept of 'real prospect' and it has been held that this does not necessarily equate to more than a 50 per cent probability (see *DKLL Solicitors* v. *Revenue and Customs Commissioners* [2007] BCC 908).

The court will, however, still be mindful to guard against the commencement of fanciful, speculative administrations, which could risk worsening the creditors' position. They will also guard against administration being improperly used to simply prevent enforcement action (see *Doltable Ltd* v. *Lexi Holdings Plc* [2006] 1 BCLC 384 where directors unsuccessfully sought to obtain a moratorium to prevent a secured creditor from realising its security over assets at a price objected to by the directors).

Each case depends on its own circumstances but it should be remembered that the court is not equipped to, and is unlikely to, indulge in speculation as to what is at heart a commercial judgment. As a result, in reaching its decision the court is likely to have primary regard to professional (expert) opinion.

As we shall see, as in the case of an out-of-court appointment, an insolvency practitioner in consenting to act, must in a prescribed form (Form 2.2B) state that in his opinion it is reasonably likely that the purpose of administration will be achieved (IR 1986, r.2.3(5)(c)).

Under the previous regime, in reaching its decision the court paid close regard to the so-called 'Rule 2.2 Report' which was provided by an insolvency practitioner (often the proposed administrator) as 'expert evidence' to the court (see *Re Colt Telecom Group Plc (No.2)* [2003] BPIR 324). This report provided specific information (much of which is now to be found in the witness statement that needs to be filed in support of the administration petition; see IR 1986, rr.2.2–2.5) and an expert assessment as to whether the purposes of the administration were likely to be achieved. This form of report is no longer required. As a result, in simple non-contested cases the court may be willing to accept the administrator's statement made in Form 2.2B alone. However, where there is likely to be a conflict (e.g. the company/directors are applying to court because a creditor is seeking a winding-up order) the applicants would be well advised to outline in some detail why it is thought that an administration order is appropriate, why it offers the best option for the creditors as a whole and show that this is supported by professional opinion. This could be achieved by attaching as an exhibit to the witness statement accompanying the application any report or letter of advice provided by an insolvency practitioner outlining his advice to the company.

Ultimately the making of the order remains a matter of discretion for the court. The court will have primary regard to the interests of the creditors as a whole. As a result, even if it were to find that the purpose of administration is reasonably likely to be achieved, if it were found that on comparable grounds other possible insolvency procedures would produce a better result and/or the creditors would be likely to reject the administrator's proposals, then the court might not make an order. It should always be remembered, however, that the cases are fact sensitive.

In *Re Land and Property Trust Co Plc (No.2)* [1991] BCLC 849 an order was refused where the creditors were likely to object to a proposed course; contrast this with *DKLL Solicitors* v. *Revenue and Customs Commissioners* [2007] BCC 908 where the largest (majority) creditor unsuccessfully objected to the order being sought.

In *The Oracle (North West) Ltd* v. *Pinnacle Financial Services (UK) Ltd* [2009] BCC 159 there was a dispute between the directors of the insolvent company and the largest creditor as to the choice of administrator. In this case the court resolved in favour of the creditor, for whose benefit the administration was being commenced. Regard to the interests and benefit of administration to the unsecured creditor was also important in *Re Kayley Vending Ltd* [2009] EWHC 904 (Ch) where the costs and expenses incurred pre-administration in the negotiation of a pre-pack sale were ordered to be paid as costs and expenses of the administration; as the sale was to an independent third party and not the existing management it was 'clearly' of benefit to the creditors as a whole.

Who may make the application?

An administration application to court may only be made by:

- the company;
- the directors of the company;
- one or more creditors of the company (including both contingent and prospective creditors);
- the justice and chief executive of the magistrates' court in the exercise of powers conferred by Magistrates Court Act 1980, s.87(A) (i.e. fines imposed on the company); or
- a combination of the persons above (IA 1986, Sched.B1, para.12(1) in compliance with IR 1986, r.2.4).

The wording of the section seems to prohibit other parties from applying to court. However as was explored in **Chapter 2**, parties other than those listed above, under a variety of statutory provisions, may apply for an administration order. Such parties will bring an application for and on behalf of the company and are specifically empowered to do so by appropriate statutory authority (e.g. a liquidator by virtue of IA 1986, Sched.B1, para.38; a supervisor of a CVA may do so pursuant to IA 1986, s.7(4)(b), see IR 1986, r.2.2(4); the FSA by virtue of Financial Services and Markets Act 2000, s.359).

While the members may, after passing the appropriate resolution, apply to court on behalf of the company for an administration order, individual members are not entitled to apply to the court for an administration order (see *Re Chelmsford City Football Club (1980) Ltd* [1991] BCC 133).

It should be noted that if the application is made by the directors, it is to be stated as being made under IA 1986, Sched.B1, para.12(1)(b), but from the date of making the application it is to be treated for all purposes as if it were an application of the company (IR 1986, r.2.3(2)).

As discussed in **2.3** an application can be made by a creditor of the company.

One or more creditors may apply for an administration order (IA 1986, Sched.B1, para.12(1)(c)) and where there are multiple creditors each must be specifically identified (IR 1986, r.2.3(4)). The court will only make an order if it is satisfied that the company is, or is likely to become, unable to pay its debts (i.e. the debtor company's insolvency) and the order is reasonably likely to achieve the purpose of administration (IA 1986, Sched.B1, para.11). The court will not make an order if there are grounds for belief that there is a genuine or substantial dispute in respect of the creditors' claim (*Re British American Racing (Holdings) Ltd* [2005] BCC 110).

There is some debate as to the standard of proof required to establish the debtor company's insolvency on a creditor's petition, as presumably it will be made in the face of opposition by the company. In *Re Colt Telecom Group Plc (No.2)* [2002] EWHC 2815, a case under the old administration regime, the applicant sought to argue that the debtor company was insolvent by reason of large contingent and prospective liabilities. The court ruled that 'likely' to be unable to pay its debts in this context meant 'more probable than not' and being 'satisfied' was measured on the balance of probabilities. As post-Enterprise Act legislation provides that it must be 'likely' that the company is unable to pay its debts and it is 'reasonably likely' that purpose of the administration will be achieved, it is suggested that a less stringent test applies to the latter than to the former.

Administration application

For a brief overview of this process see **Appendix 2** – Guide to Procedure 2.

The Insolvency Rules that govern the court appointment regime specifically provide that the administration application *shall* (emphasis added) be in Form 2.1B (IR 1986, r.2.2(1)); as a result this form should be used and amended if required.

In completing the application regard must be had to what is the appropriate court in which to issue the application. This may be guided by convenience to the applicant/company and/or regard to efficiency of the court and ability to hear the application quickly. A county court can be used where the company's share capital does not exceed £120,000 provided the company's registered office is situated in the jurisdiction of the particular court. It is common for practitioners, however, to use the High Court because of the court's greater resources, familiarity with the process and ability to check that a winding-up petition has not been issued prior to issue of the administration applications (by attendance at the Companies Court general office to search the central registry of winding-up petitions, although a search by telephone on 020 7947 7328 is now available). This is especially important in respect of an appointment by the out-of-court route where an administrator's appointment by the company/ directors will be invalid if a winding-up petition has been presented and has not been disposed of (see *Re Blights Builders Ltd* [2007] 3 All ER 776).

Practical tips on completing Form 2.1B

The numbers and letters in the list below refer to those as set out on Form 2.1B.

1. Insert the name of the company, the actual names of the directors or the creditor making the application [(a)].

45

Rule 2.2

Form 2.1B

Administration application

Name of Company	Company number

In the [full name of court]	*For court use only* Court case number

(a) Insert full name(s) of applicant(s)

*Delete as applicable

1. The application of (a) _____ being

*(i) the company, in reliance on paragraph 12(1)(a) of Schedule B1 to the Insolvency Act 1986 ("the Schedule")

*(ii) the directors, in reliance on paragraph 12(1)(b) of the Schedule

*(iii) a creditor / a creditor presenting this application on behalf of himself and the following creditors of the company: (b) _____ , in reliance on paragraph 12(1)(c) of the Schedule

(b) Name(s) of all creditors applying

*(iv) a holder of a qualifying floating charge, in reliance on paragraph 35 of the Schedule: (c)
_____

(c) Give details of charge relied on, date registered, (if any) financial limit

*(v) a holder of a qualifying floating charge, in reliance on paragraph 37 of the Schedule: (c)
_____

*(vi) the liquidator of the company, in reliance on paragraph 38 of the Schedule

*(vii) a justices' chief executive for a magistrates' court, in the exercise of the power conferred by section 87A of the Magistrates' Courts Act 1980

*(viii) the supervisor of a company voluntary arrangement, in reliance on section 7(4)(b) of the Insolvency Act 1986

(d) Insert name of company subject to application

2. (d) _____("the company") was incorporated

(e) Insert date of incorporation

on (e) _____ under the Companies Act 19   , and

(f) Insert registered number

the registered number of the company is (f) _____.

(g) Insert address of registered office

3. The registered office of the company is at (g) _____
_____

(h) Insert amount of nominal capital and how it is divided

4. The nominal capital of the company is (h) £_____ divided into ___ shares of £____ each. The amount of the capital paid up or credited as paid up is (j) £_____

(j) Insert amount of capital paid up or credited as paid up

5. The principal business which is carried on by the company is:
_____

6. The company *is / is not *an insurance undertaking / credit institution / an investment

undertaking providing services involving the holding of funds or securities for third parties / or a collective investment undertaking under Article 1.2 of the EC Regulation.

7. For the reasons stated in the *affidavit / witness statement in support of this application it is considered that the EC Regulation *will / will not apply. If it does apply, proceedings will be

(k) _____ proceedings as defined in Article 3 of the EC Regulation.

8. *The applicant(s) believe(s) that the company is or is likely to become unable to pay its debts for the reasons stated in the *affidavit / witness statement in support attached to this application.
(* Delete this paragraph if application is in reliance on paragraph 35 of Schedule B1)

9. The applicant(s) propose(s) that during the period for which the order is in force, the affairs, business and property of the company be managed by

(l) _____

_____

whose statement(s) in Form 2.2B is / are attached to this application.

10. An affidavit / witness statement in support of this application is attached.

11. The *applicant's / applicant's solicitor's address for service is (m)

_____

_____

12. The applicant(s) therefore request(s) as follows:-

(1) that the court make an administration order in relation to (d) _____

(2) that (n) _____

be appointed to be the administrator(s) of the said company

(3) (o) _____

or

(4) that such other order may be made as the court thinks appropriate.

Signed _____

          *Applicant / applicant's solicitor
          (If signing on behalf of firm or company state position or office held)

Dated _____

(p) Insert name and address
of Court/District Registry

Endorsement to be completed by the court

This application having been presented to the court on _____ will

be heard at (p) _____

_____ on

(Date) _____ at

(Time) _____ hours
(or as soon thereafter as the application can be heard)

The solicitor to the applicant is:—

Name _____

Address _____

_____

Telephone No: _____

Reference _____

[Whose Agents are:—

Name _____

Address _____

_____

Telephone No. _____

Reference _____

(b) only needs to be completed on a creditor's application in circumstances where the application is supported by other creditors.

(c) only needs to be completed if the application is by a qualifying floating charge holder. The reference to para.35 is to IA 1986, Sched.B1, para.35 which provides that a qualifying floating charge holder may apply to court (rather than appoint out of court) in special cases, perhaps where the security may be susceptible to challenge or if an administrative receiver or provisional liquidator is in office. The reference to para.37 is to IA 1986, Sched.B1, para.37, which provides that a qualifying floating charge holder has applied to court because the company is already in compulsory or voluntary liquidation, so presenting an out-of-court appointment by the qualifying floating charge holder.

2. Insert name of company subject to application [(d)]; date of incorporation [(e)]; and registered number [(f)].

3. Insert registered office [(g)]. In IA 1986, s.117(6) in regard to the issue of a winding-up petition, the place the company has its registered office is said to be where it has been longest in the last six months. This is of note in view of the practice of cross-border 'forum shopping' where a foreign company may wish to restructure its business under the UK administration process.

4. Provide details of company's nominal share capital [(h)] and paid-up share capital [(j)].

5. Provide details of the company's principal business. To obtain the information to successfully complete this section and (d) to (h) above, a company search should be obtained, including the memorandum and articles of association of the company and the last annual return.

6. Delete is/is not as appropriate. Note, however, that if the company is an insurance undertaking, credit institution, an investment undertaking providing services involving the holding of funds or securities for third parties or a collective investment undertaking under Art.1.2 of Council Regulation (EC) No.1346/2000 of 29 May 2000 on insolvency proceedings then a different insolvency regime will apply and specialist works should be consulted. Such companies will also not be subject to the EC Regulation.

7. Delete will/will not; although again if the EC Regulation does not apply then a different regime is likely to be in operation.

The proceedings [(k)] are main proceedings provided the registered office/centre of main interests lies in the UK. This will need to be expanded upon further in the witness statement in support of the application (see definition of main or secondary proceedings provided below for further details).

8. The applicant must state that he believes the company is unable to pay its debts unless the application is being made by a qualifying floating charge holder in the special cases described above.

9. Insert name and address of proposed administrators [(l)]. As Form 2.2B needs to be attached, the prospective insolvency practitioner must have reviewed the affairs of the company and concluded that administration is appropriate.

10. An affidavit/witness statement in support must be filed.

11. Insert the address for service of the applicant/applicant's solicitors [(m)]. If the directors have made the application then the registered office of the company must be used unless special circumstances described in the witness statement are shown.

12. Insert name of proposed administrator(s) [(n)].

Include any other orders being sought [(o)]; give thought to whether any issue of service needs to be specifically dealt with, any special issue regarding the commencement of administration proceedings or regard to ancillary matters such as dealing with any outstanding winding-up petitions, etc.

Witness statement to be filed with the application

The administration application in Form 2.1B must be accompanied by an affidavit/witness statement in support, which must be filed with the court and comply with IR 1986, r.2.4.

If the administration application is made by the company or by the directors, the witness statement should be made by one of the directors (IR 1986, r.2.2(2)). The director should state the basis of his authority to make the application, perhaps by reference to a board resolution which confirms both the board's decision to bring the application and the authority given to the individual to make the witness statement.

If the administration application is made by a creditor, the witness statement should be made by a duly authorised person, stating the nature of his authority and the means of his knowledge of the matters contained within the witness statement (IR 1986, r.2.2(3)).

If the application is made by a qualifying floating charge holder in the special circumstances of IA 1986, Sched.B1, para.35 (e.g. where there may be some concern as to possible challenge) sufficient details must be provided in the witness statement to allow the court to conclude that the qualifying floating charge holder would be entitled to appoint under IA 1986, Sched.B1, para.14 (IR 1986, r.2.4(3)). Presumably this could cover a situation where a floating charge holder was aware of possible challenge to the validity of the security and sought to persuade the court that the security was valid. It must be remembered that in making the order the court can have regard to all circumstances and, if it is deemed to be in the interests of the creditors as a whole, could make the order on the basis that the applicant was in any event an unsecured creditor (see *Re G-Tech Construction Ltd* [2007] BPIR 1275 for an example of how the court overcame a procedural defect where the notice of intention to appoint was in Form 2.5B as opposed to the correct form of Form 2.10B and where the court allowed a revised application to appoint to be issued).

The affidavit/witness statement in support must contain:

(a) a statement of the company's financial position, specifying to the best of the applicant's knowledge and belief, the company's assets and liabilities, including contingent and prospective liabilities;

(b) details of any securities known (or believed) to be held by creditors of the company;

(c) in a case where a security confers the power upon the shareholder to appoint an administrative receiver or an administrator, a statement as to whether an appointment has been made;

(d) details of any insolvency proceedings in relation to the company including any petition that has been presented for the winding up of the company;

(e) where more than one person is to be appointed administrator, a statement specifying the functions to be exercised for the persons acting jointly and what functions if any are to be exercised by any or all of the persons appointed (IA 1986, Sched.B1, para.100(2));

(f) any other matters which in the opinion of those making the application will assist the court in deciding whether to make an order.

The affidavit should also state whether in the opinion of the person making the application, the EC Regulation on insolvency proceedings will apply and if so whether the proceedings will be main or territorial proceedings.

The EC Regulation on insolvency proceedings (Council Regulation (EC) No.1346/2000 of 29 May 2000) came into effect throughout the EC (excluding Denmark) on 31 May 2002. The Regulation distinguishes between main and territorial (or secondary) proceedings (Art.3). This distinction is vital as main proceedings will have 'universal scope' and 'aim at encompassing all the debtor's assets' (Recital 12). Territorial/secondary proceedings have more limited scope and are subservient to any main proceedings, applying only to the debtor's assets situated in the local jurisdiction.

Main proceedings are commenced in the Member State in which the debtor's 'centre of main interests' (COMI) is situated. Unfortunately the term is not expressly defined, although in the recitals to the Regulation it is stated to be the place where the debtor conducts the administration of its interests on a regular basis. In the case of a company, there is a rebuttable presumption that this will mean the company's registered office (Art.3.1).

As a rule, therefore, for the purposes of completing an application, if the registered office of the company is situated in the UK, it can be assumed that the proceedings will be 'main proceedings'. However, further consideration might need to be had where it is thought that the 'administrative centre' of the company may be situated elsewhere.

The application must also crucially be supported by a statement from the proposed administrator consenting to act and stating that the purpose of administration is reasonably likely to be achieved (in Form 2.2B).

For Form 2.2B see **www.insolvency.gov.uk/forms/englandwalesforms. htm** or **www.companieshouse.gov.uk/forms/insolvencyForms.shtml**.

Notice of application

The application and supporting documents should be filed at court with a sufficient number of copies for service (IR 1986, r.2.5(1)) which will be sealed by the court and issued to the applicant for service (i.e. it is for the applicant to consider by reference to IA 1986, Sched.B1, para.12(2) and IR 1986, r.2.6(3) the number of parties who may require service of the proceedings) (see guidance below on who may need to be served).

As soon as reasonably practical after making the administration application, the applicant shall serve as directed by the court (IR 1986, r.2.6(2), r.2.8) the notice of application and evidence filed in support not less than five days before the hearing date on the following:

1. Any person who has appointed an administrative receiver of the company.

    It should be noted that the court must dismiss an administration application in the case where an administrative receiver is already in office (IA 1986, Sched.B1, para.39(1)) unless the appointor consents or the court is 'satisfied' that the floating charge is liable to be released or discharged under IA 1986, ss.238–240 (transaction at an undervalue and preference) or IA 1986, s.245 (avoidance provisions relating to a floating charge).

2. Any person who is, or may be, entitled to appoint an administrative receiver of the company.

    In general IA 1986, s.72A prohibits a floating charge holder from appointing an administrative receiver unless it is one of the specially listed exemptions to that section (see **Appendix 1** for a summary) or the charge was created prior to 15 September 2003. In cases where a floating charge holder still has an ability to appoint an administrative receiver notice must be given to the potential appointor, who could, providing the floating charge in question is not challengeable (e.g. under IA 1986, ss.238–240 or s.245), decide to appoint an administrative receiver, bringing into effect the consequences of IA 1986, Sched.B1, para.39(1) previously described.

3. Any person who is or may be entitled to appoint an administrator of the company.

As a result of the post-Enterprise Act restrictions in administrative receivership, in most cases the floating charge holder will no longer have an ability to prevent the company entering into administration by the appointment of an administrative receiver. However, provided that the floating charge in question is not challengeable (e.g. under IA 1986, ss.238–240 or s.245) then the charge holder will have an ability to intervene in the proceedings and make an appointment of their own nominated administrator pursuant to IA 1986, Sched.B1, para.36(1). The charge holder's nomination will be accepted by the court unless the court thinks it right to refuse the application because of particular circumstances of the case (IA 1986, Sched.B1, para.36(2)). We are still waiting to see whether there are circumstances in which a court will refuse to make an appointment where it is considered that the administrator would be too 'secured creditor friendly', e.g. where the interests/wishes of all the other creditors would prefer an administrator following an alternative strategy which may be perceived as less beneficial to the secured creditor.

Where the floating charge holder applies to court under this section he is required to produce to court the written consent of all prior floating charge holders, a written statement of consent to act and opinion as to the likely achievement of the purposes of administration from the proposed administrator (in Form 2.2B) and evidence of entitlement to appoint (IR 1986, r.2.10). This latter condition therefore requires the floating charge holder to disclose the nature of the loan agreement, the security and ability to appoint an administrator thereunder.

4. If there is a pending petition for the winding up of the company, the petitioning creditor.

It may be the case that on being provided with notice the petitioning creditor opposes the administration and seeks the winding up of the company. The court will, however, have regard to all the circumstances and the fact that the majority creditor opposes the appointment and has indicated that they would object to the proposals put forward by the administration is not in itself enough to prevent the court making an administration order (see *DKLL Solicitors* v. *Revenue and Customs Commissioners* [2007] BCC 908).

Where there is a conflict between the choice of the company's/directors' nominee as administrator and that of any other party (generally the unsecured creditors) the court will exercise its discretion after review of all the relevant circumstances. Almost certainly both proposed administrators will be seen as competent to act. The court will therefore take into account such factors as the knowledge of the case and work already carried out by one of the proposed administrators compared to the other. In *Re World Class Homes Ltd* [2005] 2 BCLC 1 prior involvement was seen as an advantage. Contrast this with *Clydesdale Financial Services* v. *Smailes* [2009] EWHC 1745 (Ch) where an administrator was removed from office as he was perceived to have been so closely involved in the negotiations of a pre-pack sale that another administrator should be appointed to conduct an independent review. See also *The Oracle (North West) Ltd* v. *Pinnacle Services (UK) Limited* [2008] EWHC 1920 (Ch) where a conflict between directors' and major unsecured creditors' choice of appointment was resolved in favour of the creditors, particularly as the administration was intended for their benefit.

5. If there is any provisional liquidation order in place, the provisional liquidator.

6. A liquidator who has been appointed in another Member State, which are main proceedings in relation to the company.

7. The person proposed to be administrator.

8. The company, if the application is made by anyone other than the company.

9. If a company voluntary arrangement is in place, the supervisor.

The applicant shall also, as soon as reasonably practicable after filing the application, give notice to any High Court enforcement officer (the formerly named 'Sheriff') or officer who to his knowledge is charged with execution or other legal process against the company or its property and any person who to his knowledge has distrained against the company or its property (IR 1986, r.2.7).

The document is served by leaving it with the recipient, or sending it by first-class post (IR 1986, r.2.8(6)). The service of the application shall be verified by an affidavit of service in Form 2.3B, specifying the date on which and the manner in which service was effected. The affidavit of service and a sealed copy of the application exhibited to it shall be filed at court as soon as reasonably practicable after service and in any event, not less than one day before the hearing of the application (IR 1986, r.2.9(2)).

For Form 2.3B see **www.insolvency.gov.uk/forms/englandwalesforms. htm** or **www.companieshouse.gov.uk/forms/insolvencyForms.shtml**.

Hearing of application

At the hearing of the administration application (and irrespective of whether the parties have been served with the application) the following may appear or be represented:

- the applicant;
- the company;
- any one or more of the directors;
- if an administrative receiver has been appointed, that person;
- any person who has presented a petition for the winding up of the company;
- any person appointed or proposed to be appointed as administrator;

- any Member State liquidator who has been appointed in main proceedings in relation to the company;
- any person who is a holder of a qualifying floating charge;
- a supervisor of any CVA in respect of the company;
- with the permission of the court, any other person who appears to have an interest justifying their appearance (IR 1986, r.2.12).

Upon hearing the application, the court may:

- make an administration order;
- dismiss the application;
- adjourn the application conditionally or unconditionally;
- make an interim order;
- treat the application as a winding-up petition and make an order to wind up the company; or
- make any other order as it thinks fit.

If the court makes an administration order it shall be in Form 2.4B.

For Form 2.4B see **www.insolvency.gov.uk/forms/englandwalesforms. htm** or **www.companieshouse.gov.uk/forms/insolvencyForms.shtml**.

The costs of the applicant and any other person allowed by the court are payable as expenses in the administration (IR 1986, r.2.12(3)). The court shall also as soon as reasonably practicable send two sealed copies of the order to the person who made the application. That applicant shall then send a sealed copy of the order as soon as reasonably practicable to the person appointed as administrator (IR 1986, r.2.14).

An interim order may be made where, for example, the company's property is considered to be in immediate jeopardy. In such cases, the court may appoint an appropriate person (who may or may not be the intended administrator) to take control of the company's property and manage its affairs pending determination of the substantive matter. In such circumstances the court may restrict the powers of the directors, or the company (IA 1986, Sched.B1, para.13(3)).

It should be noted that an application for an administration order can be treated as a winding-up petition and the court can make an order winding up the company in circumstances where the administration application is weak and unmerited. This introduces a degree of judicial intervention and some degree of uncertainty. However it is likely that the procedure will be used sparingly by the court, in cases where the company is clearly insolvent and the administration has no prospect of success. In such circumstances it would be preferable to wind up the company immediately, rather than allow a further period of uncertainty (IA 1986, Sched.B1, para.13(1)(e)). An example of the court exercising this power was in the case of a Delaware registered corporation in *Re Ci4net.com.Inc* [2005] BCC 277.

If the court makes an administration order on the application of a qualifying floating charge holder where a winding-up order is in place (IA 1986, Sched.B1, para.37) or on the application of the liquidator (IA 1986, Sched.B1, para.38) then the order shall include necessary consequential directions, including as appropriate the removal of the liquidator from office, provisions relating to release, payment of expenses, indemnity and the handling or realisation of company assets in the hands of the liquidator (IR 1986, r.2.13).

It should be remembered that an application for an administration order may not be withdrawn without permission of the court (IA 1986, Sched.B1, para.12(3)). The courts have been consistent in their attempts to dissuade creditors from using insolvency procedures as a means of debt collection or debt avoidance and an administration application will be regarded in the same light (see *Doltable Ltd* v. *Lexi Holdings Plc* [2006] 1 BCLC 384 where administration was being used to obtain a moratorium and thwart a secured creditor's enforcement action). It is a reminder that administration is a collective remedy not to be undertaken lightly and not to be used to further the interests of the applicant at the expense of the company and more importantly its creditors as a whole.

3.2 OUT-OF-COURT APPOINTMENT BY HOLDER OF FLOATING CHARGE

Following the Enterprise Act 2002 reforms, from 15 September 2003 the holder of a 'qualifying floating charge' may appoint an administrator by the out-of-court procedure set out IA 1986, Sched.B1, paras.14–21; see also IR 1986, rr.2.15–2.18.

These provisions are in large part a replacement of the previous ability of a holder of a floating charge to appoint an administrative receiver (see IA 1986, s.72(A)(1)) and offer a quick and efficient means by which a debtor company can be placed in administration. However, as we shall see there are some risks in using the procedure and disadvantages to the secured creditor (see **Appendix 1** – Summary 1). This may explain why in practice there has been some reluctance to use the process (research indicates that where there is an effective choice between a directors' or floating charge holder appointment fewer than one in five appointments are made by secured creditors).

Does the appointor possess a qualifying floating charge?

As we shall see below, the use of the out-of-court route (as the description implies) involves little or no judicial intervention. As a result, despite the fact that the due process for appointment may have been followed and all parties have assumed that the administrator's appointment is valid, if the security pursuant to which the appointment is made is not a 'qualifying floating charge' then the appointment is void *ab initio*.

To determine whether the appointor does possess a qualifying floating charge there are three important considerations:

1. Does the secured creditor possess a floating charge?
2. Is it a 'qualifying' floating charge?
3. Is the qualifying floating charge enforceable?

Each question is examined below.

What is a floating charge?

The statutory definition of a floating charge (IA 1986, s.251: 'floating charge' means a charge which as created was a floating charge) is singularly unilluminating.

In practice one will find a debenture containing both fixed and floating charges over the borrower company's assets. The statutory definition does, however, confirm that the fact that the floating charge may well become 'fixed' on crystallisation is irrelevant, as it is defined by reference to its nature as at the date of creation. It should always be remembered that whether the company's assets are secured by fixed or floating charge is a matter of substance, not form.

In determining whether an asset is subject to a fixed or floating charge, one can first look to the classic formulation, provided by Lord Justice Romer, in the case of *Re Yorkshire Woolcombers Association Ltd* [1903] 2 Ch 284. In this case a floating charge was described as one:

- which attaches to a class of assets of the company, present and future;
- where that class of assets changes from time to time; and
- where the company is entitled to carry on business and deal with those assets unless or until some step is taken by the chargee.

In the landmark decision of *National Westminster Bank Plc* v. *Spectrum Plus Ltd* [2005] UKHL 41 it was held that in determining whether a charge was fixed or floating, the court should be engaged in a two-stage process:

1. The intention of the parties in entering into the charge must be construed according to the language used. The object is not to discover whether the parties intended to create a fixed or floating charge, but to ascertain the rights and obligations which the parties intended to grant each other in respect of the charged assets.
2. Once this is determined, the court should categorise the charge by reference to those rights and obligations, not by reference to what the parties may or may not have intended. Consequently, if the parties have granted borrower's rights which were inconsistent with the nature of the fixed charge, then the charge cannot be fixed, however so described (see also *Re Brumark Investments Ltd*; sub nom. *Agnew* v. *Inland Revenue Commissioner* [2001] 2 BCLC 188).

Despite the fact that the vast majority of the company's assets may be charged under a fixed charge, providing there is a floating charge over the remainder of the assets of the company, the appointment will be as administrator (see *Re Croftbell Ltd* [1990] BCLC 844 a case concerning the appointment of an administrative receiver). Indeed it is often the case that the floating charges are often no more than so-called lightweight charges 'over all other assets of the company'. In reality, the realisable value of these 'other assets' may be negligible, but it will give the floating charge holder the option of appointing an administrator. If, however, the appointment is under the fixed charge element of the security then despite contrary description the appointment cannot be as an administrator (see *Meadrealm Ltd* v. *Transcontinental Golf Construction*, Vinelott J (unreported, 29 November 1991, ChD)).

What is a qualifying floating charge?

IA 1986, Sched.B1, para.14(2) provides that a qualifying floating charge is one which:

(a) states that IA 1986, Sched.B1, para.14 applies to the floating charge;
(b) purports to empower the holder of the floating charge to appoint an administrator of the company;
(c) purports to empower the holder of the floating charge to make an appointment which would otherwise be an appointment of an administrative receiver within the meaning given by IA 1986, s.29(2); or
(d) purports to empower the holder of the floating charge in Scotland to appoint a receiver who on appointment would be an administrative receiver.

This wide definition therefore covers 'security documentation' which:

(a) specifically refers to para.14, i.e. post-Enterprise Act 2002 terminology;
(b) specifically provides for the appointment of an administrator;
(c) contains pre-Enterprise Act terminology such as a reference to 'administrative receiver' which has not been updated and does not specifically reflect the ability to appoint an administrator; or
(d) relates to a security created before 15 September 2003 where the charge holder will have a choice of appointing either an administrator or an administrative receiver.

The security instrument (debenture, charge or other form of security) must relate to the whole or substantially the whole of the company's property and where the potential appointor holds more than one debenture, charge or other form of security, the assets secured thereunder must together relate to the whole or substantially the whole of the company's property and at least one instrument must be a qualifying floating charge (IA 1986, Sched.B1, para.14(3)).

A charge holder who possesses a charge over only part of the company's assets (which does not amount to substantially the whole of the company's property and/or who does not possess a floating charge) cannot appoint an administrator by an out-of-court route, but can apply for a court order seeking the appointment of an administrator as a 'creditor'.

Could the charge be unenforceable?

It is appropriate, where there is some doubt as to validity of the floating charge (i.e. consider effect of IA 1986, s.245 and invalidity of floating charge created within two years of the onset of insolvency save to the extent of any 'new monies' provided at the time of creation), to use the court application route for appointment rather than use the out-of-court process.

Significant difficulty can arise in circumstances where after challenge the charge may eventually be found to be unenforceable, for instance where it could also be avoided (under IA 1986, s.245), or found to be invalidly executed, or where it could be set aside (under IA 1986, ss.238–239). In such circumstances despite the administrator's appointment and performance of duties, if the charge is found to be unenforceable then the appointment will be deemed to be invalid (*BCPMS (Europe) Ltd* v. *GMAC Commercial Finance Plc* [2006] All ER 285). To avoid the significant difficulties that can arise in such circumstances an application to challenge the validity of the security/ appointment should be made promptly (*Fliptex Ltd* v. *Hogg* [2004] BCC 870). In addition, if the administrator considers that the security may be invalid then it is incumbent on them to seek immediate directions and on application by a suitable party for an administration order (e.g. the company/its directors) the court can effect the appointment of the administrator commencing the appointment from a date deemed suitable to avoid complications.

However, the risk remains that where an administrator is appointed invalidly he will be liable to the company as a trespasser. As a result of this possible liability where an appointment is made by a private debenture holder (as opposed to a major lender/bank), it is not uncommon for the insolvency practitioner to ask for an indemnity, guarantee or other form of security against such risk. It is, however, highly uncommon for a clearing bank or other mainstream financial institution to be willing to give such an indemnity. In these circumstances the purported administrator may need to apply to court for an order that the appointor indemnify him in respect of any liability which has arisen (IA 1986, Sched.B1, para.21(2)).

To avoid these complications and with due regard to the fact that the court will not have reviewed the security and 'sanctioned' the appointment, it is vital that a proper assessment is made by the appointor and the proposed administrator pre-appointment as to whether the security in respect of which the appointment is to be made is one by which the administrator will be validly appointed. See also Forms 2.5B, 2.6B and 2.7B each of which requires the appointor to state that they are the holder of a qualifying floating charge which is now enforceable. Despite the inherent risk of making/accepting the appointment without due checks, it is common practice to find that a 'security review' and assessment as to the validity of the appointment is conducted post-appointment, in some cases some weeks after appointment. Whether this is a hangover from the previous practices which developed in regard to receivership is difficult to tell.

The insolvency practitioner will, therefore, need to be assured (preferably prior to appointment) that the appointor's security is valid and enforceable. In determining this question the following should be considered:

- Does the company have the requisite capacity to borrow and create the debenture?
- Do the company's directors have the requisite power to execute the debenture?
- Was the debenture validly executed?
- Was the debenture registered within the 21-day time limit as set out in Companies Act 2006, s.860?
- Does the debenture secure the whole or substantially the whole of the company's property?
- Has the power to appoint an administrator under the debenture arisen? This may require consideration of the loan agreement, whether default has arisen and demand properly made.
- Is the debenture capable of attack by any party or by the liquidator appointed at the relevant time on any of the following grounds:
  - as a transaction undervalue (IA 1986, s.238);
  - as a preference (IA 1986, s.239);
  - as an extortionate credit transaction (IA 1986, s.244);
  - where the floating charge was created to secure past indebtedness within 12 or 24 months (depending on whether it was granted to a connected person) from the onset of insolvency (IA 1986, s.245);
  - that the transaction was entered into at an undervalue with the intention of putting assets beyond the reach of a person who was making a claim and might otherwise make a claim, or where the transaction prejudiced that party's position (IA 1986, s.423)?

Restrictions on appointment

A floating charge holder may not appoint an administrator by an out-of-court route:

- without first giving two clear days' written notice to the holder of any prior floating charge, where the holder of the prior floating charge has an entitlement to appoint an administrator or administrative receiver. The prior floating charge holder may however give consent, thereby dispensing with the need to give two days' notice (IA 1986, Sched.B1, para.15(1)(b));

- where the floating charge is not enforceable (IA 1986, Sched.B1, para.16);
- where the company is in voluntary liquidation (IA 1986, Sched.B1, para.86 – note, however, that where voluntary liquidation is proposed notice must now be provided to any qualifying floating charge holder who at that stage has an ability to appoint an administrator);
- where a provisional liquidator has been appointed (IA 1986, Sched.B1, para.17(a));
- where an administrative receiver is in office (IA 1986, Sched.B1, para.17(b));
- where an administrator is in office (IA 1986, Sched.B1, para.7).

The floating charge holder is not entitled to appoint an administrator by an out-of-court route if there is already an administrator in office, a provisional liquidator appointed or an administrative receiver in office (IA 1986, Sched. B1, para.17). The floating charge holder has, however, an ability to appoint an administrator where there has been a winding-up petition issued, unless the winding-up petition is based upon a public interest ground (IA 1986, Sched. B1, para.40(1)(b)).

Where an order for winding up has been made the qualifying floating charge holder may apply to court for an order discharging the winding-up order and making in its place an administration order, with such directions as thought fit (IA 1986, Sched.B1, para.37). In contrast, where a company is in voluntary liquidation the only party who may apply for an administration order is the liquidator (IA 1986, Sched.B1, para.38). It is for this reason that five days' notice of an intended voluntary liquidation must now be given to the holder of a qualifying floating charge who at that point retains an ability to appoint an administrator (IA 1986, s.84(2A)).

As we have seen, the existence of any of the above factors may not prevent the secured creditor from applying to court for the appointment of an administrator.

It is also worth noting that as the Enterprise Act 2002 has removed the right for most qualifying floating charge holders to appoint an administrative receiver in respect of post-15 September 2003 security (IA 1986, s.72A), the purpose of administration includes the objective of 'realising property in order to make a distribution to one or more secured or preferential creditors' (IA 1986, Sched.B1, para.3(1)(c)). If it is not reasonably practicable to achieve the other two objectives then the administrator need not act in the best interests of the creditors as a whole, but must act (which will mean there is no possibility of company rescue or return to unsecured creditors) in a way which does not unnecessarily harm the interests of the creditors.

It should be remembered that in general the holder of a floating charge may appoint an administrator out of court only if there is an existing right to exercise the powers granted by the terms of the security (which is likely to be underpinned by a default under the terms of a loan agreement/facility). It should, however, be noted that the circumstances of default in the terms of security documentation are generally very widely drawn and a charge holder can find an ability to realise their security in most cases (e.g. threat of insolvency, possible impairment of security, a petition for winding up being presented).

The situation could arise that the only creditor likely to receive any distribution is the secured creditor or alternatively in the other extreme the company may be in default of the terms of the loan agreement but otherwise solvent (e.g. in breach of a loan to value covenant). In either case the other creditors are not directly affected and in such circumstances the charge holder needs to be able to evidence that the charge is enforceable but does not need to show that the company is insolvent/has an inability to pay its debts as they fall due. As a consequence the appointment procedure available to a floating charge holder remains similar to the power to appoint an administrative receiver.

The process and procedure for out-of-court appointment by holder of a floating charge

For a brief overview of this process see **Appendix 2** – Guide to Procedure 3.

Notice to holder of prior floating charge

A floating charge holder may not appoint an administrator by an out-of-court route without first giving two clear days' written notice to the holder of any prior floating charge, where the holder of the prior floating charge has an entitlement to appoint an administrator or administrative receiver. The prior floating charge holder may, however, give consent, thereby dispensing with the need to give two days' notice (IA 1986, Sched.B1, para.15(1)(b)).

Pursuant to IA 1986, Sched.B1, para.15(1) a floating charge is deemed 'prior' if:

(a) it was created first; or
(b) it was treated as having priority by agreement of the charge holders.

As a result, the appointor needs to have regard to any agreement/deed of priority that has been entered into by the different charge holders as the interpretation of who may be a 'prior' charge holder may be dictated by such agreement.

In the absence of clear express agreement the wording 'prior' floating charge holder is open to some degree of interpretation. Does this mean that the first charge holder in time and/or as per the order contained in the register of charges at Companies House? What is the effect if a charge was created first but later ranked subservient to a later charge by virtue of the agreement in the deed of priorities?

Because of this uncertainty, if the deed of priority has granted the second charge holder priority over the first it would seem sensible to provide the second charge holder (i.e. in time) with a power of enduring attorney from the first charge holder to appoint an administrator.

As there is a delay whilst such notice pursuant to IA 1986, Sched. B1, para.15 is provided, the appointor is able to file and serve a notice of intention to appoint in Form 2.5B. On filing of a notice of intention, an interim moratorium comes into effect for five days (IA 1986, Sched.B1, para.44(2) (b)). There is, however, no requirement for the appointor to file notice of intention, which contrasts with the position of the company and its directors. If notice is given other than in accordance with Form 2.5B a moratorium will not come into effect. An interim moratorium takes effect on the filing of the notice at court, which should take place at the same time as written notice is sent to the prior floating charge holder (IR 1986, r.2.15).

If the prior floating charge holder determines that it does not wish to accept the administrator proposed by the company/its creditors, it may appoint its own choice of administrator or administrative receiver (if the security was created pre-15 September 2003). If it does not consent to the appointment of an administrator (perhaps preferring the company to pass into liquidation) the appointor is left in a difficult position. In contrast to Form 2.9B notice of appointment that is filed by the company/directors after a notice of intention has been served, which provides that the floating charge holder has not replied within five days or has consented, Form 2.6B simply provides that notice has been given. Does this mean that where the prior floating charge holder does not consent, but does not wish to appoint their own choice of nominated administrator, the subsequent charge holder can move to make the appointment? If there is no deed of priority, or it is silent, it may be the case that the prior floating charge holder should move to restrain the appointor from moving the company into administration and/or the appointor may be best advised seeking court direction in regard to the appointment.

Practical tips on completing Form 2.5B

The numbers and letters in the list below refer to those set out on Form 2.5B.

1. Insert the name and address of the holder of the floating charge [(a)].
    Insert names and addresses of the proposed administrators [(b)]. It should be noted that Form 2.2B (consent to act) does not need to be filed at this stage. However for all practical purposes the administrator should have already agreed that it is reasonably likely that the purpose of administration will be achieved and have consented to act.

Rule 2.15

Form 2.5B

Notice of intention to appoint an administrator by holder of qualifying floating charge

Name of Company	Company number

In the	*For court use only*
[full name of court]	Court case number

(a) Name and address of holder of qualifying floating charge

1. (a) _____

_____

_____ ("the appointor"), gives notice that it is the appointor's intention to appoint

(b) Give name(s) and address(es) of proposed administrator(s)

(b) _____

_____ as administrator(s) of

(c) Insert name and address of registered office of company

(c) _____

_____("the company")

in accordance with paragraph 14 of Schedule B1 to the Insolvency Act 1986.

2. The appointor is the holder of the following qualifying floating charge which is now enforceable:

(d) Give details of charge relied on, date registered and (if any) financial limit

(d) _____

_____

3. This notice has been given to the following person(s), who is / are each understood to be holder(s) of (a) qualifying floating charge(s) in respect of the company's property, the said charge(s) being (a) prior floating charge(s) in accordance with paragraph 15(2) of Schedule B1 to the Insolvency Act 1986:

(e) Insert name(s) and address(es) of holder(s) of qualifying floating charge(s) and details of charge(s) held

(e) _____

_____

4. The company *is / is not at the date of this notice subject to insolvency proceedings,

(f) Give details of any current or outstanding insolvency proceedings

(f) _____

_____

*Delete as applicable

5. The company *is / is not *an insurance undertaking / a credit institution / an investment undertaking providing services involving the holding of funds or securities for third parties / or a collective investment undertaking under Article 1.2 of the EC Regulation.

(g) Insert whether main or territorial proceedings

6. For the following reasons it is considered that the EC Regulation *will / will not apply. If it does apply, these proceedings will be (g) _____ proceedings as defined in Article 3 of the EC Regulation: _____

_____

Signed _____
(If signing on behalf of appointor indicate capacity
e.g. director/solicitor)

Dated _____

Consent of Floating Charge Holder to Appointment of Administrator
(Do not detach this part of the notice)

If, having read this notice, you have no objection to the making of this appointment you can indicate your consent either by completing the details in the box below and returning a copy of this notice as soon as possible, and within two business days from receipt of this notice, or by sending details, as set out in Rule 2.16 (5), of your consent in writing to the appointor at the following address:

(h) Appointor to insert address

(h) _____

_____

If your consent has not been given within two business days the appointor may make the appointment notwithstanding that you have not replied.

(j) Insert name and address

(j) _____

_____

_____

being the holder of the following floating charge over the company's property:

(k) Give details of charge, date registered and (if any) financial limit

(k) _____

_____

consents to the appointment of the administrator(s) in accordance with the details of this notice.

Signed _____
(If signing on behalf of a firm or company state position or office held)

Dated _____

Endorsement to be completed by the court

(l) Insert date and time

This notice was filed (l) _____

Insert name and registered office address of company subject to the appointment [(c)]. In IA 1986, s.117(6) in regard to the issue of winding-up petitions, the place the company has its registered office is said to be where it has been longest in the last six months.

2. Give details of the charge, date registered and financial limit if any [(d)]. In doing so the appointor needs to state (supported by the statutory declaration) that the charge is enforceable. This issue has been discussed at length above and may require consideration of the loan agreement/facility as well as the security. Consider whether there been a default making the security enforceable.

3. Give details, name and addresses of any holder of any prior floating charge together with details of the charge [(e)]. This will entail consideration of the register of charges and enquiries as to whether there is any priority given to any other charge holder subsequently registered in time.

4. Insert details of any current insolvency proceedings [(f)]; this would presumably be limited to the existence of a winding-up petition, as where the company is already in administration, administrative receivership, provisional liquidation or liquidation, the floating charge holder cannot use the out-of-court route.

5. Delete is/is not as appropriate. Note, however, that if the company is an insurance undertaking, credit institution, an investment undertaking providing services involving the holding of funds or securities for third parties or a collective investment undertaking under Art.1.2 of Council Regulation (EC) No.1346/2000 of 29 May 2000 on insolvency proceedings then a different insolvency regime will apply and specialist works should be consulted. Such companies will also not be subject to the EC Regulation.

6. Delete will/will not; although, again, if the EC Regulation does not apply then a different regime is likely to be in operation.

The proceedings [(g)] are 'main' proceedings provided the registered office/centre of main interests lies in the UK (see **3.1** above for further details regarding 'main' or 'secondary' proceedings).

The second part of the form deals with the notice to be completed if consent is to be granted by the floating charge holder. Alternatively, the prior floating charge holder may provide written notice of consent but this must comply with IR 1986, r.2.16(5). It is noteworthy that this contains a significant amount of detail and to ensure compliance the appointor may well prefer to use Form 2.5B to avoid ambiguity. In this section insert details of address for return of form/written consent [(h)]. This is likely to be the solicitors acting for the appointor.

- Insert name and address of appointor [(j)].
- Give details of the appointor's charge, date registered and financial limit if any [(k)].

- The endorsement [(l)] is to be left blank and is completed by the court on filing. A date and exact time are given, essential to assess when the interim moratorium comes into effect.

Notice of appointment

The appointment of an administrator takes effect when Form 2.6B is filed at court. The notice should be accompanied by two copies (the original to be retained by the court, one to be served upon the administrator and one for the appointor). Form 2.6B must be accompanied by Form 2.2B completed by the administrator (i.e. the consent to act, acknowledgement that the purpose of administration is reasonably likely to be achieved) and where there is a joint appointment this form must be accompanied by a statement as to the exercise of powers by each administrator (IA 1986, Sched.B1, para.100(2)).

Practical tips on completing Form 2.6B

The numbers and letters in the list below refer to those set out on Form 2.6B.

1. Insert the name and address of the holder of the floating charge [(a)].
     Insert names and addresses of the proposed administrators (with Form 2.2B attached) [(b)].
     Insert name and registered office address of company subject to the appointment [(c)]. In IA 1986, s.117(6), in regard to the issue of winding-up petitions, the place the company has its registered office is said to be where it has been longest in the last six months.
2. Form 2.2B needs to be attached.
3. Give details of the charge, date registered and financial limit if any [(d)]. In doing so the appointor needs to state (supported by the statutory declaration) that the charge is enforceable. This issue has been discussed at length above and may require consideration of the loan agreement/ facility as well as the security. Consider whether there has been a default making the security enforceable.
4. The appointor needs to confirm that the charge is enforceable.
5. Delete as applicable depending on whether there were prior floating charge holders, if so whether a notice of intention in Form 2.5B was filed, written notice provided and consent to the appointment obtained. If notice of intention to appoint in Form 2.5B was filed at court this needs to be attached. As discussed above it is not necessary to file Form 2.5B at court and written notice may simply have been provided; if so, this needs to be attached. In cases where a consent has been obtained, i.e. within two clear business days of service of written notice, the written consent must be attached to the Form 2.6B.

Rule 2.16   Form 2.6B

Notice of appointment of an administrator by holder of qualifying floating charge

Name of Company	Company number

In the [full name of court]	*For court use only* Court case number

(a) Name and address of holder of qualifying floating charge

1. (a) _____

_____

_____ ("the appointor")

gives notice that (b) _____

_____ is /

(b) Give name(s) and address(es) of administrator(s)

are hereby appointed as administrator(s) of (c) _____

_____ ("the company")

(c) Insert name and address of registered office of company

2. The written statement(s) in Form 2.2B *is / are attached.

3. The appointor is the holder of the following qualifying floating charge:

(d) _____

*Delete as applicable

_____

4. The above charge is enforceable at the date of this appointment.

5. + [The appointor has given at least two business days' written notice to the holder of any prior qualifying floating charge(s), and a copy of that notice, *(which was filed at _____

+Delete if not applicable

court on _____ (date)) is attached.]
OR

*Delete as applicable

+ [all the holders of any prior qualifying floating charges have consented in writing to the making of this appointment and copies of the written consents are attached.]
OR

+ [there are no prior qualifying floating charges.]

*Delete as applicable

6. The company *is / is not, at the date of this notice, the subject of insolvency proceedings:

(e) Give details of any current or outstanding insolvency proceedings

(e) _____

_____

7. The company *is / is not *an insurance undertaking / a credit institution / an investment undertaking providing services involving the holding of funds or securities for third parties / or a collective investment undertaking under Article 1.2 of the EC Regulation.

8. For the following reasons it is considered that the EC Regulation *will / will not apply. If it does apply, these proceedings will be (f) _____ proceedings as defined in Article 3 of the EC Regulation:

(f) Insert whether main or territorial proceedings

_____

9. This appointment is in accordance with Schedule B1 to the Insolvency Act 1986.

10. Where there are joint administrators, a statement for the purposes of paragraph 100(2) of Schedule B1 to the Insolvency Act 1986 is attached.

(g) Insert full name and address of person making declaration

11. I (g) _____

of _____

_____

(If making the delcaration on behalf of appointor indicate capacity e.g. director/solicitor)

do solemnly and sincerely declare that the information provided in this notice is, to the best of my knowledge and belief, true,

AND I make this solemn declaration conscientiously believing the same to be true and by virtue of the provisions of the Statutory Declarations Act 1835.

Declared at _____

Signed _____

This _____ day of _____ 20

before me _____

A Commissioner for Oaths or Notary Public or Justice of the Peace or Solicitor or Duly Authorised Officer.

Endorsement to be completed by the court

This notice and the attached documents were filed

(h) Insert date and time of filing

(h) _____

6. If appropriate, insert details and any current insolvency proceedings [(e)]; this presumably would be limited to the issue of a winding-up petition, as where the company is already in administration, administrative receivership, provisional liquidation or liquidation the floating charge holder cannot use the out-of-court route.

7. Delete is/is not as appropriate. Note, however, that if the company is an insurance undertaking, credit institution, an investment undertaking providing services involving the holding of funds or securities for third parties or a collective investment undertaking (see Art.1.2 of Council Regulation (EC) No.1346/2000 of 29 May 2000 on insolvency proceedings) then a different insolvency regime will apply and specialist works should be consulted. Such companies will also not be subject to the EC Regulation.

8. Delete will/will not; although again if the EC Regulation does not apply then a different regime is likely to be in operation.

    The proceedings [(f)] are deemed 'main' proceedings provided the registered office/centre of main interests lies in the UK (see definition of main or secondary proceedings provided in **3.1** above for further details).

9. The appointment must be in accordance with Sched.B1 (see in particular the provisions of paras.15–17 and the completion of all formalities) and the declarant is required to confirm the same.

10. Where more than one person is to be appointed administrator, a statement specifying the functions to be exercised for the persons acting jointly and what functions, if any, are to be exercised by any or all of the persons appointed (IA 1986, Sched.B1, para.100(2)) must be attached. This is of significantly greater importance where the insolvency practitioners are from different firms and the functions split between the two (e.g. management of business/marketing and sale of business and assets/ investigation and report on directors' conduct, etc.). However, in practice, while such agreement may be reached the administrators may not wish their powers to be fettered.

11. Insert details (full name and address) of the individual who is making the statutory declaration contained on the remainder of the form [(g)]. This must be someone duly authorised by the appointor such as a senior bank officer or the charge holder's solicitor. The statutory declaration must not, however, be taken lightly confirming (to the best of the declarant's knowledge and belief) that the charge is enforceable as at the date of appointment, etc.

The endorsement [(h)] is to be left blank and is completed by the court on filing. A date and exact time are given, essential to assess when the administration is deemed to commence.

Form 2.6B contains a statutory declaration. This declaration should be sworn before an independent solicitor (or commissioner for oaths, notary public, justice of the peace or officer of the court, each of whom will charge a fee of £7) and should not be made more than five business days before the date it is filed at court.

The statutory declaration will provide confirmation that:

(a) the appointor holds a qualifying floating charge over the whole or substantially the whole of the company's property;
(b) the charge is enforceable at the date of appointment;
(c) the appointment is in accordance with the Insolvency Act;
(d) notice has been provided to any prior floating charge holder.

The notice must be accompanied by the proposed administrator's written consent to the appointment in Form 2.2B containing a statement that in his opinion the purpose of the administration is reasonably likely to be achieved (see *Re Colt Telecom Group Plc (No.2)* [2003] BPIR 324 and Part 35 of the Civil Procedure Rules 1998, SI 1998/3132 for consideration of administrators' duties of independence and impartiality in providing this assessment). Where there is more than one administrator, a statement setting out the respective roles and responsibilities of each must be provided (IA 1986, Sched.B1, para.100(2)).

The appointment of the administrator will commence when the papers are filed at court (IA 1986, Sched.B1, para.19), the court endorsing on the copies of Form 2.6B the date and time of filing. One of the copies must then be served upon the administrator as soon as reasonably practicable (IR 1986, r.2.17(2)). In practice the filing of the papers is undertaken after close co-ordination with the administrator who will want to be ready to take over control and management of the company immediately on appointment. Where a company has multiple sites this can require careful planning to ensure representatives of the administrator are on hand at each site to explain the process and procedure of the administration to staff, as well as providing an early indication as to what is the intention of the administrator now in office.

Out-of-hours appointment

In exceptional circumstances it is open to the holder of a qualifying floating charge to make an appointment when the court office is closed, perhaps before 10.00 am or after 4.30 pm, or at the weekend, or on a bank holiday. It should be noted that notice to any prior floating charge holder is still required, as is the need to ensure that the administrator consents to act and is of the opinion that the purpose of administration is reasonably likely to be achieved (this, however, is endorsed upon Form 2.7B as opposed to having a separate Form 2.2B).

Form 2.7B must also be accompanied by a notice providing the full reasons why the appointment needed to be made out of hours and why it would be 'damaging to the company and its creditors not to have so acted' (IR 1986, r.2.19(8)).

Form 2.7B contains a statutory declaration which is required to be sworn by an individual duly authorised, so it should be remembered that an independent solicitor should be on hand (overnight/at the weekend) to administer the oath.

For Form 2.7B see **www.insolvency.gov.uk/forms/englandwalesforms. htm** or **www.companieshouse.gov.uk/forms/insolvencyForms.shtml**.

Form 2.7B is then sent by fax to a specially designated number provided by the Court Service (IR 1986, r.2.19(3)). It should be noted that this out-of-court and out-of-hours option is not available to the company and its directors. It is a mark of the flexibility of the UK system that in cases of extreme urgency and importance it may be possible to liaise with the court and the judge's clerk to find a judge prepared to hear an administration application outside normal court hours and possibly even outside a court room (e.g. at the judge's home).

The fax number is published on the Insolvency Service website (**www. insolvency.gov.uk**) and is currently 020 7947 6607. The appointment takes effect on the date and time of the fax transmission. On the next day the court is open, the appointor must file three copies of the notice of appointment that were faxed, together with a transmission report showing the date and time the form was faxed and all necessary supporting documents (IR 1986, r.2.19(7)).

Two sealed copies of the notice of appointment are sent to the appointor who must, as soon as reasonably practicable, send one sealed copy to the administrator. It is of crucial importance to note that an offence is committed if the appointor fails to comply with these provisions and the appointment shall cease to have effect (IA 1986, Sched.B1, para.20(b) and IR 1986, r.2.19(10)).

Court appointment sought by a holder of a floating charge

It should be noted that despite the out-of-court route available to the holder of a floating charge a court appointment may be sought where:

(a) a winding-up order is in place (IA 1986, Sched.B1, para.37);
(b) there is some doubt as to the enforceability of the security and/or ability to appoint;
(c) the company/directors have put forward a proposed administrator to whom the secured creditor objects; or
(d) a prior floating charge holder has objected to the appointment of an administrator.

3.3 OUT-OF-COURT APPOINTMENT BY COMPANY/DIRECTORS

Commencement of process

The introduction of a streamlined method for the appointment of an administrator by the insolvent company, by an out-of-court route, was one of the most radical introductions of the Enterprise Act reforms. Before 15 September 2003, a company could only be placed into administration by order of the court; since 15 September 2003 the new out-of-court route has become the most common means by which administration is commenced. It is also a feature of the post-Enterprise Act insolvency landscape that even where there is a holder of a qualifying floating charge there is often a marked preference that the process is commenced by the company and/or its directors. In some cases the secured creditor may even put pressure on the borrower company to make the appointment and insist that the company and directors choose a particular insolvency practitioner to act as administrator. The reasons for this may be in part cosmetic; unlike during the recessionary spiral of the early 1990s which saw a huge rise in receiverships (i.e. realisation of secured interests), lenders are perhaps now more conscious of the political climate and poor public relations outcome. As a result, it is only in about one in five cases where there is floating charge that the holder will make the appointment.

As we shall see, the ease, low cost and swiftness of the process has made the appointment of an administrator out of court by the company or its directors by far the most popular route of commencement and may in part account for the large growth in the number of administrations.

In **Chapter 2** we examined why the directors may determine that administration is appropriate; we shall now deal with how the company and/or its directors may put the company into administration.

The process is initiated as follows.

1. By the company:
    The members need to pass an appropriate (ordinary) resolution at a general meeting (or unanimous informal agreement as per common law, i.e. the *Re Duomatic* principle [1969] 2 Ch 365) or by written resolution (see Companies Act 2006, s.288).
2. By the directors of the company:
    The decision to appoint an administrator can be taken by the majority of directors (IA 1986, Sched.B1, para.5). The decision need not be made at a formal board meeting, as rather than referring to a resolution of the board IR 1986, r.2.22 refers to a 'decision' of the directors; however, in view of the fact that evidence of the decision needs to be filed with the requisite forms then it would remove any ambiguity or doubt as to due process for a formal resolution to be passed.

An example of a board resolution to place the company in administration is found at the end of this chapter.

There is a necessary distinction between the ability to appoint by the company and the ability to appoint by its directors, as there may be cases where the members may not wish to put the company into administration, but the management of the company is concerned with its own position (i.e. trading while insolvent). It may also be more convenient for the directors to immediately commence the procedure, rather than to call a general meeting. However, once the procedure is initiated by the directors it is treated as if it were an appointment by the company.

Restrictions on appointment

The company or its directors may only appoint an administrator if:

(a) an administrator has not been appointed by the company or its directors, nor was the company subject to a moratorium in respect of a voluntary arrangement in the previous 12 months (IA 1986, Sched.B1, para.23(2));
(b) the company is, or is likely to be, unable to pay its debts (this contrasts with an appointment made by a qualifying floating charge holder where, as we have seen, the company need not be insolvent);
(c) no petition for winding up, nor any administration application has been presented or is outstanding in respect of the company (IA 1986, Sched.B1, para.25);
(d) the company is not in liquidation or provisional liquidation;
(e) no administrator is in office;
(f) no administrative receiver is in office.

Where any of the above restrictions apply (as described in greater detail in **3.1**) it may be open to the company to apply to court for an administration order (see, however, *Chesterton International Group Plc* v. *Deka Immobilien Inv GmbH* [2005] BPIR 1103: in the absence of any circumstances rendering the security invalid or suspect, where an administrative receiver was already in office, the court felt that it lacked jurisdiction to make an administration order).

The most common prohibition against an out-of-court appointment by the directors is the prior presentation of a winding-up petition. Understandably in such circumstances the company needs to make an administration application to court, serve the petitioning creditor with the same and will need to persuade the court that irrespective of any objection by the creditor it is in the best interests of the creditors as a whole that an administration order should be made as opposed to a winding-up order.

Before commencing the administration process it is therefore essential to check that a winding-up petition has not been 'presented'. If one has been presented any purported appointment of an administrator will be invalid. The purported administrator will be deemed a trespasser liable for damages to the company (see IA 1986, Sched.B1, para.34 regarding the potential indemnity from the appointor in such circumstances).

The difficulties that can arise where a company makes an appointment were fully illustrated in the case of *Re Blights Builders Ltd* [2007] BCC 712. In this case a winding-up petition had been posted to court, it was stamped and dated but not sealed and issued for service by the petitioning creditor. In the meantime an appointment of an administrator by the company was made using the out-of-court route. After it came to light that a petition had been in existence at the time of the appointment, the administrator sought direction as to the validity of his appointment. The court held that the winding-up petition was 'presented' as and when it was filed at court. It was irrelevant that the company was unaware of the petition and that it was not registered at the central registry of petitions maintained by the Companies Court. This type of problem would be compounded yet further where the winding-up petition was filed at a county court. Although sympathetic, the court held that it could not validate the appointment.

Consequently, a search at Companies Court of the register of outstanding petitions should be undertaken and where there is a risk of an imminent winding-up petition, enquiries should be made of the creditor as to their intention. If the situation is explained to the creditor and it is indicated that an administrator will be appointed, which will be more advantageous than liquidation, the creditor may be persuaded to desist. In cases of doubt, however, the company may be well advised to make an application rather than 'risk' commencement using the out-of-court route.

The company is also prevented from using the out-of-court route for appointment where in the previous 12 months the company has already been in administration or subject to a CVA. This provision is to prevent the company/ its directors from using (and abusing) the process to obtain a moratorium solely to hinder creditor claims. In these circumstances, the company can still seek to obtain an administration order, but the application will need to be accompanied by persuasive evidence and careful explanation which is likely to be closely scrutinised.

Notice of intention to appoint

The ability of the company to make an out-of-court appointment is tempered by the requirement that before the appointment can be made at least five business days' notice of any proposed appointment must be given to the holder of any qualifying floating charge, who is entitled to appoint an administrative receiver and/or administrator (IA 1986, Sched.B1, para.26). The notice of intention shall be in Form 2.8B and on being filed at court an interim moratorium period takes effect (IA 1986, Sched.B1, para.44). The effect of the interim moratorium is discussed in more detail in **Chapter 4**, at **4.8**.

Rule 2.20

Notice of intention to appoint an administrator by company or director(s)

Form 2.8B

Name of Company	Company number

In the [full name of court]	*For court use only* Court case number

(a) Insert name and address of registered office of company

1. Notice is given that, in respect of (a) _____

_____ ("the company")

*Delete as applicable

* the company / the directors of the company ("the appointor") intend to appoint

(b) Give name(s) and address(es) of proposed administrator(s)

(b) _____

_____

as administrator(s) of the company.

2. This notice is being given to the following person(s), being person(s) who is / are or may be entitled to appoint an administrative receiver of the company or an administrator of the company under paragraph 14 of Schedule B1 to the Insolvency Act 1986:

(c) Insert name and address of each person to whom notice is given

(c) _____

_____

3. The company has not, within the last twelve months:

(i) been in administration
(ii) been the subject of a moratorium under Schedule A1 to the Insolvency Act 1986 which has ended on a date when no voluntary arrangement was in force
(iii) been the subject of a voluntary arrangement which was made during a moratorium for the company under Schedule A1 to the Insolvency Act 1986 and which ended prematurely within the meaning of section 7B of the Insolvency Act 1986.

4. In relation to the company there is no:

(i) petition for winding up which has been presented but not yet disposed of
(ii) administration application which has not yet been disposed of, or
(iii) administrative receiver in office.

*Delete as applicable

5. The company *is / is not *an insurance undertaking / a credit institution / an investment undertaking providing services involving the holding of funds or securities for third parties / or a collective investment undertaking under Article 1.2 of the EC Regulation.

(d) Insert whether main or territorial proceedings

6. For the following reasons it is considered that the EC Regulation *will / will not apply. If it does apply, these proceedings will be (d) _____ proceedings as defined in Article 3 of the EC Regulations. _____

_____

*Delete as applicable

7. Attached to this notice is *a copy of the resolution of the company to appoint an administrator / a record of the decision of the directors to appoint an administrator.

(e) Insert name and address of person making declaration

I (e) _____
(If making the declaration on behalf of appointor indicate capacity e.g. director/solicitor)

hereby do solemnly and sincerely declare that:

(i) the company is or is likely to become unable to pay its debts
(ii) the company is not in liquidation, and
(iii) the statements in paragraphs 3 and 4 are, so far as I am able to ascertain, true,

and that the information provided in this notice is to the best of my knowledge and belief true,

AND I make this solemn declaration conscientiously believing the same to be true and by virtue of the Statutory Declarations Act 1835

Declared at _____

Signed _____

This _____ day of _____ 20

before me _____

Note: This form now to be sent to all those required to be sent the form by Rule 2.20(2)

A Commissioner for Oaths or Notary Public or Justice of the Peace or Solicitor or Duly Authorised Officer.

Consent of Floating Charge Holder to Appointment of Administrator(s)
(Do not detach this part of the notice)

(f) Appointor to insert address

If, having read this notice, you have no objection to the making of this appointment you should complete the details in the box below and return a copy of this notice as soon as possible, and within five business days from receipt of this notice, to the appointor at the following address: (f) _____

If your consent has not been given within five business days the appointor may make the appointment notwithstanding that you have not replied.

(g) Insert name and address

(g) _____

being the holder of the following floating charge over the company's property:

(h) Give details of charge, date registered and (if any) financial limit

(h) _____

consents to the appointment of the administrator(s) in accordance with the details of this notice.

Signed _____ Dated _____
(If signing on behalf of a firm or company state position or office held)

Endorsement to be completed by court

(j) Insert date and time

This notice was filed (j) _____

Practical tips on completing Form 2.8B

The numbers and letters in the list below refer to those set out on Form 2.8B.

1. Insert the name and registered office of the company [(a)]. IA 1986, s.117(6) provides that in regard to the issue of a winding-up petition the place the company has its registered office is said to be where it has been longest in the last six months. This is of note in view of the practice of cross-border 'forum shopping' where a foreign company may wish to restructure its business under the UK administration process.

   Insert names and addresses of the proposed administrators [(b)]. While at this stage Form 2.2B (i.e. consent to act, etc.) does not need to filed, the fact that insolvency practitioners are named in the notice would suggest that by this stage the company/its directors should have obtained advice and agreement from an insolvency practitioner to so act. The use of Form 2.8B simply to obtain an interim moratorium and/or to file a notice of intention on multiple occasions may well amount to an abuse of process (see below), as potentially would be naming insolvency practitioners who had not (at very least in principle) agreed to act. While there are no rules governing any change of proposed administrators between the provision of the notice and then the appointment, in view of the fact that the notice is primarily one to the floating charge holder, who has the choice to object/ appoint their own nomination, in practice their consent to this change should be sought.

2. Insert name and address of qualifying floating charge holder [(c)]. The proper address for service is likely to be found in the loan agreement/ facility letter/security documentation. If this is not provided, in the case of a bank (which is likely to have multiple sites, etc.) the address should be where the company has maintained its bank account, or if no such office is known, the registered office, or if no such office, the last known usual address (IR 1986, r.2.8(5)).

3. The declarant is required to confirm that the company has not within the last 12 months: been in administration; been subject to a moratorium arising from court order pending the calling of a meeting of creditors to consider a company voluntary arrangement (at present this being available only to 'small' companies); been the subject of a company voluntary arrangement (which was obtained following a moratorium period) which has terminated early (see IA 1986, Sched.A1).

4. The declarant is required to confirm that no winding-up petition has been presented but has not been disposed of (it is therefore vital to check with the court that no petition has been issued and not yet served); no administration application has yet to be disposed of; and no administrative receiver is in office.

5. Delete is/is not as appropriate. Note, however, that if the company is an insurance undertaking, credit institution, an investment undertaking providing services involving the holding of funds or securities for third parties or a collective investment undertaking under Art.1.2 of Council Regulation (EC) No.1346/2000 of 29 May 2000 on insolvency proceedings then a different insolvency regime will apply and specialist works should be consulted. Such companies will also not be subject to the EC Regulation.

6. Delete will/will not; although again if the EC Regulation does not apply then a different regime is likely to be in operation.

   The proceedings [(d)] are deemed 'main' proceedings provided the registered office/centre of main interests lies in the UK (see definition of main or secondary proceedings provided in **3.1** for further details). The reasons why the proceedings are main proceedings must be stated on the form.

7. Attach a copy of the company's resolution to appoint, or the record of the directors' decision to appoint. Note that the resolution is in respect of the intention to appoint, it is not a resolution to file a notice of intention, again emphasising that the notice of intention is a prelude to the appointment of an administrator and should not be used solely as a means of obtaining an interim moratorium against creditor action.

   Insert details (full name and address) of the individual who is making the statutory declaration contained on the remainder of the form [(e)]. This must be someone duly authorised by the appointor such as one of the directors or the company's solicitor. The statutory declaration must not, however, be undertaken lightly, as it is a sworn declaration that none of the statutory restrictions on appointment apply (see below), that there are no outstanding insolvency proceedings (such as an outstanding winding-up petition, administration application or administrative receiver in office) and that the company is insolvent and is not in liquidation. It is an offence to make a statement that is false and/or that is not reasonably believed to be true (IA 1986, Sched.B1, para.27(4)). Because of the importance and unique nature of the knowledge pertaining to the declaration, the declarant should probably be a director or senior officer of the company duly authorised by the board to make the declaration. This declaration, which should be sworn before an independent solicitor (or commissioner for oaths, notary public, justice of the peace or officer of the court, each of whom will charge a fee of £7), should not be made more than five business days before the date it is filed at court (IA 1986, Sched.B1, para.27(2); IR 1986, r.2.21).

The second part of the form deals with the notice to be completed if consent is to be granted by the floating charge holder.

- The address of the appointor/appointor's solicitors to which the floating charge holder should apply is provided [(f)].
- (g) is for completion by the floating charge holder who should provide its name and address for service.
- (h) is for completion by the floating charge holder to give details of the charge, date registered and financial limit (if any).

In practice, sections (g) and (h) may be completed beforehand by the appointor leaving the floating charge holder to provide a duly authorised signatory to endorse the form with consent. It should be noted that the form does not provide for rejection of the proposed administrator or notice of an alternative administrator; in practice in such circumstances the appointment is likely to be contested leading to correspondence, negotiation and/or a contested court application and hearing.

The endorsement [(j)] is to be left blank and is completed by the court on filing. A date and exact time are given, essential to assess when the administration is deemed to have commenced.

It should be noted that Form 2.8B is drafted in such a way to suggest that the notice is first filed at court, endorsed and then served on the floating charge holder. In fact IA 1986, Sched.B1, para.26 provides that written notice (in the prescribed form, i.e. Form 2.8B) is first served and IA 1986, Sched.B1, para.27 provides that as soon as reasonably practicable after service of the notice a copy of the notice shall be filed at court. While an interim moratorium comes into effect on filing (and not on service) this may be of little practical consequence to the charge holder, as IA 1986, Sched.B1, para.44(7) provides that the interim moratorium does not prevent the appointment by the charge holder of an administrator by out-of-court route, or the appointment of an administrative receiver (in respect of a floating charge created pre-15 September 2003 or where a special exemption applies; see **Appendix 1** – Summary 2). It should be noted, however, that other legal processes would be prevented, so presumably the company and/or its directors may prefer to first file the notice of intention and then serve the duly endorsed copy upon the floating charge holder.

As well as to the floating charge holder, a copy of the notice of intention must also be given to:

(a) any enforcement officer who to the knowledge of the person giving the notice is charged with execution or other legal process against the company;
(b) any person who has distrained against the company or its property;
(c) any supervisor of any CVA in place in regard to the company;
(d) the company, if the company is not making the appointment (IR 1986, r.2.20(2)).

Service on the company is at its registered office, and on any other person, by delivering the requisite documents to their proper address. The proper address is that which has previously been notified as an address for service and if this is not appropriate, then delivery should be to the last known address (IR 1986, r.2.8). See *Re Sporting Options Plc* [2005] BCC 88 which rules out service by email, although regard may be had in the future to changes related to service on companies provided in Companies Act 2006.

On service of the notice of intention to appoint, the qualifying floating charge holder may agree to the appointment, or seek to appoint their own choice of administrator. It is only in respect of pre-15 September 2003 security that the floating charge holder will retain the option to appoint an administrative receiver, rather than an administrator.

Although it is not expressly stated, if the floating charge holder gives notice within the five days that they object to the administration, but do not wish to appoint an alternative administrator (perhaps because they consider that liquidation is more appropriate) this could also amount to an effective veto. The reason for this is that in the notice of appointment (Form 2.9B), the appointor is required to state that the qualifying floating charge holder has either consented or failed to reply. If the directors still wished to appoint an administrator in the face of objection from the floating charge holder, the matter would need to be resolved on application to the court; the court weighing up what would be in the best interests of the creditors as a whole. A theoretical conflict could well arise in a situation where a creditor who was fully secured wanted to realise its security via a break-up sale by a liquidator rather than see an administrator appointed who would seek to achieve the rescue of the company. In practice, the court, seeking to follow the legislature's promotion of a rescue culture, would in all likelihood look more favourably on the administration application provided that the purpose of administration was reasonably likely to be achieved (perhaps this evidence being tested by the secured creditor). In circumstances where the secured creditor objects they are more likely to appoint their own nominee as administrator who perhaps would be more likely to make proposals suitable to the charge holder. Moreover, an insolvency practitioner may be unwilling to take an appointment in the face of such opposition, for fear of reputation and also possible dispute as to the cost, expenses and fees associated with the administration in the event that there could be insufficient recovery to discharge the secured creditor in full.

If no response of any kind is received from the floating charge holder after five business days have elapsed, the appointor may move to make the appointment of the administrator no later than 10 business days after filing of the notice of intention to appoint (IA 1986, Sched.B1, para.28(2)).

Notice of appointment

Where either a notice of intention has been served as above, or where the company/directors does/do not need to serve notice of intention as the company is not subject to a qualifying floating charge, the company/its directors may proceed to appoint an administrator, such appointment taking effect upon the filing at court of the requisite documentation (IA 1986, Sched.B1, para.31).

The appointment of an administrator by a company or its directors shall be by prescribed form (Form 2.9B (prior notice of intention given) or 2.10B (no prior notice of intention)).

Practical tips on completing Form 2.9B

The numbers and letters in the list below refer to those set out on Form 2.9B.

1. Insert the name and registered office of the company [(a)]. IA 1986, s.117(6) provides that in regard to the issue of a winding-up petition the place the company has its registered office is said to be where it has been longest in the last six months. This is of note in view of the practice of cross-border 'forum shopping' where a foreign company may wish to restructure its business under the UK administration process.

    Delete the company/the directors as appropriate. See above re choice and process and procedure for each.

    Insert names and addresses of the proposed administrators [(b)].

2. Form 2.2B (i.e. consent to act, etc.) needs to filed for each administrator who is being appointed.

3. The declarant is required to confirm that the appointment is in accordance with the provisions of IA 1986, Sched.B1, para.22, namely that the company has so resolved or the directors by majority have decided to appoint the administrator. It follows that all of the statement contained within the notice of intention to appoint (Form 2.8B) remains true and accurate (e.g. no winding-up petition has been issued, no administrative receiver is in office; although owing to the fact that a moratorium came into effect on the notice of intention being filed these steps should not have occurred).

4. The appointment must be in accordance with Sched.B1 (see in particular the provisions of paras.23–30 and the completion of all formalities) and the declarant is required to confirm the same.

5. Delete is/is not as appropriate. Note, however, that if the company is an insurance undertaking, credit institution, an investment undertaking providing services involving the holding of funds or securities for third parties or a collective investment undertaking under Art.1.2 of Council Regulation (EC) No.1346/2000 of 29 May 2000 on insolvency proceedings then a different insolvency regime will apply and specialist works should be consulted. Such companies will also not be subject to the EC Regulation.

6. Delete will/will not; although again if the EC Regulation does not apply then a different regime is likely to be in operation.

Rule 2.23

Form 2.9B

Notice of appointment of an administrator by company or director(s)

(where a notice of intention to appoint has been issued)

Name of Company	Company number

In the [full name of court]	*For court use only* Court case number

(a) Insert name and address of registered office of the company

1. Notice is given that, in respect of (a)

*Delete as applicable

(b) Give name(s) and address(es) of administrator(s)

_____("the company")

* the company / the directors of the company ("the appointor") hereby appoints

(b)

*Delete as applicable

as administrator(s) of the company.

2. The written statement(s) in Form 2.2B *is / are attached.

3. The appointor is entitled to make an appointment under paragraph 22 of Schedule B1 to the Insolvency Act 1986.

4. This appointment is in accordance with Schedule B1 to the Insolvency Act 1986.

*Delete as applicable

5. The company *is / is not *an insurance undertaking / a credit institution / an investment undertaking providing services involving the holding of funds or securities for third parties / or a collective investment undertaking under Article 1.2 of the EC Regulation.

(c) Insert whether main or territorial proceedings

6. For the following reasons it is considered that the EC Regulation *will / will not apply. If it does apply, these proceedings will be (c) _____ proceedings as defined in Article 3 of the EC Regulation: _____

83

7. Where there are joint administrators, a statement for the purposes of paragraph 100(2) of Schedule B1 to the Insolvency Act 1986 is attached.

8. The appointor has given written notice of the intention to appoint in accordance with paragraph 26(1) of Schedule B1 to the Insolvency Act 1986 and a copy of that notice was filed at court on (d)

(d) Insert date

___

*Delete as applicable

and *(a) five business days have elapsed from the date of the notice, or

(e) Insert name and address of person making declaration

* (b) each person to whom the notice was sent has consented to this appointment.

I (e)

_____do

solemnly and
(If making the declaration on behalf of appointor indicate capacity e.g. director/solicitor)

sincerely declare that

(i) the information provided in this notice and
(ii) the statements made and information given in the notice of intention to appoint

are, and remain, to the best of my knowledge and belief, true,

AND I make this solemn declaration conscientiously believing the same to be true and by virtue of the Statutory Declarations Act 1835.

Declared at _____

Signed _____

This _____day of _____20

before me _____

A Commissioner for Oaths or Notary Public or Justice of the Peace or Solicitor or Duly Authorised Officer

---

Endorsement to be completed by court

(f) Insert date and time

This notice was filed (f) _____

84

The proceedings [(c)] are deemed 'main' provided the registered office/ centre of main interests lies in the UK (see definition of main or secondary proceedings provided in **3.1** for further details). The reasons why the proceedings are main proceedings must be stated on the form.

7.   Where more than one person is to be appointed administrator, a statement specifying the functions to be exercised for the persons acting jointly and what functions, if any, are to be exercised by any or all of the persons appointed (IA 1986, Sched.B1, para.100(2)) must be attached. This is of significantly greater importance where the insolvency practitioners are from different firms and the functions split between the two (e.g. management of business/marketing and sale of business and assets/ investigation and report on directors' conduct, etc.). However, in practice, while such agreement may be reached the administrators may not wish their powers to be fettered.

8.   Insert date that notice of intention was filed at court [(d)].

Insert details (full name and address) of the individual who is making the statutory declaration contained on the remainder of the form [(e)]. This must be someone duly authorised by the appointor such as one of the directors or the company's solicitor. The statutory declaration provides that the appointor may make the appointment (i.e. no restrictions apply and that therefore the information contained in Form 2.8B remains accurate), that a notice of intention has been filed and that five business days' notice have elapsed and/or consent has been obtained to the appointment. It is an offence to make a statement that is false and/or that is not reasonably believed to be true (IA 1986, Sched.B1, para.29(7)). Because of the importance and unique nature of the knowledge pertaining to the declaration, the declarant should probably be a director or senior officer of the company duly authorised by the board to make the declaration. This declaration, which should be sworn before an independent solicitor (or commissioner for oaths, notary public, justice of the peace or officer of the court, each of whom will charge a fee of £7), should not be made more than five business days before the date it is filed at court (IA 1986, Sched. B1, para.29(6); IR 1986, r.2.21).

The endorsement [(f)] is to be left blank and is completed by the court on filing. A date and exact time are given, essential to assess when the administration is deemed to commence.

Practical tips on completing Form 2.10B

The numbers and letters in the list below refer to those set out on Form 2.10B.

1.   Insert the name and registered office of the company [(a)]. IA 1986, s.117(6) provides that in regard to the issue of a winding-up petition the

Rule 2.23   Form 2.10B

Notice of appointment of an administrator by company or director(s)
(where a notice of intention to appoint has not been issued)

Name of Company	Company number

In the [full name of court]	For court use only Court case number

(a) Insert name and address of registered office of the company

1. Notice is given that, in respect of (a) _____

_____

_____ ("the

company")

* Delete as appropriate

* the company / the directors of the company ("the appointor") hereby appoints

(b) Give name(s) and address(es) of administrator(s)

(b) _____

_____

as administrator(s) of the company.

*Delete as applicable

2. The written statement(s) in Form 2.2B * is / are attached.

3. The appointor is entitled to make an appointment under paragraph 22 of Schedule B1 to the Insolvency Act 1986.

4. This appointment is in accordance with Schedule B1 to the Insolvency Act 1986.

5. The company has not, within the last twelve months: -

(i) been in administration
(ii) been the subject of a moratorium under Schedule A1 to the Insolvency Act 1986 which has ended on a date when no voluntary arrangement was in force
(iii) been the subject of a voluntary arrangement which was made during a moratorium for the company under Schedule A1 to the Insolvency Act 1986 and which ended prematurely within the meaning of section 7B of the Insolvency Act 1986.

6. In relation to the company there is no:

(i) petition for winding up which has been presented but not yet disposed of
(ii) administration application which has not yet been disposed of, or
(iii) administrative receiver in office.

*Delete as applicable

7. The company *is / is not* an insurance undertaking / a credit institution / an investment undertaking providing services involving the holding of funds or securities for third parties / or a collective investment undertaking under Article 1.2 of the EC Regulation.

8. For the following reasons it is considered that the EC Regulation *will / will not apply. If it does apply, these proceedings will be (c) _____ proceedings as defined in Article 3 of the EC Regulation:

(c) Insert whether main or territorial proceedings

_____

Form 2.10B continued

*Delete as applicable

9. Attached to this notice is *a copy of the resolution of the company to appoint an administrator / a record of the decision of the directors to appoint an administrator.

10. Where there are joint administrators, a statement for the purposes of paragraph 100(2) of Schedule B1 to the Insolvency Act 1986 is attached.

(d) Insert name and address of person making declaration

I (d) _____
(If making the declaration on behalf of appointor indicate capacity e.g. director/solicitor)

hereby do solemnly and sincerely declare that:

(i) the company is or is likely to become unable to pay its debts
(ii) the company is not in liquidation, and
(iii) the statements in paragraphs 5 and 6 are, so far as I am able to ascertain, true,

and that the information provided in this notice is to the best of my knowledge and belief true,

AND I make this solemn declaration conscientiously believing the same to be true and by virtue of the Statutory Declarations Act 1835.

Declared at _____

Signed _____

This _____ day of _____ 20____

before me _____

A Commissioner for Oaths or Notary Public or Justice of the Peace or Solicitor or Duly Authorised Officer

---

Endorsement to be completed by the court
(e) Insert date and time   This notice was filed (e) _____

87

place the company has its registered office is said to be where it has been longest in the last six months. This is of note in view of the practice of cross-border 'forum shopping' where a foreign company may wish to restructure its business under the UK administration process.

Delete the company/the directors as appropriate. See above re choice and process and procedure for each.

Insert names and addresses of the proposed administrators [(b)].

2. Form 2.2B (i.e. consent to act, etc.) needs to be filed for each administrator who is being appointed.
3. The declarant is required to confirm that the appointment is in accordance with the provisions of IA 1986, Sched.B1, para.22, namely that the company has so resolved or the directors by majority have decided to appoint the administrator.
4. The appointment must be in accordance with Sched.B1 (see in particular the provisions of paras.23–30 and the completion of all formalities) and the declarant is required to confirm the same.
5. The declarant is required to confirm that the company has not within the last 12 months: been in administration; been subject to a moratorium arising from court order pending the calling of a meeting of creditors to consider a company voluntary arrangement (at present this being available only to 'small' companies); been the subject of a company voluntary arrangement (which was obtained following a moratorium period) which has terminated early (see IA 1986, Sched.A1).
6. The declarant is required to confirm that no winding-up petition has been presented but has not been disposed of (it is therefore vital to check with the court that no petition has been issued and not yet served); no administration application has yet to be disposed of; and no administrative receiver is in office.
7. Delete is/is not as appropriate. Note, however, that if the company is an insurance undertaking, credit institution, an investment undertaking providing services involving the holding of funds or securities for third parties or a collective investment undertaking under Art.1.2 of Council Regulation (EC) No.1346/2000 of 29 May 2000 on insolvency proceedings then a different insolvency regime will apply and specialist works should be consulted. Such companies will also not be subject to the EC Regulation.
8. Delete will/will not; although again if the EC Regulation does not apply then a different regime is likely to be in operation.

The proceedings [(c)] are main proceedings provided the registered office/centre of main interests lies in the UK (see definition of main or secondary proceedings provided in **3.1** for further details). The reasons why the proceedings are main proceedings must be stated on the form.

9. Attach a copy of the company's resolution to appoint, or the record of the directors' decision to appoint.

10. Where more than one person is to be appointed administrator, a statement specifying the functions to be exercised by the persons acting jointly and what functions, if any, are to be exercised by any or all of the persons appointed (IA 1986, Sched.B1, para.100(2)) must be attached. This is of significantly greater importance where the insolvency practitioners are from different firms and the functions split between the two (e.g. management of business/marketing and sale of business and assets/ investigation and report on directors' conduct, etc.). However, in practice, while such agreement may be reached the administrators may not wish their powers to be fettered.

    Insert details (full name and address) of the individual who is making the statutory declaration contained on the remainder of the form [(d)]. This must be someone duly authorised by the appointor such as one of the directors or the company's solicitor. The statutory declaration provides that the appointor may make the appointment (i.e. none of the statutory restrictions on appointment apply, that there are no outstanding insolvency proceedings (such as an outstanding winding-up petition, administration application or administrative receiver in office) and that the company is insolvent and is not in liquidation. It is an offence to make a statement that is false and/or that is not reasonably believed to be true (IA 1986, Sched. B1, para.29(7)). Because of the importance and unique nature of the knowledge pertaining to the declaration, the declarant should probably be a director or senior officer of the company duly authorised by the board to make the declaration. This declaration, which should be sworn before an independent solicitor (or commissioner for oaths, notary public, justice of the peace or officer of the court, each of whom will charge a fee of £7), should not be made more than five business days before the date it is filed at court (IA 1986, Sched.B1, para.29(6); IR 1986, r.2.21).

The endorsement [(e)] is to be left blank and is completed by the court on filing. A date and exact time of filing is endorsed, essential to assess when the administration is deemed to have commenced.

Form 2.2B (the administrator's statement) must contain the following:

- consent to the appointment;
- a statement that in his opinion the purpose of the administration is reasonably likely to be achieved;
- the disclosure of any prior professional relationship with the company.

This latter provision is one the administrator will consider where there is a potential conflict and he has acted in accordance with regulatory provisions in taking such an appointment. An appointment cannot be taken up if the firm has been auditor to the company and/or provided material advice and services apart from recent advice on insolvency issues.

In making the statement, the administrator is entitled to rely upon the information supplied by the directors of the company, unless he has reason to doubt its accuracy. Although the insolvency practitioner no longer has to provide evidence that his appointment would be likely to achieve one of the purposes of administration (as was the case under the old administration regime, which required the preparation and filing of a so-called Rule 2.2 Report by the insolvency practitioner), the administrator must go through many of the steps that were previously required to satisfy himself that the administration is reasonably likely to achieve the purpose of the administration. This will require investigation of the company's affairs and an assessment of the merits of administration against other insolvency processes in the light of how this will affect the creditors as a whole.

As soon as reasonably practicable thereafter, the appointor should notify the administrator and other prescribed persons of the appointment (IA 1986, Sched.B1, para.32). Further details of the notice provisions and other steps to be taken after appointment are dealt with in **Chapter 5** which details the administration process.

EXAMPLE OF BOARD RESOLUTION TO PLACE COMPANY IN ADMINISTRATION

[*NAME OF COMPANY*] LIMITED

(Company No. [ ])

(the 'Company')

Minutes of a meeting of the board of directors of the Company held at [*place*]

On [*date*]

Present

[*Name*]   [*Position*]
[Apologies for absence received from]

1. Chairperson

[*Name*] was appointed chairperson of the meeting.

2. Notice and quorum

The Chairperson reported that due notice of the meeting had been given and that a quorum was present. Accordingly the Chairperson declared the meeting open.

3. Declaration of interest

3.1 [The relevant directors declared the nature and extent of their interest in the matters to be considered at the meeting in accordance with section 177 of the Companies Act 2006 and the Company's articles of association; as follows]

[Provide details of such if any direct or indirect interests had in the proposed administration]

OR

[Each director confirmed that they had no direct or indirect interest in any way in the proposed transaction [and other arrangements] to be considered at the meeting which they were required to disclose in accordance with section 177 of the Companies Act 2006 and the Company's articles of association.]

3.2 It was noted that the articles of association of the Company entitled a director to be counted in the quorum of directors and to vote on any matter on disclosing the nature and extent of his material interest.

3.3 It was further noted that, among his other duties, a director is required by statute to act in the way he considers, in good faith, would be most likely to promote the success of the Company for the benefit of its members as a whole, having regard, among other things, to the matters listed in section 172(1) of the Companies Act 2006.

4. Business of the meeting

The Chairperson reported that the business of the meeting was to consider the financial affairs of the Company and to determine whether to take steps to place the Company into administration.

5. Resolutions

5.1 After consideration of the financial affairs of the Company the Board concluded that the Company was insolvent in that it had an inability to pay its debts as they fell due. Following further consideration of advice provided by *[name of insolvency practitioner]* on the options available to the Company and to the matters referred to in section 172(1) Companies Act 2006 IT WAS RESOLVED that such steps as prove necessary should be taken immediately to place the Company into administration.

5.2 IT WAS FURTHER RESOLVED that *[name of insolvency practitioner]* be authorised to do all such acts and agree to execute on behalf of the board and/or on behalf of the Company all necessary documentation including but not limited to the preparation and filing at court of a notice of intention to appoint administrators.

6. Close

There being no further business the Chairperson declared the meeting closed.

....
Chairperson

....
Dated

CHAPTER 4

The effect of administration

In this chapter the effect and consequences of a company entering into administration are considered.

4.1   INTRODUCTION OF A STATUTORY MORATORIUM

The central feature of the administration process is the commencement of a statutory moratorium preventing certain prescribed creditor actions. This moratorium provides the administrator with a window of opportunity in which to assess the viability of the business and make proposals to the company's creditors. During this time, the administrator is provided breathing space, free from attempts by creditors to enforce claims against the company. An individual creditor's rights are thus necessarily prejudiced in the cause of the collective good of the creditors as a whole. As we shall see there are checks and balances to ensure that an individual creditor is not 'unfairly' prejudiced, although as discussed in **Chapter 1** the moratorium has very different implications for a creditor where the administrator has conducted a pre-pack sale of the business and assets on or soon after appointment.

It must be kept at the forefront of one's mind that the moratorium does no more than suspend the enforcement of a creditor's rights against the debtor company; it does not destroy the creditor's rights. Unless otherwise provided for within the contract, a contractual obligation on the part of the company in administration is not revoked by the commencement of the administration, it is only the ability of the contracting party to enforce any rights that might derive from a breach of contract by the insolvent company that are affected.

The effect of the moratorium can also be relaxed with the consent of the administrator, or permission of the court, as a means to avoid potentially unfair treatment to specific creditors/contractual parties. The moratorium is also limited to provide protection only in regard to the debtor company and its property, not guarantors and other third parties.

The fact that there is a suspension (rather than destruction or crystallisation) of rights also has an important consequence for a creditor. In theory it is entirely possible that the company could enter administration and, with the advantages afforded by the moratorium period, restructure its affairs, return to profitability and exit administration by a return of control and management to the owners of the company. As the moratorium comes to an end, so the creditors' rights to take proceedings are re-established. It should be noted, however, that despite the existence of the moratorium any relevant Limitation Act 1980 provisions continue to apply to creditor claims against the company (see *Re Cosslett (Contractors) Ltd* [2004] EWHC 658 (Ch)). As a result, if a creditor is approaching a Limitation Act expiry period for a claim (not established as a payable debt), consent of the administrator or permission of the court to commence proceedings should be obtained as a means of safeguarding the creditors' position. It is often the case that the proceedings can be issued and then stayed by consent, acting as a protective claim pending determination of the administration.

Ultimately where the administration has been completed the claimant can continue with the litigation. In the more likely circumstances where another insolvency procedure follows (e.g. liquidation) it is the nature of the subsequent insolvency procedure which will determine the ability and worth of the claimant continuing with those proceedings. It should be noted that a creditor cannot prove for a debt (perhaps in a subsequent liquidation following administration) which is statute barred.

While the most significant effect of administration is that a statutory moratorium comes into force, other important consequences arise.

4.2 THE EFFECT OF ADMINISTRATION UPON ANY WINDING-UP PETITION

A petition for the winding up of a company will be dismissed if an administration order is made (IA 1986, Sched.B1, para.40(1)). Unlike receivership, save for the limited exemption detailed below, administration cannot run concurrently with liquidation, as both are collective processes that deal with the company *and* its assets, not solely the assets.

As we have seen in **3.1** where an administration application is issued (IR 1986, r.2.6(3)(b)) the application needs to be served on any creditor petitioning for the winding up of the company, who may make representations at the hearing (see *DKLL Solicitors* v. *Revenue and Customs Commissioners* [2007] EWHC 2067 (Ch) for an example of a case concerning a contested administration application and how the court may have regard to all the circumstances and not just the wishes of the majority creditor). As a result, it would be advisable for any applicant seeking an administration order to ensure that any court application is heard before, or perhaps listed with, the hearing of the winding-up petition. If the winding-up petition is to be heard first it would be prudent for the applicant to attend the hearing of the winding-up petition to ensure the court is made aware of the administration application and therefore adjourns or stays the winding-up petition. The costs incurred by the petitioning creditor in seeking a winding-up order will generally be ordered to be an expense of the administration.

Where the administrator has been appointed by a floating charge holder by an out-of-court route, the winding-up petition will be suspended during the course of the appointment (IA 1986, Sched.B1, para.14). Where there is an outstanding winding-up petition and the administrator's proposals are accepted by the creditors, the administrator may apply for directions (IA 1986, Sched.B1, para.63) and/or seek dismissal of the petition. It may be inadvisable to leave the petition suspended, as on discharge of the administration it could be revived, which may prejudice the restructured company or the consequent proposals to put the company into voluntary liquidation/seek its dissolution.

Where a winding-up petition is presented under IA 1986, s.124A (public interest grounds), IA 1986, s.124B (petition for winding up of a Societas Europaea – see European Public Limited-Liability Company Regulations 2004, SI 2004/2326) or under Financial Services and Market Act 2000, s.367 (i.e. a petition by the Financial Services Authority) it is possible for the company to be concurrently in administration and liquidation. As a result, in these circumstances IA 1986, Sched.B1, paras.40(1)(a) and 42(3) will not have effect.

4.3 THE EFFECT OF ADMINISTRATION ON RECEIVERS/SECURED CREDITORS

When an administration order is made, any administrative receiver of the company shall vacate office (IA 1986, Sched.B1, para.41(1)); in addition, an administrative receiver of the company cannot be appointed once the company is in administration (IA 1986, Sched.B1, para.43(6A)). An administrator and administrative receiver fulfil the same role of control and management of the company and therefore cannot both be in office at the same time.

However, it should be remembered that an administration application will be dismissed unless:

(a) the floating charge holder consents to the administration appointment; or
(b) the court thinks the security under which the appointment of the administrative receiver has been made may be released or discharged under IA 1986, ss.238, 240 or 245.

Furthermore, the out-of-court routes of appointment are unavailable where there is an administrative receiver in office.

As a consequence, administration cannot be used as a means to take control and management of the company away from an administrative receiver, save where the validity of the security is in doubt.

Where a secured creditor has appointed a receiver over part of the company's property, the administrator may require that the receiver vacates office (IA 1986, Sched.B1, para.41(2)).

It should also be borne in mind that any step to enforce security (including the appointment of a receiver) over the company's property requires the consent of the administrator, or permission of the court (IA 1986, Sched.B1, para.43(2)). As a result, in theory at least, the power of the secured creditor and any receiver remaining in office will be severely curtailed. In practice, however, the position and the 'balance of power' may be very different, with the administrator recognising that to deal with the assets subject to the fixed charge, the rights of that secured creditor cannot be prejudiced and to realise the secured asset, a release will be required from the secured creditor. In those circumstances the proposed administrator is likely to work closely with the secured creditor and is likely to accede to a request to leave the asset in the hands of the receiver, or where the secured creditor agrees that the administrator takes control and management of the secured asset it will only be on the basis that this offers a realistic chance of better realisation of their security. In addition, it should be remembered that where a secured creditor has already taken control of the company's principal asset (e.g. the company's business premises) it may have the practical effect of making the purpose of administration unachievable.

Where a receiver or an administrative receiver vacates office, the receiver's right to remuneration is charged and paid (ahead of any claim by the security holder appointing him) from any property in his custody and control immediately before he vacates office (IA 1986, Sched.B1, para.41(3)(a)). This right is, however, tempered by the effects of the statutory moratorium (see IA 1986, Sched.B1, para.41(4)(c)) so cannot be enforced except with consent of the administrator.

As outlined above, the secured creditor cannot take steps to enforce security over the company's property except with consent of the administrator or permission of the court (IA 1986, Sched.B1, para.43(2)). IA 1986, s.248 widely defines 'security' to include any mortgage, charge, lien or other security. 'Other security' has been held to include:

- security arising from operation of law (*Re Euro Commercial Leasing Ltd* v. *Cartwright & Lewis* [1995] BCC 830);
- a contractual provision, where there was a right to look to the debtor's property by detention in settlement of a debt (*Bristol Airport Plc* v. *Powdrill* [1990] Ch 744);
- commercial arrangements having an effect equivalent to security (see *March Estates Plc* v. *Gunmark Ltd* [1996] 2 BCLC 1, although subsequent cases which followed this stressed the need for the security (whether consensual or non-consensual) to be 'security' in a stricter legal sense; see *Razzaq* v. *Pala* [1997] 1 WLR 1336 and *Clarence Café Ltd* v. *Comchester Properties Ltd* [1999] L&TR 303);
- a repairer's lien regardless of any demand for delivery up by the administrator (see *London Flight Centre (Stansted) Ltd* v. *Osprey Aviation Ltd* [2002] BPIR 1115).

It remains unclear whether a demand for payment is deemed to be the 'taking of steps' to enforce security (in *Re Olympia & York Canary Wharf Ltd (No.1)* [1993] BCLC 453 it is noted that this question was specifically not being dealt with). It is proffered that as the moratorium is concerned with enforcement of rights against the company and more importantly its property (not the destruction of rights) the issue of a demand, which might be a necessary prelude to the enforcement of security, would not in any way hamper the ability of the administrator to carry out his functions. Indeed in many cases it is the commencement of the administration as an insolvency proceeding that triggers the secured creditor's enforcement rights in any event. This trigger does not mean, however, that the secured creditor can exercise those rights and it is contended that a demand for payment should be regarded in the same vein. In practice the issue may not have reached court because an administrator faced with a demand (against the company) by a secured creditor will almost certainly negotiate with them and ascertain their intention as regards their security.

It should also be noted that where the secured creditor holds a floating charge the creditor will have been given notice of the intended appointment and therefore had an opportunity to appoint an administrative receiver or a receiver prior to the commencement of the administration. In regard to a secured creditor holding a fixed charge over a significant asset of the company it would also not be unusual to find that the proposed administrator has conducted initial negotiations with the secured creditor, so avoiding conflict once the administration has commenced.

4.4 MORATORIUM ON INSOLVENCY PROCEEDINGS

While the company is in administration the company cannot enter into voluntary or compulsory liquidation; as a result no resolution may be passed by the members or order made by the court to commence the liquidation (IA 1986, Sched.B1, para.42(2), (3)).

This prohibition does not apply to a winding-up order sought under IA 1986, s.124A (public interest grounds), IA 1986, s.124B (petition for winding up of a Societas Europaea – see European Public Limited-Liability Company Regulations 2004, SI 2004/2326) or under Financial Services and Market Act 2000, s.367 (i.e. a petition by the Financial Services Authority).

If the administrator becomes aware that a public interest winding-up petition has been presented during the course of the administration the administrator shall apply for directions under IA 1986, Sched.B1, para.63 (see IA 1986, Sched.B1, para.42(5)). The court will consider whether both the liquidator and the administrator should remain in office, perhaps because the former is undertaking investigations leading to possible proceedings against former owners/management, while the latter is seeking to realise the business and assets of the company on a going concern basis.

4.5   MORATORIUM ON OTHER LEGAL PROCESSES

Enforcement of security

As discussed in **4.3**, IA 1986, s.248 widely defines 'security' to include any mortgage, charge, lien or other security. As a result of the moratorium a secured creditor cannot take any step to enforce security except with consent of the administrator or permission of the court (IA 1986, Sched.B1, para.43(2)). In granting permission to allow the secured creditor to take steps the court may also impose a condition on, or a requirement in connection with, the transaction (IA 1986, Sched.B1, para.43(7)).

Repossession of goods under a hire purchase agreement

No step can be taken by a lessor exercising rights under a hire purchase agreement (such as repossession in event of insolvency and/or non-payment) without the consent of the administrator or permission of the court (IA 1986, Sched.B1, para.43(3)).

In addition, 'any hire purchase agreement' also includes conditional sales agreements and chattel leasing agreements. Where goods remain in the possession of the debtor company the 'owner' of the goods is prevented from recovering them even where the agreement to hire/lease, etc. has been terminated prior to the commencement of the administration (*Re David Meek Plant Ltd* [1993] BCC 175).

Importantly, a creditor possessing a retention of title over goods supplied to the debtor is also prevented from exercising rights that may have been retained under the contract of supply, such as the right to go on to the debtor's premises and take back unpaid-for stock.

As we shall see, in practice it will be incumbent on the administrator to quickly come to some agreement with lessors of equipment under hire purchase agreements or suppliers with the benefit of possible retention of title, as such creditors should not be unfairly harmed and/or the administration process should not be used simply to hamper their rights. Particularly in regard to goods subject to retention of title, a not uncommon arrangement is for an agreement to be reached which allows the administrator to sell to a third party and to hold the proceeds in escrow to be paid to the supplier if the retention of title clause is ultimately found to be effective. In other cases the administrator selling to a third party will do so without representation or warranty as to title and will require that the third party purchaser retains and holds goods subject to possible retention of title and/or indemnifies the administrator against loss and damage suffered by claims from the supplier.

Landlord's right to forfeit

A landlord cannot take any steps to forfeit a lease by peaceable re-entry for non-payment of rent once a tenant company is in administration except with consent of the administrator or leave of the court (IA 1986, Sched.B1, para.43(4)). The landlord also cannot distrain for rent or sue for non-payment although both actions are covered by 'other legal process' discussed below.

In recent years nowhere has the tension between the individual right of an individual creditor (in this case the landlord) and the collective best interests of the creditors as a whole been more evident than in the interplay between the tenant company, the administrator and landlord.

While it is often the case that the insolvent company's problems mean that it cannot continue to meet its leasehold obligations, during the recession and fall in property market from mid-2007 onwards, many tenants have found that they are paying rent way in excess of market rate and there is a perception that administration (or at least the threat of administration) has been used as a process to negotiate more favourable terms. The reason for this is that rent is not necessarily payable as a cost and expense of the administration process, much depending on the particular circumstances of the case (see *Innovate Logistics Ltd* v. *Sunberry Properties Ltd* [2009] BCC 164 although contrast to *Goldacre (Office) Ltd* v. *Nortel Networks UK Ltd* (In Administration) [2009] EWHC 3389 (Ch)). As a result, during the period of administration, the landlord may find that rent is not paid on an ongoing basis.

To compound the situation the administrator may well find it expedient to grant an unlawful licence to occupy (as far as the tenant company's leasehold obligations are concerned) to a third party/buyer of the tenant company's business and assets. This is almost certainly the case where a pre-pack administration sale is contemplated and there is a fear that prior notice of the proposal to the landlord would cause the landlord to take action. The landlord in such circumstances faces a fait accompli, with no immediate ability to enforce rights against the tenant company in administration and an unlawful occupier who perhaps will wish to renegotiate terms as opposed to negotiating an assignment of the existing lease. Where the occupier is a new corporate vehicle controlled and managed by the previous owner-managers of the tenant company, feelings of injustice on the part of the landlord may be magnified.

Each case will, of course, be fact sensitive and it may be the case that the administrator will seek to negotiate with the landlord over the terms of occupation during the course of the administration, perhaps paying rent on a reduced basis, perhaps weekly in arrears as opposed to quarterly in advance. With such breathing space the administrator may be able to restructure the company and/or introduce the landlord to a potential new tenant company who would be willing to take an assignment of the lease. In such circumstances it might be to the advantage of the landlord if the administrator remains in occupation, particularly in a case where the premises might be unoccupied, where no new tenant can be found and the local authority's demand for business rates (which would fall upon the landlord if the property were taken back) will remain a 'liability' of the tenant company in administration.

We shall explore further the circumstances where the landlord may wish to forfeit and might wish to seek to obtain the court's permission to enforce rights in **4.6** below.

Commencement or continuation of any legal process

No legal process (including legal proceedings, execution, distress and diligence) may be instituted or continued against the company or property of the company except with consent of the administrator or permission of the court (IA 1986, Sched.B1, para.43(6)).

Originally restricted to the enforcement of debt and not quasi-judicial proceedings (see *Air Ecosse Ltd* v. *Civil Aviation Authority* (1987) 3 BCC 492) in recent years this provision has been very widely interpreted to include:

- employment tribunal claims (*Re Divine Solutions (UK) Ltd* [2004] BCC 325);
- a tenant's application for a new lease under Landlord and Tenant Act 1954, Part II (*Somerfield Stores Ltd* v. *Spring (Sutton Coldfield) Ltd* [2009] EWHC 2384 (Ch));
- revocation of a patent (*Biosource Technologies Inc* v. *Axis Genetics Plc* [2000] 1 BCLC 286);
- advertisement of a winding-up petition (*Re a Company (No.001992 of 1988)* [1989] BCLC 9);
- reference of a building contract dispute to a statutory arbitration procedure (*A Straume (UK) Ltd* v. *Bradlor Developments Ltd* [2000] BCC 333);
- criminal proceedings (*Re Rhondda Waste Disposal Ltd* [2001] Ch 57).

4.6 COURT'S PERMISSION TO TAKE LEGAL PROCEEDINGS

As discussed above if the court is willing to grant permission for a creditor to take any of the above steps, it may impose a condition on, or a requirement in connection with, the proceeding/transaction (IA 1986, Sched.B1, para.43(7)).

The court exercises a discretionary power in considering whether to give a creditor permission to take proceedings. Each case is therefore entirely fact sensitive and the court will carefully balance the interests of the individual creditor, who will necessarily be prejudiced (i.e. they cannot exercise their rights) against the interests of the creditors as a whole. See *Somerfield Stores Ltd* v. *Spring (Sutton Coldfield) Ltd* [2009] EWHC 2384 (Ch) for discussion on the harm caused to the applicant outweighing the benefit to the administrator and the creditors as a whole.

The court will in particular take account of the administrator's proposals and whether there is a reasonable prospect of achieving the purpose of the administration if permission is granted to a particular creditor (see *Royal Trust Bank* v. *Buchler* [1989] BCLC 130). Clearly the more likely it is that the purpose of administration will be prejudiced if a creditor is granted permission to exercise a right (e.g. if a landlord is permitted to forfeit the company's lease the company will be deprived of a property in which to continue business) the more likely it is that permission will be refused.

The leading authority in this area remains the case of *Re Atlantic Computer Systems Plc* [1990] BCC 859. The Court of Appeal made it clear that the court should retain flexibility and should not stick too rigidly to precedent and automatic rules of application. The Court of Appeal, however, provided some guidance as to the type of factors it would take into account when considering the question of whether to grant permission:

- In every case it is for the person seeking permission to make out a case; the burden of proof is on the applicant.
- If granting permission to an owner of land or goods to exercise proprietorial rights to repossess their land or goods is unlikely to impede the purpose of the administration, permission should normally be granted.
- In any other case, the court should balance the interests of the applicant against those of the company's other creditors and consider whether the refusal to grant permission would be inequitable.
- In carrying out the balancing exercise, great weight should be given to the applicant's proprietorial or secured interests.
- The administration procedure should not be used to unfairly prejudice the rights of secured creditors.
- The adequacy of the security and the prejudicial effect of delay may be relevant.
- The benefits obtained by the unsecured creditors should not be at the expense of the secured creditors, except where it is limited and unavoidable.
- If significant loss would result to the applicant, it would normally be appropriate to grant permission; conversely where little to no loss would result to the applicant then permission may be inappropriate.
- Permission may, however, be granted in the case where the loss caused to other creditors substantially outweighs the loss caused to the lessor.
- In considering the likely loss to both the applicant and other creditors, the court should have regard to, inter alia:
  - the financial position of the company in administration;
  - the company's ability to pay interest, charges and arrears to the applicant;
  - the administrator's proposal and prospect of success for the administration;

- the period during which the administration has already run and what period is left;
- the conduct of the parties; and
- the effect on all parties should permission be granted.

After considering all of the above, the court may impose such terms and conditions upon the exercise of the lessor's rights as it thinks fit. Likewise the court may impose conditions upon the administrator, if the creditor is refused permission. The court will not seek to adjudicate any dispute regarding security unless it is a short point of law and it is convenient to do so.

In conclusion, the burden of proof in obtaining permission is therefore upon the applicant who must show that the granting of permission would not defeat the purpose of the administration (*Royal Trust Bank* v. *Buchler* [1989] BCLC 130) and that on balance it is right that the proprietary right of the creditor is allowed to be exercised (e.g. where significant loss will be incurred by the creditor: *Scottish Exhibition Centre Ltd* v. *Mirestop Ltd* [1993] BCC 529). The court will not grant permission if the effect is to prefer one unsecured creditor over another (*Re TBL Realisations Plc* [2004] BCC 81).

In practice to avoid an application for permission, or even an application brought by a creditor alleging unfair harm (IA 1988, Sched.B1, para.74), the administrator should quickly assess the affairs of the company paying particular regard to the interests of any landlord, secured creditor and owner of property/goods in the possession of the company. The administrator should assess whether equipment, goods and/or the premises occupied or held by the company are essential for the continuation of the company's business and/or whether their continued retention is uneconomic. If it is uneconomic (i.e. the costs of retention, such as rent, mean that the administrator cannot continue the business of the company without loss) then the equipment or property should be returned to the lessor immediately.

Often the administrator will be proposing a sale of the company's business and/or its assets and consequently may need to consider whether any leasehold interest of the company could be assigned for value. Careful negotiation with the landlord of the premises, or lessor of the equipment, is essential once a potential purchaser has been identified. The landlord and lessor will also be likely to wait for proposals to be put forward before considering whether to exercise their rights and/or consent to any assignment. It should, however, be remembered that while the moratorium has the effect of preventing proceedings being commenced by the landlord, the terms of the lease will almost certainly provide that the administrator cannot 'force' a new tenant upon the landlord.

Before commencing the administration therefore the administrator should have properly assessed the probable costs and expenses of the company's continued operation and consequently assessed the possibility of whether the purpose of administration is reasonably likely to be achieved. If a sale is likely and a possible premium obtained for the company's leasehold interests then the insolvency practitioner is likely to have accounted for the costs of rental, etc. and will be assured that on appointment ongoing rent will be paid. In a normal case if the rent is to be paid on an ongoing basis then it is unlikely, even taking into account other breaches of leasehold covenant that may have resulted (indeed the fact of tenant administration may give rise to a right of forfeiture), that the landlord would be granted permission to forfeit in the short to medium term.

However, the uncertainty as to the payment of costs such as rent and the possible reaction of creditors is one of the factors behind the increase in use of pre-pack administrations. In such cases it may well be the case that the individual creditor's rights are very significantly prejudiced, i.e. the injury has been caused and the creditor's ability to negotiate and bargain with the administrator has been removed. For example the grant to a third party of an unlawful licence to occupy the company leasehold premises, or the sale to a third party of goods subject to potential claims may have deprived the creditor of an effective remedy.

The greater preponderance of pre-pack administrations has therefore altered the balance of power between creditors, as an individual creditor may well be excluded from the planning process of the administration and the first they may know of the change in situation is sometime later (change in business ownership in the occupier of the premises). The landlord creditor may well find they are then negotiating with a well-funded third party who has acquired the business and assets of the former contracting party and who is willing to drive a hard bargain regarding continued occupation/retention of property.

4.7 POWERS OF DIRECTORS

The making of an administration order also has the effect of suspending the directors' powers of management over the company (IA 1986, Sched.B1, para.64). The directors may, however, exercise management power with the consent of the administrator, which may be given generally, or in relation to specific matters (*Re P&C and R&T (Stockport) Ltd* [1991] BCLC 366).

Irrespective of any loss of management power the directors are still liable to perform their statutory duties in relation to the company, fulfilling any required obligations under law, such as the filing of annual returns.

The administrator also has the power to remove the directors from office (IA 1986, Sched.B1, para.61) and may appoint a director whether to fill a vacancy or not. A director removed from office in this manner has no rights other than those that may exist under any service contract for loss of office (*Newtherapeutics Ltd* v. *Katz* [1991] Ch 226).

Often the administrator may find that the continued involvement of the directors is essential to ensure the smooth running of the company during the administration process. The directors may, therefore, be called upon by the administrator to deal with suppliers, creditors and employees and many of the day-to-day issues of management, leaving the administrator free to deal with strategy, restructuring and/or sale of the business. In some instances the situation may require the administrator to compel the directors to assist and co-operate. The powers of the administrator and duties and obligations of the directors in this regard are dealt with further in **Chapter 6**.

The directors may also remain in operational control of the business, where they wish to bid for the business and/or assets of the company from the administrator. In such circumstances one practice that has grown up is for the administrator to enter into a business management/operating licence with the directors/proposed purchasers who will carry on the business for and on behalf of the administrator, while the business and assets are marketed or perhaps restructured to make the business more attractive to a potential purchaser. The management fee for this service may be any operating profit obtained, but the administrator will be sure to have retained appropriate controls over the management of the business and obtained indemnities for any loss or damage that may result from the period of business operation.

4.8   INTERIM MORATORIUM

An interim moratorium will come into effect where:

(a) the administration application has been issued, but not heard;
(b) an administration application has been granted, but the administration order has yet to take effect; or
(c) notice of intention to appoint an administrator has been filed at court (IA 1986, Sched.B1, para.44).

An interim moratorium will not take effect if there is an administrative receiver in office, unless the administrative receiver and appointor of the administrative receiver have consented to the making of an administration order (IA 1986, Sched.B1, para.44(6)). This provision is necessary as the holder of a floating charge has an effective veto over any attempt to appoint an administrator by court order (IA 1986, Sched.B1, para.39(1)(a) unless the security is liable to be set aside as a transaction at an undervalue, preference or avoided under IA 1986, s.245).

The interim moratorium has the same consequences as the statutory moratorium coming into effect on the commencement of the administration. However, for obvious reasons until the appointment is made, the consent of the administrator cannot be obtained to exercise rights that are otherwise prohibited by the statutory moratorium (IA 1986, Sched.B1, para.44(6)).

The effect of the interim moratorium and its continuation for a period of up to 10 business days (IA 1986, Sched.B1, para.44(2)) does mean that it can be used by the company/its directors to halt possible enforcement action by creditors. Indeed there is nothing in the legislation that expressly prohibits the filing of successive notices of intention to appoint, which could have the effect of extending this 10-day period. Where there is a legitimate reason for the filing of successive notices, such as change in circumstances and the need for final planning/calculation by the proposed administrator prior to commencement of the administration proper this might be seen as excusable. However, improper use and/or the filing of multiple notices could well be seen as an abuse of process.

For the duration of the interim moratorium, permission of the court is not required for:

(a) the presentation of certain petitions for the winding up of the company (IA 1986, s.124A (public interest petition) and Financial Services and Markets Act (FSMA) 2000, s.367 (FSA petition));
(b) an appointment of an administrator by the floating charge holder;
(c) an appointment of an administrative receiver by the floating charge holder; or
(d) the carrying out by an administrative receiver (whenever appointed) of his functions.

Once the permanent statutory moratorium has come into effect as we have seen, save for the special exemption winding-up petitions, the actions listed above cannot be taken. This presents the floating charge holder with a short window of opportunity on being served the notice of intention, or notice of application, in which to act and make their own appointment, if they deem it appropriate and in their interests to do so.

CHAPTER 5

The administration process

The process of administration from appointment to the initial creditors' meeting and thereafter to exit is identical whichever method of appointment was used and whoever appointed the administrator. In this chapter we look at the process of administration following appointment of an administrator covering publicity, the initial notice to creditors, proposals, the initial creditors' meeting and the requirements for further reporting. Summaries of the process can be found in **Appendix 3**.

5.1 INITIAL STEPS FOLLOWING APPOINTMENT

Publicity

While a company is in administration, every business document (meaning invoice, order for goods and services, business letter and order form) issued by and on behalf of the company must state:

(a) the name of the administrator; and
(b) that the affairs, business and property of the company are being managed by the administrator (IA 1986, Sched.B1, para.45(1)).

This publicity requirement now also extends to 'all the company's websites' (see Companies (Trading Disclosures) (Insolvency) Regulations 2008, SI 2008/1897).

An administrator, an officer of the company and also, interestingly, the company commit an offence if without reasonable excuse, they permit contravention of this section. The penalty for non-compliance on summary conviction is a fine of up to one-fifth of the statutory maximum (IA 1986, Sched.10). (The statutory maximum is £5,000 Criminal Justice Act 1982, s.74, as read with Magistrates' Courts Act 1980 s.32(9) (for England and Wales) and the Criminal Procedure (Scotland) Act 1995 s.225(8) (for Scotland), both as amended by the Criminal Justice Act 1991 s.17.)

The importance of publicity is to ensure that those contracting with the company are aware that their rights against the company in administration are limited. It is, however, entirely open for these parties to propose such terms of trading as they think fit. For instance, a supplier may be unwilling to supply goods on credit and instead demand cash on delivery. This has important practical implications for the success of the administration. The administrator must take into account the likely squeeze on cash flow and sufficient funding must be in place or contingency plans available, such as finding alternative suppliers, if the administration is to have any chance of success.

Advertisement of administrator's appointment

As soon as reasonably practicable, the administrator shall:

(a) send a notice of his appointment to the company;
(b) publish a notice of his appointment in the London Gazette; and
(c) advertise his appointment as he thinks appropriate.

The notice of appointment in Form 2.11B shall be 'gazetted' and may be advertised in such manner as the administrator thinks appropriate (IR 1986, r.2.27(1)). Prior to 6 April 2009 (Insolvency (Amendment) Rules 2009, SI 2009/642) the administrator was required to advertise his appointment in such newspaper as he thought appropriate in order to ensure the appointment came to the notice of the company's creditors; this often led to advertisements in both the national and local press. Now the administrator may in the exercise of his discretion decide whether and how best to advertise his appointment. In response to this change websites offering to advertise appointments (and other services such as advertising the business and assets for sale) have sprung up.

For Form 2.11B see **www.insolvency.gov.uk/forms/englandwalesforms. htm** or **www.companieshouse.gov.uk/forms/insolvencyForms.shtml**.

Within seven days of appointment (meaning the date of order, or date that the administrator receives notice of his appointment if the out-of-court route is followed) notice must be sent to the registrar of companies (IA 1986, Sched. B1, para.46(4)).

As soon as reasonably practicable (rather than within 28 days under the old pre-Enterprise Act regime) the administrator must obtain a list of the company's creditors and send notice in Form 2.12B to each creditor of whose claim and address he is aware (IA 1986, Sched.B1, para.46(3)). In the case of *Re Sporting Options Plc* [2005] BCC 88 it was held that the notification of appointment could not be made by email.

Notice must also be sent to:

(a) any appointed receiver or administrative receiver;
(b) if there is a pending petition for the winding up of the company, the petitioner;
(c) a provisional liquidator, if one has been appointed;
(d) any High Court enforcement officer (sheriff) who to the administrator's

knowledge has been charged with execution or other legal process against the company;

(e) any person who to the administrator's knowledge has distrained against the company or its property; and

(f) the supervisor of any CVA which is in place.

This notice should also be in Form 2.12B (IA 1986, Sched.B1, para.46(5) and IR 1986, r.2.27(2)).

For Form 2.12B see **www.insolvency.gov.uk/forms/englandwalesforms. htm** or **www.companieshouse.gov.uk/forms/insolvencyForms.shtml**.

While the phrase 'as soon as reasonably practicable' is used to denote the time in which certain announcements should be made, and as such, specific time limits for service/advertisement are no longer prescribed, it would be prudent for the administrator to take all steps that must be taken as swiftly as possible and, in any event, within the previous time limits. Accordingly, it would be advisable for the advertisement to be within a day or two of appointment and notice to creditors and other prescribed parties to be sent within a week or two. However, it is possible for the court to direct that notice may be dispensed with altogether or for a different time period to apply (IA 1986, Sched.B1, para.46(7)). This should only be considered in exceptional circumstances where an administrator considers it unlikely that he will be able to comply with the usual practice and procedures.

An administrator commits an offence if he fails to comply without a reasonable excuse with any of the requirements of this paragraph (IA 1986, Sched.B1, para.46(9)). A fine of one-fifth of the statutory maximum and a daily fine of one-fiftieth of the statutory maximum can be imposed (currently £1,000 and £100 respectively) (IA 1986; Sched.B1, para.46(9), Sched.10).

5.2 STATEMENT OF COMPANY'S AFFAIRS

As soon as reasonably practicable after appointment, the administrator must send notice to one or more 'relevant persons' to provide a statement of affairs of the company (IA 1986, Sched.B1, para.47(1)). This seemingly mandatory requirement must be reviewed, however, in light of IA 1986, Sched.B1, para.48(2)(a) which provides that an administrator may revoke a requirement under IA 1986, Sched.B1, para.47(1) (see also IR 1986, r.2.31(1) making it clear that this is an issue to be exercised in the discretion of the administrator).

A 'relevant person', as defined by IA 1986, Sched.B1, para.47(3), is a person:

(a) who is or was an officer of the company;

(b) who took part in the formation of the company during the period of one year ending with the date on which the company entered into administration;

(c) who was employed by the company (either through a contract of employment or a contract for services) during that period; or

(d) who is or was during that period an officer or employee of a company which has or has been during that year been an officer of the company.

Notice to the relevant person must be in Form 2.13B and the administrator must provide each recipient with the requisite forms for the preparation of the statement of affairs (IR 1986, r.2.28(4)).

For Form 2.13B see **www.insolvency.gov.uk/forms/englandwalesforms. htm** or **www.companieshouse.gov.uk/forms/insolvencyForms.shtml**.

Pursuant to IR 1986, r.2.28(3) the notice to the relevant person must inform each person of:

(a) the names and addresses of others (if any) to whom the notice has been sent;

(b) the time within which the statement must be delivered;

(c) the effect of non-compliance with the notice and the penalty arising; and

(d) the duties under IA 1986, s.235 to provide information and to attend the administrator if required.

The person upon whom notice is served must provide a statement of affairs within 11 days unless the administrator agrees, or where the person applies to be released from the obligation, the court otherwise orders (IA 1986, Sched. B1, para.48(1), (2) and (3); IR 1986, r.2.31). Any person failing to comply with the notice is liable on summary conviction for a fine of up to the statutory maximum (at present £5,000) or on indictment to an unlimited fine (IA 1986, Sched.B1, para.48(4)).

The statement of affairs must be provided in Form 2.14B and must be verified by a statement of truth (IR 1986, r.2.29(1)). A person providing a statement of truth in which he has no reasonable belief commits an offence. The statement of affairs must:

(a) give particulars of the company's assets, debts and liabilities;

(b) give the names and addresses of the company's creditors;

(c) specify the security held by each and every creditor; and

(d) state the date upon which any security was granted.

See IA 1986, Sched.B1, para.47(2).

For Form 2.14B see **www.insolvency.gov.uk/forms/englandwalesforms. htm** or **www.companieshouse.gov.uk/forms/insolvencyForms.shtml**.

The administrator may also require any other relevant person to submit a statement of concurrence (in Form 2.15B – see IR 1986, r.2.29(2)) verified by a statement of truth. That person is required to do so within five business days unless agreement to extend has been obtained from the administrator (IR 1986, r.2.29(4)).

Any statement of concurrence shall be filed together with the statement of affairs with the court (in Form 2.16B) and must also delivered to the registrar of companies (IR 1986, r.2.29(7)).

For Forms 2.15B and 2.16B see **www.insolvency.gov.uk/forms/ englandwalesforms.htm** or **www.companieshouse.gov.uk/forms/insolvency Forms.shtml**.

A person preparing a statement of affairs or making a statement of concurrence may be paid such expenses as the administrator considers reasonable, from administrator's receipts (IR 1986, r.2.32). Although any decision on this issue is capable of appeal by the court, it is clear that the obligation to provide the statement of affairs is not removed or limited by any dispute over payment of fees (IR 1986, r.2.32(3)). It must also be remembered that the obligation to provide a statement of affairs applies irrespective of the size and complexity of the business. It may therefore be the case that a director will require the support of the company's former internal accounts department, or even external accountants, to provide a meaningful statement. In such circumstances the issue of expenses is clearly much more relevant.

Where the administrator thinks it will prejudice the conduct of the administration if either the whole or a part of the statement of the company's affairs were to be disclosed, the administrator may apply to court for an order limiting disclosure (IR 1986, r.2.30(1)). On application, the court may order that the statement of affairs, or part of it, shall not be filed with the registrar of companies (IR 1986, r.2.30(2)). As soon as the order is made, the administrator shall file Form 2.16B together with the order and the statement of affairs (limited to the extent provided by the order) with the registrar of companies, together with copies (IR 1986, r.2.30(3)). A creditor may apply to court for disclosure of the statement of affairs, or part of it where an order of limited disclosure has previously been granted (IR 1986, r.2.30(4)).

5.3 ADMINISTRATOR'S PROPOSALS

Having taken control of the management of the company, considered the statement of affairs and conducted his own investigations, the administrator must make a statement setting out his proposals for achieving the purpose of the administration (IA 1986, Sched.B1, para.49(1)). This must be as soon as reasonably practicable and in any event no later than eight weeks after the company has entered into administration (IA 1986, Sched.B1, para.49(5)).

The eight-week time limit may only be extended by permission of the court, or creditors' agreement obtained in writing or at a creditors' meeting (IA 1986, Sched.B1, para.49(8)). Creditors' consent is obtained by a majority of unsecured creditors in value who respond and from every secured creditor. If the administrator considers the distribution will only be made to secured and preferential creditors and IA 1986, s.176A does not apply, it is only the consent of each secured creditor and of at least 50 per cent (in terms of value) of the preferential creditors who respond that must be obtained (IA 1986, Sched.B1, paras.107, 108).

An extension obtained by creditors' consent:

(a) can be agreed only once;
(b) may not be for more than 28 days;
(c) cannot be used to extend any court deadline; and
(d) may not be used to extend the period after expiry (IA 1986, Sched.B1, para.108(5)).

On application to the court, an extension can be obtained and may be granted more than once and/or after expiry (IA 1986, Sched.B1, para.107(2)). Where the court orders an extension of time, the administrator must send notice (in Form 2.18B) to:

(a) the registrar of companies;
(b) each and every creditor of the company who is claiming a debt and of whom the administrator is aware; and
(c) every member of the company of whose address he is aware (IR 1986, r.2.33(4)).

For Form 2.18B see **www.insolvency.gov.uk/forms/englandwalesforms. htm** or **www.companieshouse.gov.uk/forms/insolvencyForms.shtml**.

The primary purpose of the proposals is to inform the creditors how the administrator intends to achieve the purpose of administration. The proposals should therefore contain a statement dealing with why administration is considered appropriate (i.e. the purpose of administration) and explain, as appropriate to the circumstances, why the administrator does not consider it reasonable and practicable for the company to be rescued, and/or if appropriate, why it is not reasonably practicable for the company's creditors as a whole to achieve a better result than would be applicable if the company were to be wound up (IR 1986, Sched.B1, para.49(2)(b)).

These provisions ensure that the administrator must not only have regard to company rescue as the pre-eminent objective in fulfilling the purpose of administration, but also highlight to the creditors the reasoning and justification as to why the administrator considers company rescue cannot be achieved, if that is the case.

The statement of administrator's proposals must be sent to the registrar of companies in Form 2.17B (IR 1986, r.2.33(1)) and to the company's creditors and members (so far as the administrator is aware of these). Although notification of appointment cannot be sent by email, in certain circumstances the administrator may be permitted to provide copies of his proposals by email or provide the creditors with reference to a website (*Re Sporting Options Plc* [2005] BCC 88). The administrator may also dispense with the need to send proposals to the members if he publishes a notice (advertised as he thinks fit; see IR 1986, r.2.33(7)) undertaking to provide a copy of the statement of proposals free of charge to any member who applies in writing to a specified address (IA 1986, Sched.B1, para.49(6)).

In accordance with the provisions of IR 1986, r.2.33(2) the statement of proposals shall also include the following information:

(a) details of the court where the proceedings were initiated and the relevant court reference number;

(b) the full name, registered address, registered number and any other trading names of the company;

(c) details relating to the appointment, including the date of appointment and manner of appointment;

(d) the names of the directors and secretary of the company and details of any shareholdings that they may have;

(e) an account of the circumstances giving rise to the appointment of the administrator;

(f) a copy of the company's statement of affairs (or summary) with administrator's comments;

(g) if any order limiting disclosure of the statement of affairs has been made, a statement dealing with this;

(h) in the circumstances where a statement of affairs has not been provided, the names and addresses of creditors including details of any security held;

(i) if no statement of affairs has been provided, details of the financial position of the company at the latest practical date, including a list of the company's creditors, names and addresses and details of debt and an explanation as to why no statement of affairs has been provided;

(j) the basis upon which it is proposed that the administrator's remuneration should be fixed under IR 1986, r.2.106;

(k) to the best of the administrator's knowledge and belief, an estimate of the value of the prescribed part (i.e. the sum derived from floating charge realisations pursuant to IA 1986, s.176A) and an estimate of the value of the company's net property; and if it is not proposed to make any distribution to secured creditors pursuant to IA 1986, s.176A(5) (i.e. if the company's net property is less than the prescribed minimum and the administrator thinks the cost of making a distribution to unsecured creditors would be disproportionate to the benefit or alternatively, where the administrator is to seek a court order for the same), this must be stated;

(l) how it is envisaged the purpose of the administration will be achieved and how it is proposed the administration shall end. If a creditors' voluntary liquidation is proposed, details of the proposed liquidator must be provided together with a statement that the creditors may nominate a different person as the proposed liquidator;

(m) where the administrator has decided not to call a meeting of creditors, the administrator must set out his reasons;

(n) the manner in which the affairs and business of the company have since the date of appointment been managed and financed, including details of any disposals and the terms of such disposals and the manner in which the business affairs of the company will be continued to be managed, if the administration proposals are approved and how they will be financed;

(o) whether the EC Regulation on insolvency proceedings (Council Regulation (EC) No.1346/2000) applies and, if so, whether they are main proceedings or territorial proceedings;

(p) such other information as the administrator thinks necessary to enable the creditors to decide whether or not to vote on the proposals.

The administrator may propose either a CVA or a scheme of arrangement (one of the two previous pre-Enterprise Act purposes of the administration) as a means of achieving the purpose of the administration (IA 1986, Sched.B1, para.49(3)). This is logical, as both are methods of achieving the purpose of the administration (rather than purposes in their own right). Both also offer the opportunity for the unsecured creditors to achieve a higher return and/or the opportunity that the company may be rescued.

The administrator's proposals may not include any action which would:

(a) affect the rights of the secured creditors to be paid their full security;

(b) result in a preferential debt being paid otherwise than in priority to non-preferential debts; or

(c) result in one preferential creditor being paid a smaller proportion of the debt than another.

The proposals may, however, provide for such eventualities if the relevant creditors' approval is first obtained, or the proposal involves the company entering into either a CVA or a scheme of arrangement.

5.4 MEETING TO CONSIDER THE ADMINISTRATOR'S PROPOSALS

In all cases (except where IA 1986, Sched.B1, para.52(1) applies, i.e. the statement of proposals provides that unsecured creditors will be paid in full or not at all) the administrator's statement of proposals will be accompanied by an invitation to an initial creditors' meeting (IA 1986, Sched.B1, para.51(1)). At least 14 days' notice of the meeting should be given to the creditors (IR 1986, r.2.35(4)), notice of the meeting being in Form 2.20B (IR 1986, r.2.35(2)).

For Form 2.20B see **www.insolvency.gov.uk/forms/englandwalesforms. htm** or **www.companieshouse.gov.uk/forms/insolvencyForms.shtml**.

The initial creditors' meeting should be held as soon as reasonably practicable and in any event within 10 weeks beginning on the date upon which the company enters into administration (IA 1986, Sched.B1, para.52(2)). This provision may only be varied by court order or with the consent of the creditors (see above) (IA 1986, Sched.B1, paras.51(4), 107). Where the court orders an extension, notice in Form 2.18B shall be sent to every person entitled to notice of the meeting (IR 1986, r.2.34(3)).

For Form 2.18B see **www.insolvency.gov.uk/forms/englandwalesforms. htm** or **www.companieshouse.gov.uk/forms/insolvencyForms.shtml**.

Notice of the meeting must also be sent to those past and present directors of the company and such other officers of the company whose presence the administrator thinks is required, using Form 2.19B (IR 1986, r.2.34(2)). It should be remembered that at least one director wishing to place a company into liquidation needs to be present at a creditors' meeting; this is not the case in administration. However, often the administrator will find the presence of the directors of assistance in answering questions posed by creditors from the floor, although it should be remembered that the initial creditors' meeting is convened to consider the proposals and not conduct an analysis of the prior conduct of the directors and assessment of why the company failed.

For Form 2.19B see **www.insolvency.gov.uk/forms/englandwalesforms. htm** or **www.companieshouse.gov.uk/forms/insolvencyForms.shtml**.

In fixing the venue for the meeting the administrator is to have regard to the convenience to the creditors and the meeting must be held between 10.00 am and 4.00 pm on a business day unless the court directs otherwise (IR 1986, r.2.35(3)).

Notice of the initial creditors' meeting must be published in the Gazette and may be advertised in such manner as the administrator thinks fit (IR 1986, r.2.34(1)).

The meeting may be adjourned once, for no more than 14 days, by the chairman and must be adjourned on resolution of the meeting in circumstances where there is no requisite majority for approval of the proposals (IR 1986, r.2.34(4)).

5.5 BUSINESS AND RESULT OF CREDITORS' MEETING

At the initial creditors' meeting, the creditors shall consider the administrator's proposals and may approve them with or without modification (IA 1986, Sched.B1, para.53(1)).

The meeting is chaired by the administrator, or in his place, some other insolvency practitioner or sufficiently experienced employee of the administrator's firm (IR 1986, r.2.36).

If a modification is proposed and approved by the creditors, the administrator must also consent to the modification (IA 1986, Sched.B1, para.53(1)(b)). This is important as the administrator must act in accordance with the proposals save where any revision to those proposals is not considered substantial (IA

1986, Sched.B1, para.68(1)). As a result, if the modification is one that the administrator thinks is unworkable he is not required to accept it. If this means that the proposals are not accepted then the administrator will report to the court, which may make such order as thought appropriate (IA 1986, Sched. B1, para.55) (whether this means that the court could in theory impose a set of proposals on the creditors is a moot point although see *DKLL Solicitors v. Revenue and Customs Commissioners* [2007] BCC 908 and the obiter comment made with regard to steps that an administrator could take in the face of a dissenting majority creditor).

In the case of opposition the administrator may well adjourn the meeting and put forward revised proposals or perhaps defer the more contentious decisions to a creditors' committee, which may be formed at any creditors' meeting (IA 1986, Sched.B1, para.57). In practice, however, by the time of the creditors' meeting, even though held much sooner than previously, the 'heat' from creditors may have dissipated and the proposals are often 'uncontentious' and drafted in a very general manner to provide the administrator with wide powers of management, control and decision making, to be exercised at his discretion. In addition, one sometimes sees a 'take it or leave it' set of proposals, with one proposed resolution for acceptance or rejection of the proposals as a whole, as opposed to a preferred list of steps to be voted on and approved as separate resolutions by the creditors. Such a practice has been discouraged by insolvency practitioner regulatory bodies in their reports and guidance to members.

A resolution is passed when a majority (in value) of those present and voting in person or by proxy vote in favour of it (IR 1986, r.2.43(1)). A resolution is invalid if those voting against it include more than half the value of creditors to whom notice of the meeting was sent and who are not to the best of the chairman's belief connected with the company (IR 1986, r.2.43(2)).

A creditor is entitled to vote if he has lodged with the administrator (not later than 12.00 pm on the day before the meeting) written details of the debt claimed, or as otherwise permitted by the administrator and the claim has been duly admitted by the administrator (IR 1986, r.2.38(1)). The administrator is entitled to call for documents and other evidence to substantiate a claim (IR 1986, r.2.38(3)). The votes are calculated according to the claims as at the date of administration (less any subsequent payment or adjustment for set-off in accordance with IR 1986, r.2.85).

A creditor possessing an unliquidated claim is not entitled to vote unless the administrator agrees to puts a value on the claim and, unlike in liquidation (IR 1986, r.1.17(3)), there is no requirement to fix such a claim with a minimum sum of £1 (IR 1986, r.2.38(5)).

The chairman has a power to admit or reject creditor claims, for the purposes of voting at the meeting. He may mark claims as objected to but allow the creditor to vote subject to a final later determination. Any decision in regard to the admission or rejection of claims is subject to appeal, which must be made not later than 14 days after the date of receipt of the administrator's report (IR 1986, r.2.39). In practice the effect of these provisions is likely to have most impact where a creditor purporting to have a majority claim is rejected and the proposals as approved set out a course of action opposed by that creditor. In the circumstances injunctive relief may be brought to restrain the administrator from acting in a prejudicial manner (perhaps selling the business and assets of the company) pending a determination on the administrator's decision.

Secured creditors are not entitled to vote save where they have valued their security and an estimated unsecured balance remains (IR 1986, r.2.40). However, if the administrator has given notice that he does not think that any distribution will be made to unsecured creditors apart from the prescribed part payment (i.e. pursuant to IA 1986, Sched.B1, para.52(1)(b)) but a meeting has still been requisitioned by creditors, the secured creditor is entitled to vote in respect of the full value of the debt without deduction of the value of his security (IR 1986, r.2.40(2)).

A creditor with a debt on or secured by a current bill of exchange or promissory note is not entitled to vote unless he treats as secured the liability to him on that bill or note of every person who is liable on it antecedently to the company, estimates the value of the security and, for the purpose of his entitlement to vote, deducts it from his claim; in such instances the creditor may be entitled to vote for the estimated unsecured balance (IR 1986, r.2.41).

An owner of goods under a hire purchase or chattel leasing agreement, or a seller of goods under a conditional sale agreement, is entitled to vote in respect of the debt due and payable on the date the company entered into administration (IR 1986, r.2.42).

At the conclusion of the meeting, the administrator must as soon as practicable report the decision of the meeting to the court, the registrar of companies and the creditors (IA 1986, Sched.B1, para.53(2)).

Pursuant to IA 1986, Sched.B1, para.52 the administrator is not obliged to call an initial meeting of creditors if he states in his proposals that:

(a) the company has sufficient property to enable creditors to be paid in full;
(b) the only distribution to unsecured creditors will be pursuant to IA 1986, s.176A(2)(a) (i.e. the prescribed part); or
(c) the company cannot be rescued, nor a greater realisation than on winding up achieved (i.e. the appointment of the administrator is being made solely in order to realise property in order to make a distribution to one or more secured or preferential creditors).

Despite the administrator determining that a meeting should not be held as described above, he may be required to summon an initial creditors' meeting if requested to do so by the creditors of the company whose debts exceed 10 per cent of the total debt of the company (IA 1986, Sched.B1, para.52(2)). The request for the meeting must be in Form 2.21B and made within 12 days of the proposals being sent out. A meeting so requisitioned shall be held within 28 days and security for the cost of summoning and holding the meeting must be deposited by the requisitioner. This deposit may be repaid where the meeting resolves that the expenses of summoning it should be payable as an expense of the administration (see IR 1986, r.2.37). This is a high-risk strategy for an unsecured creditor not otherwise financially interested in the outcome of the administration.

For Form 2.21B see **www.insolvency.gov.uk/forms/englandwalesforms. htm** or **www.companieshouse.gov.uk/forms/insolvencyForms.shtml**.

The requirement to hold any creditors' meeting may be satisfied by a course of correspondence (IR 1986, r.2.48). Correspondence can be by telephonic and/or other electronic means and notice must be sent in Form 2.25B to every creditor who is entitled to notice.

For Form 2.25B see **www.insolvency.gov.uk/forms/englandwalesforms. htm** or **www.companieshouse.gov.uk/forms/insolvencyForms.shtml**.

For votes to be counted, the administrator must receive the vote by 12.00 noon on the closing date specified in Form 2.25B which must be accompanied by a statement in writing on the creditor's entitlement to vote (IR 1986, r.2.48(2)).

The closing date set by the administrator is at his discretion, but must not be less than 14 days from the date of issue of notice (IR 1986, r.2.48(4)).

For the business to be transacted by correspondence, at least one valid form must be returned by a creditor by the time of the closing date (IR 1986, r.2.48(5)).

At the conclusion of the meeting of creditors and, as soon as reasonably practicable, notice of the result of the meeting in Form 2.23B and a copy of the proposals must be sent to:

(a) each creditor who received notice of the meeting and any person who received a copy of the original proposals;
(b) the court;
(c) the registrar of companies; and
(d) any creditor who did not receive notice of the meeting (IA 1986, Sched. B1, para.53; IR 1986, r.2.46).

For Form 2.23B see **www.insolvency.gov.uk/forms/englandwalesforms. htm** or **www.companieshouse.gov.uk/forms/insolvencyForms.shtml**.

5.6 REVISION OF ADMINISTRATOR'S PROPOSALS, FURTHER MEETINGS AND CREDITORS' COMMITTEE

Once the proposals have been agreed, the administrator cannot make any substantial amendment to the proposals without first obtaining the creditors' consent obtained at a further creditors' meeting (IA 1986, Sched.B1, para.54(1)).

What amounts to a 'substantial' amendment may be questionable and hence directions of the court could first be sought by the administrator before going to the cost and expense of calling another meeting (IA 1986, Sched.B1, para.63).

The administrator's statement of revised proposals must be in Form 2.22B and contain information broadly in line with that required in the original proposals (see IR 1986, r.2.45(2)). These revised proposals must be sent to the creditors and may be advertised as the administrator thinks fit (IR 1986, r.2.45(4)).

The administrator may act in accordance with any revision to proposals not considered to be substantial (IA 1986, Sched.B1, para.68(1)(b)). If a creditor felt aggrieved with any changes to the proposals being undertaken by the administrator without approval, he could use the procedures contained in IA 1986, Sched.B1, para.74 (unfair harm) or para.75 (misfeasance).

After the approval of the proposals the administrator may summon further meetings of creditors (IA 1986, Sched.B1, para.62) and shall do so if required by requisition from creditors holding at least 10 per cent of the total debt or where directed to do so by the court (IA 1986, Sched.B1, para.56). The requisitioning of a meeting is subject to the same rules as apply where a meeting is requisitioned following the administrator's determination not to call an initial creditors' meeting (see IR 1986, r.2.37).

As opposed to the calling of a number of creditors' meetings during the course of the administration it may be more expedient to propose to the creditors that a creditors' committee is formed (IA 1986, Sched.B1, para.57). The powers and functions of a creditors' committee are of less importance in the UK than in other jurisdictions (particularly in contrast to the US Chapter 11 procedures) but such committees are often used to sanction company proceedings, the sales processes and the remuneration of the administrators, so their role should not be underestimated.

5.7 PROGRESS REPORT

A progress report (as defined in IR 1986, r.2.47) shall be sent to the creditors, the court and registrar of companies covering the six-month period commencing on the date the company entered into administration and every subsequent period of six months. The report needs to be in Form 2.24B and must be sent to creditors within one month of the end of the period covered by the report. An extension of time in which to file the report can only be obtained on court application (IR 1986, r.2.47(5)).

For Form 2.24B see **www.insolvency.gov.uk/forms/englandwalesforms. htm** or **www.companieshouse.gov.uk/forms/insolvencyForms.shtml**.

The progress report must include:

(a) details of the court where the proceedings have been commenced/filed and the relevant court reference number;
(b) details of the company's name, address and registered office and registered number;
(c) the administrator's name and address, date of appointment and circumstances of the appointment;
(d) details of any extension to the initial period of appointment;
(e) details of progress made during the period of the report, including a receipts and payments account;
(f) details of any assets that remain to be realised; and
(g) any other relevant information to be provided to creditors.

Commercially sensitive information can be excluded, but only if a limited disclosure order is first obtained (IR 1986, r.7.31(5)).

The receipts and payments account must state the assets that have been realised, for what value and what payments have been made to creditors. The account is to be in the form of an abstract showing receipts and payments during the period of the report (IR 1986, r.2.47(2)).

The process adopted at the conclusion of the administration and exit method from administration are dealt with in **Chapter 7**.

CHAPTER 6

The role, functions and powers of an administrator

In this chapter the role, functions and powers of the administrator to be exercised during the course of the administration are outlined. This covers areas such as the treatment of contracts entered into pre- and post-administration, the costs and expenses of administration, as well as the possibility of distributions to be made to creditors. Further detail on the issue of creditor payments and the effect of the prescribed part can be found in **Appendix 4**. Also discussed in **6.5** are the methods by which an administrator's conduct may be challenged.

6.1 THE ROLE OF THE ADMINISTRATOR

In **Chapter 1** the nature of administration and the administrator's role were briefly outlined. To reiterate, the administrator however so appointed:

- is an officer of the court (IA 1986, Sched.B1, para.5);
- is a statutory office holder of the company;
- acts as an agent of the company (IA 1986, Sched.B1, para.69);
- must perform his functions to achieve the statutorily defined objective of administration (IA 1986, Sched.B1, para.3);
- subject to one small caveat, must perform his functions in the interests of the creditors as a whole (IA 1986, Sched.B1, para.3(2));
- in fulfilling his role, will owe fiduciary duties to the company (see *Oldham v. Kyrris* [2004] BPIR 165 and IA 1986, Sched.B1, para.75(3)(c)); and
- must perform his functions as quickly and efficiently as reasonably practicable (IA 1986, Sched.B1, para.4).

In addition, the administrator may do anything necessary and expedient for the management of the affairs, business and property of the company (IA 1986, Sched.B1, para.59(1)).

It is the addition of the word 'affairs' that indicates that an administrator's powers are wider than the directors' powers, which are confined to the management of the business.

The general power of management is augmented by widely drawn specific powers outlined in IA 1986, Sched.1 as follows:

- Power to take possession of, collect and get in property of the company and, for that purpose, to take such proceedings as may seem to be expedient.
- Power to sell or otherwise dispose of the property of the company by public auction, private auction or private contract.
- Power to raise or borrow money, or grant security over the property of the company.
- Power to appoint a solicitor, accountant or other professionally qualified person to assist in the performance of the administrator's functions.
- Power to bring or defend any action or other legal proceedings for and on behalf of the company.
- Power to refer to arbitration any question affecting the company.
- Power to effect and maintain insurances in respect of the business and property of the company.
- Power to use the company's seal.
- Power to do all acts and execute in the name and on behalf of the company any deed, receipt or other document.
- Power to draw, accept, make and endorse any bills of exchange or promissory notes in the name and on behalf of the company.
- Power to appoint any agent to do any business which the administrator is unable to do himself and which may be more conveniently done by an agent.
- Power to employ and dismiss employees.
- Power to do all such things (including the carrying out of works) as may be necessary for the realisation of the property of the company.
- Power to make any payment that is necessary or incidental to the performance of the administrator's functions.
- Power to carry on business of the company.
- Power to establish subsidiaries of the company.
- Power to transfer to subsidiaries of the company, the whole or any part of the business and property of the company.
- Power to grant or accept surrender of a lease or tenancy of any of the property of the company and to take a lease or tenancy of any property required or convenient for the business of the company.
- Power to make any arrangement or compromise on behalf of the company.
- Power to call up any uncalled capital of the company.
- Power to rank and claim in the bankruptcy, insolvency, sequestration or liquidation of any person indebted to the company and to receive dividends and to accede to trust deeds for the creditors of any such person.
- Power to present or defend a petition for the winding up of the company.
- Power to change the company's registered office.
- Power to do all such other things as fall to the exercise of the foregoing powers.

Any person dealing with an administrator in good faith and for value need not enquire whether the administrator is acting within his powers (IA 1986, Sched.B1, para.59(3)). The administrator acts as agent of the company and consequently in addition to this statutory protection, third parties receive adequate protection through rules of agency (IA 1986, Sched.B1, para.70(3)).

In addition to the powers outlined above, the legislation also provides an administrator with the following specific powers:

(a) to remove or appoint a director of the company (IA 1986, Sched.B1, para.61);
(b) to call a meeting of members or creditors of the company (IA 1986, Sched. B1, para.62);
(c) to apply to court for directions in connection with the carrying out of his functions (IA 1986, Sched.B1, para.63); and
(d) to make a distribution to creditors of the company (IA 1986, Sched.B1, paras.65(1) and 66).

This last power is subject to the administrator's obligations under IA 1986, s.175 (i.e. payment of preferential debts). If payment is made to an unsecured creditor (including payment of the prescribed part under s.176A; see *Re Airbase (UK) Ltd* [2008] BCC 213 and **Appendix 4** – Summary 5), the administrator may only do this with permission of the court and/or where the administrator thinks it is likely to achieve the purpose of the administration.

The ability to pay a secured, preferential or even an unsecured creditor is an interesting development of the reformed administration process. It may be used where an 'essential' creditor makes it a condition of future supply that arrears are paid. If the administrator considers it is likely that the continued supply of a good or service is essential for the company to continue to trade, a payment can be made (*Re Rover Espana SA* [2006] BCC 599). The power to make such payments, if thought conducive to the running of an administration, has always been permitted (IA 1986, s.14(3)). However, under the former provisions it was held that where payments did not assist the administration, distributions could not be made to unsecured creditors, even if it offered a more cost-effective and efficient method of distribution (*Re Designer Room Ltd* [2005] 1 WLR 1581). It was, however, subsequently held in *Re Crompton's Leisure Machines Ltd* [2006] EWHC 3583 (Ch) that distributions could be made to creditors who would be preferential creditors in any subsequent liquidation and in *Re Lune Metal Products Ltd* [2007] BCC 217 that distributions would be permitted if they were ancillary to an application to discharge the administration order (IA 1986, s.18(3)).

The provisions following the Enterprise Act 2002 reforms provide that an administrator may make a distribution where it is likely to assist the purpose of the administration (IA 1986, Sched.B1, para.66). While it has been held that the administrator's power to make payments to secured or preferential creditors is unrestricted (*Re Collins & Aikman Europe SA* [2006] BCC 861). However, can distributions regularly be made to unsecured creditors by the administrators?

In para.4.5.14 of the Administration Guidance Notes issued by the Insolvency Service in 2003 it is stated that:

> The administrator … can also make a distribution to the unsecured creditors out of realised assets, but … only with the permission of the court. Distributions in administration will be made in the same way that a liquidator distributes realisations to creditors, but in those cases where sufficient assets have been realised to allow a distribution to be made to unsecured creditors it is anticipated that the company will usually move from administration into a creditors' voluntary liquidation, in order that a voluntary liquidator can make the distribution(s).

It is therefore suggested that it remains the case that it is not the role of the administrator to make distributions to creditors generally; this remains the role of a liquidator. However, in special circumstances with permission of the court, such payments may be possible. In *Re GHE Realisations Ltd* [2006] BCC 139 it was held that the court needed to be satisfied that the distribution was in the best interests of the creditors as a whole, considering whether a distribution in this manner had been included in the proposals, the value of the monies held and whether a creditors' voluntary liquidation had been proposed as an exit route. See also *Re Kaupthing Singer & Friedlander Ltd (In Administration)* [2009] EWHC 2308 (Ch) for an example of an administrator's application for distribution to creditors and how the set-off provisions contained in IR 1986, rr.2.85–2.88 should be applied.

The administrator shall on appointment take custody and control of all property to which he thinks the company is entitled (IA 1986, Sched.B1, para.67). Thereafter, the administrator will manage the affairs and business of the company in accordance with:

(a) any proposals approved by the creditors;
(b) any revisions to those proposals which the administrator does not consider to be substantial;
(c) any revisions to the proposals approved by the creditors (IA 1986, Sched. B1, para.68(1)).

The court may give directions to the administrator regarding the management of the company's business and affairs if one of the following applies:

(a) no proposals have been approved;
(b) the directions sought are consistent with the proposals or agreed revised proposals;
(c) the court considers the directions are necessary to reflect the change in circumstances, since the approval by the creditors of the proposals or agreed revised proposals; or
(d) the court considers directions are desirable to clear up any misunderstanding in the proposals or agreed revised proposals (IA 1986, Sched.B1, para.68(3)).

These provisions make it clear that the administrator's functions are to be exercised in accordance with the creditors' proposals. It is not for the administrator to action a frolic of his own without seeking creditor or court approval of the same. It may also be difficult to assess whether the action being mooted is a substantial departure from agreed proposals. In cases of doubt the administrator may be best advised to seek directions from the court (IA 1986, Sched.B1, para.63).

Following the case of *Re Transbus International Ltd* [2004] EWHC 932, it has been held that prior to proposals being approved, the administrator can take immediate steps to restructure the company and/or sell its business or assets and need not seek court approval. In the case, Mr Justice Lawrence Collins stated that: 'The Enterprise Act 2002 reflects a conscious policy to reduce the involvement of the court in administrations where possible.'

The *Transbus* case followed the pre-Enterprise Act authority of *T&D Industries Plc* [2000] 1 WLR 646. Previously there had been some doubt as to whether an administrator should seek leave of the court to sell the business or assets of a company prior to a meeting of creditors. In *T&D Industries*, Mr Justice Neuberger held that an immediate sale was an option open to an administrator in suitable circumstances. The administrator has a wide discretion to act and the court would not act as a 'bomb shelter' from creditor criticism. While the timescale for preparing a statement of proposals and leading the creditors' meeting (i.e. to take place within 12 weeks) may mean that there is less need for the administrator to proceed with the sale of the company ahead of the creditors' meeting, quick sales are often necessary prior to the creditors' meeting. The case also emphasised the fact that the court will not intervene in cases which are a matter of commercial judgment for the administrator.

It should be remembered, however, that the creditors or members of the company may apply to the court claiming that an administrator is acting or proposes to act in a manner that will unfairly harm the interests of the applicant (whether alone or with some other members or creditors – IA 1986, Sched.B1, para.74(1)). It is this revised power that is likely to be used by the creditors should they strongly disagree with the administrator's decision to sell the business and assets of the company ahead of the creditors' meeting and proposals being agreed.

The administrator also has various statutory powers of investigation common to all office holders (see IA 1986, s.234 (getting in the company's property), s.235 (duty to co-operate with office holder), s.236 (inquiry into company's dealings, etc.).

6.2 ADMINISTRATOR'S POWER TO DEAL WITH CHARGED PROPERTY

The administrator may dispose of or take action relating to property which is subject to a floating charge as if it were not subject to the charge (IA 1986,

Sched.B1, para.70(1)). The floating charge holder will, however, continue to enjoy such rights of priority over the proceeds of sale or acquired property as previously existed. Acquired property means property of the company which is either directly or indirectly represented by the property disposed of.

The court may also grant an administrator permission to dispose of property which is subject to a fixed charge as if it were not subject to that security, but will only do so where the disposal of the property is likely to promote the purpose of the administration (IA 1986, Sched.B1, para.71(1)). An order may be made by the court, subject to the condition that there will be applied towards discharging the sums secured by the security:

(a) the net proceeds of sale; and
(b) if there is a shortfall, any additional sums that are required to be paid to the secured creditor to produce a total return to the secured creditor that is equal to the sale price of the secured property at market value.

These provisions ensure that the secured creditor will not be financially prejudiced by the court's approval of the administrator's proposal to dispose of secured property. However, in practice the administrator will usually work in conjunction with the secured creditor and obtain the relevant consent before dealing with the secured creditor's property. From a practical point of view the potential control of the costs that can be recovered by the administrator is a powerful incentive for the administrator to reach agreement with the secured creditor.

A significant amount of case law has grown up regarding the court's approach to an administrator's ability to deal with secured assets (see *Re ARV Aviation Ltd* (1988) 4 BCC 708; *Re Consumer and Industrial Press Ltd (No.2)* (1988) 4 BCC 72). The court will weigh up the interests of the secured creditors against the likelihood of success of the administrator's proposals and the benefit to the creditors as a whole. As the secured creditor may need to be compensated at market value, a valuation of the property in question must be obtained before the court undertakes this exercise. Where the court makes an order under this section, the administrator is required to file at Companies House a copy of the order within 14 days (IA 1986, Sched.B1, para.71(5)); failure to comply is punishable with a fine of up to one-fifth of the statutory maximum and a daily rate of one-fiftieth of the statutory maximum (as at 30 April 2007 the statutory maximum was £5,000).

6.3 ADMINISTRATOR'S POWER TO DEAL WITH PROPERTY SUBJECT TO A HIRE PURCHASE AGREEMENT

An application may be made by the administrator to obtain permission to dispose of goods that are in the possession of the company under a hire purchase (HP) agreement, as if the property were owned by the company (IA

1986, Sched.B1, para.72(1)). The court will make such an order only if it considers the disposal of the property is likely to promote the purpose of the administration.

An order made in respect of property held under a HP agreement is subject to the same conditions as would apply where a property is subject to a fixed charge. Therefore, on the sale of the goods, the net proceeds of disposal of the goods are applied to the lessor under the HP agreement and additional money may be required to be added to the net proceeds so as to produce an amount determined by the court to be the amount that would have been realised for the goods at market value.

If the administrator is successful in his application, a copy of the order must be filed at Companies House within 14 days of the date of the order. An administrator commits an offence if he fails to comply with this requirement.

This section was subject to some considerable debate during passage of the Enterprise Bill through Parliament. It was argued that the requirement for the lessor to apply to court for relief was inappropriate in cases of low value goods such as photocopiers and certain IT equipment. A proposal put forward to compel the administrator to pay for goods held under HP agreements was, however, rejected. The Government determined that the court was best able to balance the various competing interests (see *Re Atlantic Computer Systems Plc* [1992] Ch 505). It should be noted, however, that even if an application is granted it would not stop the aggrieved creditor challenging the administrator's conduct on grounds of unfair harm (IA 1986, Sched.B1, para.74(5)).

6.4 PROTECTION FOR SECURED OR PREFERENTIAL CREDITORS

An administrator's statement of proposals may not include any action which:

(a) affects the rights of secured creditors of a company to enforce the security;
(b) results in preferential debts of the company being paid otherwise than in the usual order of priority; or
(c) would result in one creditor of the company being paid a smaller proportion of the debt than another (IA 1986, Sched.B1, para.73).

However, the administrator can take any of the actions listed above if the creditor consents, or, if applicable, a CVA or scheme of arrangement is put forward and approved by the requisite majority of creditor(s) so affected.

6.5 CHALLENGE TO ADMINISTRATOR'S CONDUCT OF THE COMPANY

A creditor or member of the company in administration may apply to court claiming that the administrator has acted or proposes to act in a way which has harmed, or will harm his interests (whether alone or in common with some other members or creditors) (IA 1986, Sched.B1, para.74(1)). The legislation in place prior to 15 September 2003 provided a right of challenge on the grounds of 'unfair prejudice'.

The 'new' legislation is not confined to the actual management of the company by the administrator, but could include any conduct of the administrator, which would seem to open up the administrator to a wide degree of challenge (see *Re Charnley Davies (No.2)* [1990] BCC 605 which discusses in detail the scope and limitation of IA 1986, s.27 as unamended). As a consequence, it would seem that the creditor may be able to challenge the decision of the administrator even if he is acting within the scope of his powers of management, e.g. to sell part of the business prior to the meeting of creditors.

It will also be a matter of judicial interpretation as to whether there is any significant difference between 'unfair prejudice' and 'unfair harm'. The Oxford English Dictionary's definition of prejudice is 'harm or injury to a person that results or may result from a judgment or action, especially one where his or her rights are disregarded'. This contrasts with the definition of harm, which is 'hurt, injury, damage, mischief'. Prejudice, therefore, tends to denote a loss of right or interest, which may or may not be accompanied by actual loss. Harm seems to suggest actual loss or damage. As a consequence, it may be the case that there is a wider ability to challenge the decisions and conduct of the administrator, but in such circumstances, the creditor may need to show that in addition to loss of rights, he has suffered actual harm, loss or damage. This may restrict the number of challenges that are made.

It is not appropriate under this section for the court to review decisions taken by the administrator that are taken reasonably, even if they were subsequently proved wrong/mistaken (*Unidare Plc* v. *Cohen* [2005] BPIR 1472). It is also not enough to argue that harm is being caused to the financial interests of the creditors – this is likely to arise in most cases; what needs to be shown is that it is 'unfair' harm. The court will also not allow the section to be used to give directions as to day-to-day conduct of the administration (see *Re Lehman Brothers International (Europe) (In Administration); * sub nom. *Four Private Investment Funds* v. *Lomas* [2009] 1 BCLC 161 where creditors sought unsuccessfully to compel the administrator to provide them with information in advance of the proposals).

A creditor or a member of the company in administration may also apply to the court if the administrator is not performing his functions as quickly or efficiently as reasonably practicable (IA 1986, Sched.B1, para.74(2)). It should be remembered that the administrator is under a positive legal duty to perform quickly and efficiently (IA 1986, Sched.B1, para.4).

On application, the court may:

- grant relief;
- dismiss the application;
- adjourn the hearing conditionally or unconditionally;
- make an interim order;
- regulate how the administrator will exercise his functions;
- require the administrator to do or desist from a specific action or course of conduct;
- compel the calling of a meeting of creditors for a specific purpose; or
- remove the administrator from office or make any other order or consequential provision as deemed appropriate.

It is permissible for the application to be accompanied by an application to remove the administrator under IA 1986, Sched.B1, para.88 (*Sisu Capital Fund Ltd* v. *Tucker* [2006] BPIR 154).

An order will not be made by the court if it would impede or prevent the implementation of:

- an approved CVA;
- a sanctioned scheme of arrangement; or
- an approved administrator's proposal, if the challenge is not made within 28 days of that proposal (IA 1986, Sched.B1, para.74(6)).

These provisions prevent a creditor and/or members circumventing existing rights of challenge, or seeking to overturn a CVA or scheme of arrangement. Where the creditors have agreed the administrator's proposals, the individual creditor's right to challenge these proposals must be exercised within a 28-day period.

The court may also examine the conduct of the administrator or purported administrator on the application of the official receiver, the administrator (in the case of a purported administrator), liquidator, creditor or contributory (IA 1986, Sched.B1, para.75(2)).

The grounds of potential challenge are that the administrator has:

- misapplied or retained money or property of the company;
- become accountable for money or property of the company;
- breached fiduciary or other duties in relation to the company; or
- been guilty of misfeasance.

The court may examine the conduct of the administrator or purported administrator and order the repayment of monies and/or interest or order an account for monies. In cases of misfeasance, a compensatory sum may be ordered to be paid to the company.

This section enables the challenge to be made where an administrator has been invalidly appointed by a floating charge holder (perhaps by reason of an invalidity of the security) and subsequently, that appointment is challenged. The purported administrator would be required to pay any sums held to the validly appointed administrator. It should be remembered that an administrator appointed invalidly by the floating charge holder would be entitled to an indemnity from the appointor.

Any recovery made pursuant to this section will be for the general benefit of creditors rather than for individual creditors (*Oldham* v. *Kyrris* [2004] BCC 111).

6.6 ADMINISTRATOR'S LIABILITY FOR CONTRACTS

The administrator is liable for any contract entered into during the course of the administration and any liability arising thereon shall be payable from property within the administrator's custody and control, payable prior to the claims of the floating charge holder and in priority to the administrator's own remuneration (IA 1986, Sched.B1, para.99(4)).

This is an important provision that ensures that an administrator will look carefully at the necessity of entering into any contracts following his appointment, such as taking on new supplies, etc. The provision does not, however, cover contracts entered into by the company pre-administration (see *Re Salmet International Ltd* [2001] BCC 796 and *Centre Reinsurance International Co.* v. *Freakley* [2006] 1 WLR 2863 and **6.7** below).

Any liability arising out of any contracts of employment that were adopted by the former administrator shall act as a charge on the property under the administrator's custody and control (see IA 1986, Sched.B1, para.99(5)). Briefly, these provisions provide that:

(a) any action taken within a period of 14 days after the administrator's appointment shall not be taken into account or contribute to the adoption of the contract;

(b) no account is taken of any liability that arises with reference to anything done or which occurred before the adoption of the contract of employment; and

(c) the administrator will only be liable for wages and salaries accrued after the adoption of the contract.

These provisions follow the former IA 1986, s.19(4) and (5), which was extensively amended pursuant to Insolvency Act 1994. The provisions were hurriedly introduced by Parliament as a result of the decision of the Court of Appeal in *Powdrill* v. *Watson*; sub nom. *Re Paramount Airways Ltd (No.3)* [1994] 2 All ER 513.

It should be noted that the making of an administration order does not automatically bring to an end an employee's contract of employment or indeed any other contractual liability.

It should therefore be remembered that the performance and general obligations of a contract entered into prior to administration between the company in administration and another company always remains a matter of contractual agreement between the contracting parties. It is often the case that the contract specifically provides that, in the event of the insolvency of one party to the contract (such as an administration) the contract is terminated. This, however, should not be taken as read and other contractual law principles (e.g. frustration, repudiatory breach, anticipatory breach) may need to be considered.

6.7 ADMINISTRATOR'S LIABILITY FOR EXPENSES INCURRED POST-ADMINISTRATION

The issue of an administrator's liabilities and expenses arising during the course of the administration was brought into sharp focus by the decision of *Exeter City Council* v. *Bairstow*; sub nom. *Re Trident Fashions Ltd* [2007] EWHC 400 (Ch) and is an issue referred to in greater depth in **Chapters 1** and **8**.

This case concerned a claim by a local authority that non-domestic rates were payable as an expense of the administration by the administrator in respect of property occupied by the company at the commencement of the administration. The case rested on the interpretation of IR 1986, r.2.67 which was introduced after the Enterprise Act reforms to deal with the expenses and priorities in administration (in turn required because the reforms had introduced the possibility of an administrator making distributions to unsecured creditors with leave of the court).

While IA 1986, Sched.B1, para.99 is modelled on the former IA 1986, s.19 and therefore allows the flexible approach to expenses as per *Re Atlantic Computer Systems Plc* [1992] Ch 505; IR 1986, r.2.67 is modelled on the liquidation expenses rules in IR 1986, r.4.128 which provide for a more rigid approach. This clash of interpretation was 'remedied' by IR 1986, r.2.67(4) (introduced on 1 April 2005 by Insolvency (Amendment) Rules 2005, SI 2005/527) which provides that: 'For the purposes of paragraph 99(3), the former administrator's remuneration and expenses shall comprise all those items set out in paragraph (1) of this Rule.'

As a result, when considering the claim by the local authority David Richards J saw no alternative but to accept that the Insolvency Service, by introducing IR 1986, r.2.67(4), had intended to follow the determination of liquidation expenses, and as the House of Lords in *Re Toshoku Finance UK Plc* [2002] 3 All ER 961 had held that post-liquidation tax liability was an expense of the liquidation, then non-domestic rates for both occupied and unoccupied premises (and therefore other taxes) were an expense of the administration.

Following the decision, the non-domestic rating legislation was amended to provide that where the premises were unoccupied the administrator (like a liquidator) would not be liable for the rates as a cost and expense of the administration. This has led to the unusual situation in the current recession of landlords 'hoping' that the company stays in administration, taking into account that the lease cannot be disclaimed, and the rates do not fall upon the landlord.

Despite this reform the problem of IR 2.67(4) remains, which could see claims being brought by a wider range of creditors (not just the tax collecting bodies). If the court does not have the ability to exercise the flexibility and balancing of the interests of the single creditor against the interests of the creditors as a whole found in *Re Atlantic Computer Systems Plc* [1992] Ch 505, the successful use of administration as a process of company rescue will be in doubt. As seen in the recent case of *Innovate Logistics* v. *Sunberry Properties* [2009] BCC 164 there is some indication that the court has due regard to this issue and will exercise its discretion carefully, adopting the more flexible case-by-case approach of *Re Atlantic Computer Systems*. This more flexible approach should, however, be contrasted with the stricter analysis found in the decision in *Goldacre (Office) Ltd* v. *Nortel Networks UK Ltd (In Administration)* [2009] EWHC 3389 (Ch) in December 2009.

CHAPTER 7

Ending administration

Prior to the Enterprise Act reforms administration was often criticised for the length of time taken to complete the process and the procedural difficulties caused in making distributions to creditors. This area of the administration process was therefore substantially reformed, ensuring that the process was one which should be conducted as quickly and efficiently as reasonably practicable (IA 1986, Sched.B1, para.4). The exit from administration must now be at the forefront of the insolvency practitioner's mind on commencement of the process (indeed, forming part of the proposals put to creditors: IR 1986, r.2.33(2)(m)).

The reforms have left a number of ways in which administration can come to an end:

- automatically after 12 months;
- on application to court by the administrator (which may be allied to a winding-up petition);
- on filing of notice that the purpose of administration has been achieved (out-of-court appointment application only);
- following court order (e.g. appointment of administrator was for an improper purpose or on challenge to administrator's conduct);
- where a winding-up order is made on a 'public interest' petition (IA 1986, ss.124A, s.124B, or FSMA 2000, s.367);
- on the commencement of a creditors' voluntary liquidation following administration by notice;
- on the dissolution of the company.

An administrator's appointment will generally cease as a result of either the success or the failure of the administration (i.e. the purposes of the administration have been achieved, or are no longer capable of being achieved).

In theory, the company could have been stabilised during the period of moratorium and returned to profitability. The control and management of the company could then be passed back to the directors and shareholders. However, unfortunately this is not a common occurrence. More likely than not, the business and assets of the company will have been realised by the administrator, by selling the business as a going concern, or as part of a restructuring of the business. The realisation of assets may enable the creditors of the company to be satisfied in full or, more likely, to be paid a proportion of their debts. As a consequence, there needs to be some thought as to what insolvency procedures should follow: liquidation, CVA or scheme of arrangement?

The most likely consequence of administration is therefore the liquidation of the original company. While an administrator can make distributions to secured and preferential creditors during the course of the administration (and with permission of the court to unsecured creditors), such payments may only be made if they are likely to achieve the purpose of the administration (see *GHE Realisations Ltd* [2006] BCC 139 where it was held that distributions to unsecured creditors could be made if it were in the interest of the creditors as a whole).

In general a distribution to unsecured creditors after the purpose of the administration has been achieved is unlikely to be viewed as permissible. As explained in **6.1** above, it appears to be the intention of Parliament that distributions to unsecured creditors should remain within the remit of a liquidator. As a result while an administrator could propose a company voluntary arrangement, or petition for the compulsory winding up of the company, a more common route may be to use the new procedures to move straight into voluntary liquidation. This is explored in greater depth in **7.8**.

7.1 AUTOMATIC END OF ADMINISTRATION

The appointment of an administrator ceases to have effect at the end of one year beginning on the date upon which the appointment took effect (IA 1986, Sched.B1, para.76(1)). As a result, simply through elapse of time the company will cease to be in administration (IA 1986, Sched.B1, para.1(2)(c)) by whatever method the administrator was appointed. This is one of the key Enterprise Act reforms of the administration process and although calls for the automatic vacation of office as little as three months after the date of commencement (following the Australian model) were rejected, it is a strict measure ensuring that administration is not unnecessarily prolonged without some form of creditor and/or judicial scrutiny.

The one-year period can be extended by court order (as long as the court thinks necessary) or with consent from the appropriate creditors (for a period not exceeding six months) (IA 1986, Sched.B1, para.76(2)). It should be noted, however, that after the automatic end of the administration the creditors cannot consent to an extension (IA 1986, Sched.B1, para.78(4)(c)) nor can the court order an extension (IA 1986, Sched.B1, para.77(1)(b)). Failure to extend the period during the course of administration cannot be rectified by use of 'the slip rule' in IR 1986, r.7.55 (for further limitations on use of the slip rule provision in regard to out-of-court appointments of administrators see *Re G-Tech Construction Ltd* [2007] BPIR 1275). However, in *Re TT Industries Ltd* [2006] BCC 372 exceptional circumstances (i.e. error by the court staff in listing the matter) were held to merit an order being granted to extend the administration period after the end of the 12-month period.

If the administration were to come to an end as a result of an oversight the consequences are severe. The error cannot be rectified by an out-of-court appointment by the company/directors owing to the prohibition on successive administrations in a 12-month period (see IA 1986, Sched.B1, para.23). The insolvent company would thus be passed back to its directors/shareholders and be open to creditor action, leading to potential claims against the former administrator for breach of duty and loss and damage to the company/creditors (see IA 1986, Sched.B1, para.75). While an application to court for a 'new' administration could be made, the possibility of damage to the company in the interim period remains and in any event it could be the case that the court refuses to make an order.

In order to avoid the effects of this provision it was a relatively common practice after the new provisions came into effect for administrators to seek creditor consent to an extension within the initial proposals, i.e. at the beginning of administration. In guidance issued by the Insolvency Service (*Dear IP* No.37 October 2008) the efficacy of this practice was questioned and a view expressed that such a provision in the initial proposal should be included only where absolutely necessary.

7.2 EXTENSION BY CREDITORS' CONSENT

The period of administration can be extended by obtaining creditors' consent (in writing, which includes email (IA 1986, Sched.B1, para.111) or at a meeting) at any time prior to the expiry of the initial term. The term of administration may, however, be extended only once in this manner, it cannot follow an extension granted by the court and can be for no greater period than six months (see IA 1986, Sched.B1, para.78).

Consent is required from:

(a) all secured creditors; and
(b) creditors holding 50 per cent of the total unsecured debt disregarding debts of any creditor who abstains or does not respond (IA 1986, Sched. B1, para.78(1)).

However, if the administrator has provided a statement (pursuant to IA 1986, Sched.B1, para.52(1)(b)) that:

(a) the company had insufficient property to pay all creditors;
(b) unsecured creditors will receive no payment other than the prescribed part (IA 1986, s.176A(2)(a); see also **Appendix 4** – Summary 5); and

(c) the only possible objective that the administration is capable of achieving is a distribution to secured creditors;

consent may be obtained from all secured creditors and if appropriate, where distribution to preferential creditors is to be made, the consent of the preferential creditors holding at least 50 per cent of the total debts.

As soon as reasonably practicable after the administrator's appointment is extended by consent, the administrator must file notice of extension with the court and notify the registrar of companies (IA 1986, Sched.B1, para.78(5)). An administrator who fails to comply with this section without reasonable excuse commits an offence (IA 1986, Sched.16). The penalty is a fine of one-fifth of the statutory maximum and a daily rate fine of one-fiftieth of the statutory maximum.

7.3 EXTENSION BY COURT ORDER

An order extending the administration period can be sought from the court at any time before the expiry of the initial period and for any period thought necessary (see IA 1986, Sched.B1, paras.76(2)(a) and 77(1)).

The application must be accompanied by a progress report (IR 1986, r.2.112(1)) which details the progress made towards achieving the purpose of administration including a receipts and payments account (IR 1986, r.2.47). The court will have regard to the statutory responsibility of the administrator to act as quickly and efficiently as possible and will seek to assess whether the proposals being put forward by the administrator will be successful and for the general benefit of the creditors as a whole. The courts are at the very least likely to require assurances and evidence from the administrator that the purpose of the administration remains reasonably likely to be achieved, and that no unfair prejudice to creditors would result from an extension of the administration period. In exercising its discretion the court is likely to have regard to the same sort of factors as had when making an initial administration order.

7.4 DETERMINATION OF ADMINISTRATION ON APPLICATION TO COURT BY AN ADMINISTRATOR

The administrator may make an application to court for his appointment to cease to have effect from a specified time (IA 1986, Sched.B1, para.79(1)) and shall apply to court if:

(a) he thinks the purpose of the administration cannot be achieved in relation to the company; or

(b) he thinks the company should not have entered into administration; or
(c) a resolution is passed at a creditors' meeting requiring him to make an application (IA 1986, Sched.B1, para.79(2)).

The use of the word 'shall' imposes a mandatory requirement (see discussion of the use of 'shall' in regard to an application under IA 1986, Sched.B1, para.68(2) in *Re Transbus International Ltd* [2004] 1 WLR 2654). There may also be other circumstances requiring the administrator to make an application to court (e.g. where a compulsory winding-up order is to be made: *Re J Smiths Haulage Ltd* [2007] BCC 135; see also *Re TM Kingdom Ltd* [2007] BCC 480).

On application, the court may:

(a) adjourn the hearing conditionally or unconditionally;
(b) dismiss the application;
(c) make an interim order; or
(d) make any order as thought appropriate.

The orders that may be made include a direction dealing with the treatment of creditor claims such as by means of a liquidation where it would be usual for the administrator to petition for compulsory winding up where the administration has failed (see *Oakley Smith* v. *Greenberg* [2003] BPIR 709). There is, however, no requirement that administration should be followed by another insolvency process and the control and management of the company could be returned to the directors, perhaps where the company has been rescued and is no longer insolvent or where a CVA or scheme of arrangement has been put in place compromising creditor claims.

Where the administration has commenced following the making of an administration order, the administrator must apply to court if he thinks the purpose of the administration has been sufficiently achieved in relation to the company (IA 1986, Sched.B1, para.79(3)).

Alternatively, if a court-appointed administrator considers that it is appropriate to move from administration to creditors' voluntary liquidation (IA 1986, Sched. B1, para.83) or to seek the dissolution of the company (IA 1986, Sched.B1, para.84) it has been confirmed by the court that the administrator does not need to apply to court for the administration to come to an end (*Re Ballast Plc* [2005] BCC 96 and *Re GHE Realisations Ltd* [2005] EWHC 2400 (Ch)).

Where an administrator reports to court that the creditors have failed to approve the proposals put forward or have proposed a revision which is unacceptable to the administrator, the court may order that the appointment ceases to have effect (IA 1986, Sched.B1, para.55). It remains a moot point as to whether the court could order the administration should continue in light of majority creditor objection but the case of *DKLL Solicitors* v. *Revenue and Customs Commissioners* [2007] BCC 908 would seem to indicate that this is a possibility.

Where the court decides the appointment should come to an end, the court will discharge the administration order and the administrator must send a copy of the order to the registrar of companies within 14 days, beginning with the date of the order (IA 1986, Sched.B1, para.86). He commits an offence if he fails to comply with this section.

7.5 TERMINATION OF ADMINISTRATION WHERE OBJECTIVE ACHIEVED

If the administrator thinks that the purpose of the administration has been sufficiently achieved, and where the appointment has been made by the floating charge holder, or by the company or its directors by the out-of-court route (IA 1986, Sched.B1, paras.14 or 22), he may file a notice in prescribed Form 2.32B with the court and the registrar of companies together with a copy of the final progress report (IA 1986, Sched.B1, para.80; IR 1986, r.2.113(1)).

For Form 2.32B see **www.insolvency.gov.uk/forms/englandwalesforms. htm** or **www.companieshouse.gov.uk/forms/insolvencyForms.shtml**.

The word 'sufficiently' is not defined but whether the purpose of the administration has been 'sufficiently achieved' would seem to rest on the administrator's assessment of whether the steps outlined in the proposal have generally been achieved. In the vast majority of cases the administration is followed by another insolvency procedure or dissolution of the company. In such circumstances, rather than use this procedure the administrator may think it appropriate to apply to court under IA 1986, Sched.B1, para.79 as described above for directions. As a result, the procedure is probably best limited to circumstances where the company has been rescued.

Two copies of the notice must be filed at court and a copy of the notice sent to the registrar of companies. The court shall endorse each copy with a date and time of filing and the administrator's appointment shall cease to have effect upon that date and time (IR 1986, r.2.113(3)).

The administrator's discharge takes effect at a time appointed by resolution of the creditors' committee, or if none by the creditors. An administrator can avoid the need to call a creditors' meeting for this purpose if there is not going to be a distribution to unsecured creditors (except for the prescribed part pursuant to IA 1986, s.176A) and the consent of the secured creditors (and if applicable the preferential creditors) is obtained.

An administrator may also seek his discharge from liability under IA 1986, Sched.B1, para.98(2)(c) from the court on application for termination of the administration. If taking this step, the administrator should inform the creditors of this intention in the final progress report (IR 1986, r.2.114).

The administrator shall, as soon as reasonably practicable and within five business days, send a notice of the end of the administration and accompanying reports to every creditor of the company of whose claim he is aware and every person who was notified of the appointment and also to the company (IR 1986, r.2.113(5)). The administrator shall, however, be taken to have complied with this requirement if within five business days of filing the notice, he publishes a notice in the London Gazette undertaking to provide a copy of the notice of the end of the administration to any creditor who applies for the same; such notice may also be advertised as the administrator sees fit (IR 1986, r.2.113(6A)).

7.6   COURT ENDING ADMINISTRATION ON APPLICATION OF CREDITOR

On the application of a creditor of the company, the court may provide that the appointment of the administrator shall cease to have effect at a specified time (IA 1986, Sched.B1, para.81(1)).

An application under this section must allege that the appointment was by reason of an improper motive on the part of the applicant for the administration order, or the appointor by an out-of-court route (IA 1986, Sched.B1, para.81(2)).

This provision should be contrasted with a creditor's right to have the conduct of the administrator examined on the basis of unfair harm (IA 1986, Sched.B1, para.74). Instead the provisions contained in para.81 attack the motive behind the appointment, not the conduct of the administrator, and as a consequence, it is not necessary to show that the creditor has actually suffered loss or harm as a result of the appointment.

The appointor, the holder of a floating charge, the administrator and applicant can all be represented at the hearing, of which five days' notice must be given. In practice, the application may also be preceded by injunctive relief seeking to restrain the administrator from acting (and in particular disposing of the business and assets of the company by a pre-pack sale).

There is no statutory guidance given to the meaning of 'improper motive' and the section itself is a new one following the Enterprise Act reforms.

In the case of *Doltable Ltd* v. *Lexi Holdings Plc* [2006] 1 BCLC 384 it was held that an improper purpose was shown where the appointment of an administrator by the directors of an insolvent company was to prevent a secured creditor taking action, even though they argued that this action was taken in the best interests of the creditors as a whole by seeking to ensure that a higher price for the business was obtained than would have been the case if the bank's nominated administrator took control of the sale.

In contrast, in *Re British American Racing (Holdings) Ltd* [2005] BCC 110 it was held it was not an abuse and improper purpose for a creditor and 89 per cent shareholder to appoint an administrator, thereby excluding the minority creditors who opposed a sale of the business, as the sale of the business was of benefit to the creditors as a whole.

For an administrator's appointment to be successfully challenged almost certainly some element of bad faith on the part of the appointor will need to be established. For example, this could be where the directors are clearly using the administration process to avoid the payment of creditors by setting up a 'phoenix company', stripping the original company of its assets and transferring them to the new company solely in order to avoid creditor claims. The provision might also be used if the directors are seeking to avoid the attention of creditors at a s.98 meeting (i.e. a meeting of creditors on the winding up of a company).

Upon application under this provision, the court may make such order as it thinks appropriate, whether in addition to, in consequence of, or instead of the order applied for (IA 1986, Sched.B1, para.81(3)).

7.7 CESSATION OF APPOINTMENT ON PUBLIC INTEREST WINDING-UP PETITION

An administrator's appointment will cease to have effect upon the winding-up order being made by the court on a petition presented in the public interest (IA 1986, s.124A), or on application of the Secretary of State in accordance with Council Regulation (EC) No.2157/2001 on the statute for a European company (location of head office and registered office), introduced by European Public Limited-Liability Company Regulations 2004, SI 2004/2326 and otherwise known as a 'Societas Europaea "SE" petition' (IA 1986, s.124B), or by the Financial Services Authority pursuant to FSMA 2000, s.367. The same effect occurs where a provisional liquidator is appointed in such circumstances.

It is however possible for the administrator's powers to be varied and/ or limited on direction by the court, which thus provides the only means whereby an administrator could hold office concurrently with a liquidator or provisional liquidator (IA 1986, Sched.B1, para.82).

7.8 MOVING FROM ADMINISTRATION TO CREDITORS' VOLUNTARY LIQUIDATION

While it is possible that the company could have been stabilised during the period of moratorium and returned to profitability and thereby 'rescued', in practice this is rare (estimated to occur in less than five per cent of cases and even in such cases a process such as a CVA or scheme of arrangement is likely to have been the cause of the 'rescue').

A more likely result of administration is that the business and assets of the company will have been realised by the administrator, by selling the business as a going concern, or by selling its assets, which may result in the restructuring of the business, but not the company. The realisation of assets will hopefully result in a better return to creditors and indeed the appropriate process for effecting distribution to creditors is something that the administrator should have had in mind in making the original proposals to the creditors (see **Appendix 4** – Flowchart 4).

As we have seen in **Chapter 6**, while an administrator can make distributions to secured and preferential creditors during the course of the administration (and with permission of the court to unsecured creditors), such payments may only be made if they are likely to achieve the purpose of the administration (see *Re GHE Realisations Ltd* [2006] BCC 139 where it was held that distributions to unsecured creditors could be made if it were in the interests of the creditors as a whole).

As a result, a distribution by an administrator to unsecured creditors, to be made after the purpose of the administration has been achieved, is unlikely to be permitted by a court. Accordingly, an administrator could propose a Companies Act scheme of arrangement, a company voluntary arrangement or petition for the compulsory winding up of the company in order to effect the distribution. A more common means of exit and thereby distribution is the use of the procedures introduced in the Enterprise Act reforms to move the company straight from administration into voluntary liquidation (IA 1986, Sched.B1, para.83).

Where an administrator of the company thinks that the total amount which each secured creditor of the company is likely to receive has been paid or set aside and that a distribution will be made to unsecured creditors, notice should be sent to the registrar of companies in Form 2.34B, attaching a final progress report, which must include details of the assets to be dealt with in the liquidation (IR 1986, r.2.117(1)).

In practice, a situation can arise whereby further realisations (such as book debt realisations) can equally be made in liquidation and as a consequence the administrator must consider the cessation of the appointment. However, it could be the case that at the time the administrator will not be able to pass over funds to the liquidator thereby 'guaranteeing' that funds are to be distributed to unsecured creditors and that returns will instead be dependent on the liquidator's realisations. Can the administrator use the process to move from administration to liquidation?

In the case of *Unidare Plc* v. *Cohen* [2006] 2 WLR 974 consideration was given to the use of the word 'thinks' in the context of the administrator's decision; it was held that provided the administrator's decision had been reached through a rational thought process, it was not open to the applicant to challenge the decision on objective grounds. The case supports the wider proposition that the courts will be highly reluctant to intervene in cases of professional/commercial judgment exercised by an administrator rationally and in good faith. Consequently, it is proffered that where the administrator thinks that a return will be made as a result of the further work to be undertaken by the liquidation, he could use this method.

As soon as reasonably practicable, the administrator must send a copy of the notice and documents to those who received notice of his appointment, to the court and the registrar of companies. On registration of the notice, the appointment of the administrator shall cease to have effect and the company shall be wound up as if a resolution for voluntary winding up had been passed on that day (IA 1986, Sched.B1, para.83) meaning the winding up will be deemed to have commenced as from the preceding midnight.

This procedure is available whether the administration was commenced by an out-of-court route or following court order (*Re Ballast Plc* [2005] BCC 96) and offers a seamless transition from one procedure to another (see *Re E-Squared Ltd* [2006] BCC 379 where notices were not registered until after expiry of the administrator's term of office (i.e. the 12-month automatic cessation) but the court held that the company had been wound up on the date of registration and that as at that date the former administrator would be viewed as its liquidator).

The liquidator will generally be the former administrator, although the creditors may nominate a different person to be the liquidator (IA 1986, Sched.B1, s.83(7)).

Alternatively (and commonly) the company can enter liquidation where it forms part of the administrator's original or revised proposals. The proposals must give the details of the proposed liquidator (generally being the same as the administrator) and inform the creditors that they are free to nominate a different person to act as liquidator. The appointment takes effect by the creditors approving the proposed administrator's proposals or revised proposals (IR 1986, r.2.117(3)).

If the administration moves to voluntary winding up without any intervening period the company is deemed to enter into creditors' voluntary liquidation as if an appropriate resolution has been passed on that date. This means that a meeting of creditors pursuant to IA 1986, s.98 is not required to initiate the process and as a result the relevant date of insolvency (which may be important for the calculation of certain claims, e.g. those of preferential creditors) remains the date of the commencement of the administration.

7.9 MOVING FROM ADMINISTRATION TO DISSOLUTION

Where the administrator thinks that the company has no property that might permit a distribution to its creditors, notice of that fact should be sent to the registrar of companies (IA 1986, Sched.B1, para.84). Unless the court orders otherwise the company will be dissolved and struck off the register three months later (IA 1986, Sched.B1, para.84(6)).

In the case of *GHE Realisations Ltd* [2006] BCC 139 it was confirmed that despite the literal wording of the statute such notice may also be provided under this provision where there has already been a distribution of all the company's property during administration. This generally arises where there has been a payment to secured and preferential creditors and after the costs and expenses of administration are taken into account there will be no further distribution to creditors. As we have seen where the only payment to be made to unsecured creditors is the prescribed part (IA 1986, s.176A, see **Appendix 4** – Summary 5) then in order to avoid the need to move into creditors' voluntary liquidation, an application by the administrator to make this payment will be required. Following such payment the administrator could then use this route as the appropriate exit route to administration.

The notice must also be served as soon as reasonably practicable upon the court and on each creditor, accompanied by a final progress report in Form 2.35B.

For Form 2.35B see **www.insolvency.gov.uk/forms/englandwalesforms. htm** or **www.companieshouse.gov.uk/forms/insolvencyForms.shtml**.

The administrator or any interested party can apply to court to extend or suspend the period or apply for an order that the dissolution should not take effect (IA 1986, Sched.B1, para.84(7)). Where an order is made to extend, suspend or disapply the dissolution, the administrator shall as soon as reasonably practicable notify the registrar of companies in Form 2.36B.

For Form 2.36B see **www.insolvency.gov.uk/forms/englandwalesforms. htm** or **www.companieshouse.gov.uk/forms/insolvencyForms.shtml**.

This provision may be relied upon where the administrator or creditor(s) consider that despite there being no assets, further investigation is required, such as into the conduct of the directors or into antecedent transactions entered into by the company. The company could therefore move from administration to liquidation, although thought would need to be given as to how the liquidator would be funded, or alternatively whether the proposed liquidator (and potentially the legal team that may be required) would act on the basis of some form of conditional fee arrangement, recovering fees from realisations. Such arrangements are not uncommon.

In general however the provisions of IA 1986, Sched.B1, para.84 provide a swift and easy exit route from administration (by whatever means the company entered into administration see *Ballast Plc* [2005] BCC 96) in circumstances where there are no assets or further assets to distribute, there is no future for the insolvent corporate shell, and/or where the expenses and costs of liquidation cannot be justified.

It should be noted that should it later transpire that for instance the company had realisable assets, an application to restore the company to the register will be required. As there is no power to restore the administration (IA 1986, Sched.B1, para.84(4)) a petition to wind up the company in parallel to its restoration would be required (Companies Act 2006, s.1029). It is however difficult to envisage circumstances where after dissolution and then restoration, administration would result in a more favourable outcome than liquidation.

7.10 RESIGNATION OF AN ADMINISTRATOR

The administrator may resign from office in limited prescribed circumstances (IA 1986, Sched.B1, para.87). These are set in IR 1986, r.2.119 namely:

(a) ill health;
(b) the intention to cease being in practice as an insolvency practitioner;
(c) a conflict of interest or change in personal circumstances, which precludes or makes impracticable the discharge of his duties; or
(d) other grounds where permitted by the court.

The administrator must provide at least seven days' written notice in Form 2.37B of his intention to resign or to apply to court for permission to resign, such notice being sent to:

• the court, if administrator appointed by the court;
• the floating charge holder, if administrator appointed pursuant to the out-of-court route provided in IA 1986, Sched.B1, para.14;
• the company, if administrator appointed pursuant to the out-of-court route provided in IA 1986, Sched.B1, para.22(1);
• the directors, if administrator appointed pursuant to the out-of-court route provided in IA 1986, Sched.B1, para.22(2).

For Form 2.37B see **www.insolvency.gov.uk/forms/englandwalesforms.htm** or **www.companieshouse.gov.uk/forms/insolvencyForms.shtml**.

The notice of intention to resign must be in Form 2.38B; this must be filed at court and a copy sent to the registrar of companies within five days of filing at court (IR 1986, r.2.121).

It must also be served on any prescribed party as set out above.

For Form 2.38B see **www.insolvency.gov.uk/forms/englandwalesforms. htm** or **www.companieshouse.gov.uk/forms/insolvencyForms.shtml**.

On ceasing to be qualified to act as an insolvency practitioner (IA 1986, Sched.B1, para.89), the insolvency practitioner must give notice to the court, the holder of a floating charge or the company or directors, depending on his mode of appointment, in Form 2.39B.

For Form 2.39B see **www.insolvency.gov.uk/forms/englandwalesforms. htm** or **www.companieshouse.gov.uk/forms/insolvencyForms.shtml**.

7.11 REPLACEMENT OF AN ADMINISTRATOR

Where an administrator dies, resigns, is removed from office by court order, or vacates office on ceasing to be qualified to act as an insolvency practitioner in relation to the company, he may be replaced (IA 1986, Sched.B1, paras.91–95). Such application must be accompanied by a written statement in Form 2.2B by the person proposed to be the replacement (IR 1986, r.2.125(1)).

In practice such replacements are often done in a single 'block transfer' application (see *Re Equity Nominees Ltd* [2000] BCC 84 and *Donaldson* v. *O'Sullivan* [2009] BCC 99 in regard to an unsuccessful challenge as to the lawfulness of the procedure).

Where the administrator was appointed by court order, the administrator may only be replaced on application to court by:

- the creditors' committee;
- the company;
- the directors of the company;
- one or more creditors of the company; or
- the remaining administrator(s) still in office.

An application will also be granted if the court is satisfied that the creditors' committee or any remaining administrator in office is not taking reasonable steps to find a replacement, or the court is satisfied for another reason that it is right for a replacement application to be made (IA 1986, Sched.B1, para.91(2)).

Where the administrator was appointed by the floating charge holder, the appointor retains the power to replace the administrator (IA 1986, Sched. B1, para.92). The holder of a prior qualifying floating charge in respect of the company's property may apply to the court for the administrator to be replaced by an administrator nominated by themselves (IA 1986, Sched.B1, para.96(2)). It should be noted however that there does not necessarily need to be a vacancy in office for the prior floating charge holder to apply to court.

Where the administrator was appointed by the company or its directors and notice of intention has been served on the holder of a floating charge, the administrator can only be replaced if:

(a) the holder of the qualifying floating charge consents; or
(b) if the consent is withheld, the court grants permission (IA 1986, Sched. B1, para.94).

If there is no qualifying floating charge holder and the administrator has been appointed by the company and its directors, the administrator may be replaced by requisite resolution at a duly convened creditors' meeting (IA 1986, Sched. B1, para.97). The unsecured creditors can also ensure, by application to the court, that any administrator chosen by the company or directors is removed from office if they consider the administrator is not acting in their best interests, or perhaps not acting as quickly and efficiently as reasonably practicable (for an example of IA 1986, Sched.B1, para.88 allied to an application under IA 1986, Sched.B1, para.74(2) see *Sisu Capital Fund Ltd* v. *Tucker* [2006] BPIR 154).

7.12 THE EFFECT OF VACATION OF OFFICE

Where a person ceases to be in office and/or where he is replaced, he is under a duty to deliver up the assets of the company (after deduction of properly incurred expenses), its books and records as soon as reasonably practicable; default leading to possible fine (IR 1986, r.2.129).

The administrator removed from office is discharged from liability in respect of any action taken as administrator (IA 1986, Sched.B1, para.98(1)).

The discharge takes effect as follows:

1. In the case of an appointment by the company/directors, discharge is effected on the passing of a resolution by the creditors' committee or by resolution of the creditors.
2. Where an administrator has died, discharge takes effect on the filing at court of notice of his death.
3. If an administrator thinks the company has insufficient property to make a distribution to the unsecured creditors, except for the payment of the prescribed part (IA 1986, s.176A) and makes a statement to that effect (IA 1986, Sched.B1, para.52(1)(b)) a resolution approving his discharge can then be passed by the secured creditors and if appropriate, the majority of the preferential creditors so voting.
4. In the case of appointment by court order, the court will sanction discharge (IA 1986, Sched.B1, para.98(2)(c)).

Although the administrator is discharged from any liability accrued before the discharge takes effect, it does not prevent the court from exercising the right to examine the conduct of the administrator in respect of any potential misfeasance, although any claim of this nature can only be after permission of the court is obtained (IA 1986, Sched.B1, para.75(6)). The discharge may also be postponed if the court thinks that investigation into the administrator's conduct is necessary (see *Re Sibec Developments Ltd* [1993] BCC 148 and *Re Newscreen Media Group Plc* [2009] 2 BCLC 353, where it was confirmed that while the court had jurisdiction to set aside the administrator's release it would do so rarely, such as in cases of the release being obtained by fraud; if a creditor felt there were irregularities in the conduct of the administration the appropriate remedy was the use of IA 1986, Sched.B1, para.75).

7.13 ADMINISTRATOR'S REMUNERATION

The former administrator's remuneration and expenses and any sum payable in respect of a debt or liability arising out of any contract entered into by him in connection with the appointment will be:

(a) charged on and payable out of the property of the company of which the former administrator had custody and control immediately prior to the time he ceased to be the company's administrator; and

(b) payable in priority to any debts secured by the floating charge (IA 1986, Sched.B1, para.99).

The administrator is entitled to receive remuneration for his services (IR 1986, r.2.106(1)) fixed either as a percentage of the total of the property or on a time costs basis. This is determined by the creditors' committee, or where there is none by the meeting of creditors. In the absence of creditor agreement it is to be fixed by application to court. The draft Insolvency (Amendment) (No.3) Rules 2009 set to come into force on 6 April 2010 also propose that the remuneration for insolvency practitioners can be on a fixed-fee basis.

Where there are insufficient monies to pay unsecured creditors anything other than payment under IA 1986, s.176A (the prescribed part), agreement regarding remuneration is required from each secured creditor. If distribution is to be made to preferential creditors, the consent of those preferential creditors with debts exceeding more than 50 per cent of the preferential debts of the company is required.

The basis of the remuneration is often dealt with in the initial proposals sent to creditors at the outset of the administration, allowing the administrator to draw down fees on an interim basis.

If the administrator considers that the remuneration fixed by the creditors/creditors' committee is insufficient, he may request that it be increased by resolution of the creditors (IR 1986, r.2.107) or by application to the court (IR 1986, r.2.108).

Any creditor of the company with the concurrence of at least 25 per cent of the value of the creditors may apply to court for an order that the administrator's remuneration be reduced on the grounds that they are in normal circumstances excessive (IR 1986, r.2.109). If the court considers the application to be well founded, it may make an order fixing the remuneration at a reduced amount or rate.

In assessing office holder remuneration (see *Re Cabletel Installations Ltd* [2005] BPIR 28) the court will have regard to:

(a) the main categories of work undertaken and whether the time spent was justified;

(b) the level at which the work was done;

(c) the benefit of the work done and whether it was necessary;

(d) the proportionate value of the work.

See also the guiding principles to be considered by the court as set out in *Practice Statement (Ch D: Fixing and Approval of Remuneration of Appointees)* [2004] BPIR 953. Both the *Cabletel* decision and the Practice Statement indicate that the courts will subject office holders' remuneration to the degree of scrutiny associated with a solicitors' inter-partes costs assessment, although regard will be had to the administrator's role as an 'officer of the court' and the 'public' collective function being fulfilled by the office holder.

CHAPTER 8

The future for administration

8.1   INFINITY AND BEYOND

The 'New Labour' Government of 1997 was somewhat unusual in placing the reform of insolvency law as one of its priorities on coming into office. While reform in this area may not be seen as a natural vote winner, after the lessons of the recession of the early 1990s, it was made clear that the incoming Government saw the reform of insolvency law as an integral part of its broader stated aim to develop an enterprise culture. The Government's vision was the establishment of a new business culture, one that would encourage entrepreneurial activity, allowing businesses and individuals a second chance to try and succeed following financial difficulty.

The genus of this policy is said to have originated from the then Secretary of State, for the then named Department of Trade and Industry, Peter Mandelson. On his fact-finding mission to the US he was said to have been much influenced by the more debtor-friendly approach to insolvency found in the US. This was evident and seen to be particularly beneficial in Silicon Valley, which at that time was still undergoing the last years of the dot.com boom. Here entrepreneurial innovation was driving forward the growth of a developing industry at a tremendous rate of speed and while business failure in such a developing sector was inevitable it was not necessarily frowned upon; indeed in some quarters the experience of bankruptcy was viewed as part of a successful businessman's financial education. Parallels were being drawn between the dot.com boom and the nineteenth-century boom in the railways, whereby over 400 railway companies trading during that century were consolidated, merging into a small handful of successful companies by the century's end. An insolvency regime that facilitates this process of innovation and economic development was seen as a vital boon to the economy as a whole.

It was also felt that the perceived fear of financial failure, and the consequential sanctions that could be imposed, inhibited reasonable entrepreneurial risk taking. As a result, the removal of the stigma of financial failure and the development of a regime more debtor-friendly and in line with US Chapter 11, one less driven by 'self-interested' secured lenders, were the aims driving a series of radical proposals. These proposals were the subject of a consultation process from 1999 onwards. While ultimately somewhat watered down, at least in part because of strong representation from the banking industry, the consultation process did lead to the significant reform of insolvency legislation in the Enterprise Act 2002, and as we have seen reform of the administration process.

The development of UK insolvency law at this time was also seen against a background of increasingly complex corporate debt structures, where companies often have multiple capital providers and stakeholders, who may have very different agendas when considering their investment. The relaxation in the regulation of the banking and financial services industries, beginning in the 1980s, also saw a move away from the traditional model of bank lending and indeed banks' own capitalisation. Historically a bank would manage the company's facility often through a single branch office and, save for the shareholders, remain the only source of capital. Corporate finance and credit facilities were of course more difficult to obtain, but a restricted system did ensure that the appointment of a receiver was the option of last resort for the bank, which would intimately know the affairs of its customers. A move to multi-party lending and the trading in debt itself has seen an ever-increasing number of different stakeholders involved in corporate insolvencies and has caused a fundamental shift in the needs of the UK insolvency regime. No longer could corporate rescue be dependent on the actions of a single (secured) creditor to initiate a process; instead one needed to develop alternative processes which could be led by the debtor company and yet be flexible enough to deal with the demands of multiple stakeholders. The replacement of administrative receivership with administration and the reforms of the latter process were certainly intended to achieve this aim.

The centrepiece of the corporate insolvency law reform provisions was thus the significant reform of the administration process, leaving it as the primary process of corporate rescue. Just by viewing the number of administrations before and after the introduction of the Enterprise Act reforms, on 15 September 2003, one could say that the reforms have been a resounding success. When introduced by the Insolvency Act 1986 administrations ran at a level of a few hundred a year; on the first year after the introduction of the reformed process there were 1,602 administrations. By 2008 this had risen to 4,822 and accounted for 22 per cent of all corporate insolvency law processes.

8.2 IT'S RESCUE JIM ... BUT NOT AS WE KNOW IT

Despite the huge increase in use of the administration procedure, it is arguable that a fundamental shift towards a culture of company rescue has not been achieved. Directors, and particularly equity stakeholders, do not see administration as a means to provide necessary shelter from creditor action and breathing space to restructure its debts, akin to the US Chapter 11 procedure. Negative attitudes towards the process do appear fixed and indeed as we shall see one of the key features of the post-September 2003 insolvency regime has been the marked failure to use administration as a process to facilitate company rescue (achieved in less than five per cent of cases). As a result, while undoubtedly administration has grown in use and developed to act as an alternative way of realisation of assets outside a liquidation process, its use may see the rescue of the business, but seldom of the company.

It is also of note that the reforms of insolvency law were being undertaken at the beginning of a spectacular and prolonged period of growth in the world economy, driven by what has now turned out to be unsustainable levels of demand for goods and services, fuelled by the supply of readily available 'cheap' credit for businesses and individuals across the globe. In times of plenty it is easy to see insolvency law as being a burdensome and bureaucratic interference in commercial activities. The argument runs that parties are free to contract and make their own decisions as to the provision of credit, the free market libertarian arguing that this should simply be a case of 'creditor beware'. Insolvency is thus seen as an unavoidable by-product of the necessity for credit in a free market economy. As a result, the insolvency regime should be one that is 'debtor-friendly' and allow those who have encountered financial failure a chance of rehabilitation, providing a swift and easy means by which individuals and businesses can get back to economic activity. The greater good to economy as a whole of such a cycle outweighs the potential loss to individual creditors.

The credit crunch of 2007 leading to a recession in the UK from 2008, which at the time of writing has not yet officially ended, has tested the new regime. This testing has led to certain developments in practice and procedure, which in turn has led to criticism. It should, however, be borne in mind that in the wake of any economic downturn there will almost inevitably be criticism of the insolvency regime, as insolvency by its very nature will create tension, conflict and disappointment as between debtor and creditor and as between creditors. In a downturn it is natural for the concerns of creditors to be given more prominence and lead to calls that creditors should receive better returns. In turn these calls are likely to be accompanied by criticism of any professionals involved in the process who are seen to be 'profiting' from the insolvency; and it is of note that in November 2009 the Office of Fair Trading launched an investigation into insolvency practitioner fee levels.

At the time of writing it is therefore not altogether surprising that creditor concerns, voiced through the media, are currently inclined to paint the new insolvency regime as a 'debtor's charter' encouraging owners and managers to walk away from debt responsibility and allowing 'phoenix trading' to the disadvantage of all. It is argued that the focus of the insolvency law regime should be less on debtor rehabilitation (and the rescue of businesses and jobs) and more upon the return and treatment of creditors. In the forefront of this debate is one development of the new regime, which is responsible for more ire than perhaps any other, namely the growth of the 'pre-pack administration'.

It is contended, however, that the growth of the pre-pack administration has less do with any fundamental flaw in the insolvency regime but more to do with the continued negative perceptions associated with the initiation of the administration process. Despite its intended design, administration is not seen as company rescue process, nor is it greatly used for that purpose. Why is this?

The first reason and perhaps most significant is the attitude of creditors and suppliers towards a debtor company's administration. Creditors and suppliers to the insolvent business are often fearful of further loss and will naturally be sceptical of any insolvency process that is initiated by the management of the company. Often intentionally kept in the dark for fear of provoking action, creditors and suppliers can therefore be shocked that an administration process has been commenced, was somehow foisted upon them and is one where the management appears in cahoots with the administrator. Creditor anger at the management of the business, perhaps which was growing during the run up to the initiation of the process can cloud commercial judgments. On appointment the administrator's difficulty in obtaining support from creditors and suppliers during the rescue process can all but extinguish any ability to trade during administration and instead leave the insolvency practitioner with little option but to effect an agreement to sell the business and assets of the company immediately upon appointment.

A more recent trend flowing from the loss of Crown preferential status since September 2003 has also been a hardening of attitude by HMRC to corporate debt recovery. It is of note that Value Added Tax Act 1994, Sched.11 provides HMRC with an ability to demand security for payment of VAT which may be or become due. Over 2,000 demands were made in 2009 and particular attention was focused on those owner-managers who had left or proposed to leave VAT debt in a debtor company, and who were proposing to acquire the debtor's company's business and assets from an administrator.

At the same time HMRC has been increasingly willing to pursue actions against directors through the insolvency process using conditional fee arrangements with the insolvency practitioner and their lawyers. This action is often more driven by public policy considerations and as a means of policing conduct. This has an indirect consequence of making 'honest' directors fearful of insolvency and the criticism and investigations that will follow. As a result, since administration is seen as primarily an insolvency process, it is fatally delayed.

At the time of writing the approach HMRC is taking to debt recovery is changing still further. Traditionally HMRC is responsible for the majority of creditor petitions to wind up insolvent companies. During the beginning of the recession for fear of worsening the general economic situation HMRC was seen to be more lenient. However, the ending of the HMRC Business Payments Support Service, set up in November 2008 to allow a quick and easy ability to negotiate a 'time to pay arrangement', will see in 2010 over 250,000 corporate tax debts falling due and the collection of deferred tax liability of well over £4 billion. With the need for the Treasury to balance the budget and maximise tax revenues, the attitude of HMRC to debt (and its recovery) will be central.

Putting to one side the position of HMRC there also remains the problem of general creditor scepticism in regard to any insolvency process and the unwillingness of corporate funders to 'throw good money after bad'. As we have seen in **Chapter 1**, in the consultation process following the Budget of 2009, calls for super-priority funding were rejected (at least for the time being); the broad conclusion drawn from the consultation process was that funding was not generally seen as an issue preventing business rescue. That may be the case for larger companies but in the mid-market and for the owner-managed businesses it leaves little option for the administrator other than to effect a sale of the business and assets upon or soon after appointment. It is therefore true that funding may not be an issue preventing business rescue, as a buyer of the business free from debt burden is likely to present a more attractive funding proposition. However, the funding of the insolvent company itself and therefore company rescue and reconstruction remains problematic. These problems in turn are a major contributory factor to the growth of pre-pack administration sale.

We shall look further at the vexed issued of contractual obligations following administration shortly, but while it may be a trite point it is nevertheless true that a supplier cannot be forced to supply to an insolvent business. Even where there is an existing contract of supply, the parties' fundamental freedom of contract allows the parties to provide for the circumstances of termination which may include an 'insolvency event' including administration. Despite assurances that orders placed during the course of administration will be met as a cost and expense of the administration, suppliers are often unwilling to provide credit terms and will demand cash on delivery. Those providing services such as a credit card facility and/or seeking rent may demand a personal indemnity from an administrator to allow the continued use of the facility or premises, which in practice will only rarely be granted. The cash call from suppliers, 'ransom' creditors and demands made upon the administrator for personal indemnities mean that where administration is an option, a pre-pack may be viewed as being of significantly less risk.

In addition to creditor perceptions of insolvency further reasons for the infrequent use of administration as a company rescue procedure are the debtor company's own views and prejudices towards the procedure. Particularly evident in the mid-market, owner-managers of businesses often leave seeking advice until too late in the day when there is little prospect of company rescue. They do so as they fear that the business will be lost to them, the management and control taken over by the administrator and his team and they view the commencement of the process as being the death-knell of the company. Unfortunately when administration is left too late this becomes a self-fulfilling prophecy.

8.3   HOW DO YOU SOLVE A PROBLEM LIKE ... ADMINISTRATION?

While a change in attitude towards administration would be important to future development, there are some structural and procedural problems with administration that continue to cause difficulties and prevent its greater use as an effective company rescue tool.

A trading administration, whereby an administrator takes over the management and control of the company carrying on its business as a going concern pending reconstruction or sale of business and assets, has unfortunately become less attractive to insolvency practitioners. The reason for this is the risk of loss occurring during the course of the administration. This is due to a problem that has been a constant refrain throughout this book, namely the difficulty in assessing what is, and is not, an administration expense. The uncertainty in this regard has given rise to concern as to the initiation of a trading administration and the encouragement of the use of the 'less risky' route of a pre-pack sale.

Pre-Enterprise Act administrators would have taken some comfort in knowing that the costs and expenses incurred during the administration process were ones that they had agreed to undertake. If a creditor disagreed with the determination of the administrator as to what should be treated as an administration expense and therefore remained unpaid, it was for that creditor to apply to court for permission to take such enforcement action as available to them.

Post-Enterprise Act, the addition of a prescriptive set of rules as to administration expenses (akin to liquidation expenses) has led to a problem of assessing what company liabilities incurred pre-insolvency will continue post-insolvency. It should, however, be noted that unlike a liquidator, the administrator has no option other than to carry on performing (or at least incurring liability for) the company's obligations. While it is a fair point to say that the insolvency practitioner should always assess these ongoing costs and liabilities to determine whether the administration is more attractive than liquidation, it is not always clear what these pre-insolvency company commitments are.

While, in an ideal world, an administrator would discuss with creditors and suppliers, pre-administration, the terms of continuing trade post-administration, in practice it is often the case that an administrator is called into a situation of corporate distress at very short notice. As a result, prior 'warning' to creditors will not be provided because of the concern that these very same creditors will take entirely understandable but self-interested enforcement action, which may damage the prospects of better returns to the creditors as a whole. For instance, if one sought to negotiate with the landlord over a rent reduction or rent holiday during the proposed administration period, the landlord fearing default and the restrictions on action post-administration may well seek to forfeit the lease or distrain over company property. As a result, often such creditors are not informed of any proposed action pre-insolvency and therefore the administrator will take office and immediately have to begin negotiations with creditors and suppliers, some of whom, for the reasons outlined above, will not be willing to compromise their position.

It must, however, be remembered that the costs and the expenses of administration are set out in order of priority and consequently contractual liabilities undertaken by the administrator will have a first call on available funds and be paid prior to the remuneration to be received by the insolvency practitioner. It is perhaps not surprising, therefore, that the insolvency practitioner may not wish to risk the uncertainty of what are to be treated as costs and expenses, and the criticism that will result if the trading of the business results in loss.

Trading administrations have therefore become more difficult and are often only undertaken should an indemnity be provided by a third party, such as a parent company or a potential purchaser. In some instances the administrator may grant a business management operating licence to a party willing to carry on the company's business pending restructuring and/or sale. This management licence is likely to provide for indemnity against the costs and expenses incurred, if there is any trading loss, but such indemnity only remains as good as the strength of covenant provided by the third party.

Some of those who call for more radical reforms would follow the example provided in some other jurisdictions and allow administrators to 'pick and choose' which contractual liabilities they will undertake. The ability to disclaim onerous contracts would be part of the company's ability to restructure. This, of course, would result in a significantly more debtor-friendly regime than is the traditional model in the UK, which places greater store on freedom and certainty of contract/investment.

There are two other issues touched on throughout this book which also explain why administration is failing to be the company rescue technique envisaged. The first factor lies in a significant difference in the treatment of owner-managers in administration compared to say US Chapter 11. In Chapter 11 proceedings 'debtor in possession' means that the existing management remains in control during the restructuring of the business during the moratorium period. Importantly in the UK the management and control of the business pass to the administrator. As a result, it is often the case that directors in the UK are reluctant to use administration for fear of disenfranchisement. Unfortunately administration is seen as ending the directors' involvement and even responsibility for the company and its creditors.

It is interesting to note that at the current time to counter this problem the Government is proposing to introduce reforms to make company voluntary arrangements more attractive. This would include measures such as the extension of the moratorium prior to the creditors' meeting for all companies, not just small companies, and relaxing some of the more onerous responsibilities of the nominee to scrutinise and supervise the affairs of the company prior to the meeting. These proposals have been made against the background of interesting developments in the use of the CVA by retailers with large expensive leasehold property portfolios, to compromise the claims of creditors/landlords where they wished to close certain stores (for example, the restructuring of JJB Sports, Focus DIY and Blacks). The CVA proposal has been made on the basis that should the landlords of the closed stores refuse, the company would be forced into a pre-pack administration (see example of Stylo Plc/Barrett Shoes earlier in 2009). The 'threat' of the pre-pack has thus encouraged the 'consensual' CVA.

It is additionally of note that the Conservative Party is also suggesting reforms to the insolvency regime which would 'take the best bits of Chapter 11'. This appears to be aimed at providing for a moratorium period allowing the company and its directors time and breathing space to formulate a plan of rescue. Whether this will be some form of 'light-touch' administration, reformed CVA or new process remains unclear. The calls for reform, however, would seem to indicate that both Government and opposition think that administration is not acting as the intended tool of corporate company rescue. Reforms in the future may instead see the increased use of the CVA as a means of company rescue and administration used (as now) primarily as a means of business rescue.

A further issue, very much tied to that of expenses, is the problem of funding. In US Chapter 11 proceedings the company has an ability to obtain funding that can, with leave of court, be given 'super-priority funding' status. In the UK if a company enters into administration, often the business faces very significant cash flow difficulties. As we have seen suppliers may well demand cash on delivery and restrict credit terms. With the administrator's obligations to ensure payment of ongoing expenses it may well be the case that additional funding is required.

While the introduction of some form of super-priority funding was considered prior to the Enterprise Act 2002 reforms and again in 2009, it was concluded on both occasions that in the UK it is for the banking industry and those who lend to companies to judge best whether administration will be of benefit and effect greater realisation. If they are willing to lend this shows confidence in the strength of the post-administration business plan and they are likely to support those that are robust and justifiable. This seems an unfortunate lost opportunity. Not only is it the case that in the post-credit crunch period there is more restricted bank lending, the analysis misses a very fundamental point that in the mid-market, at least, it is often the case that secured creditors are neutral as to whether the company goes into administration, particularly if they are fully secured in the event of the business being liquidated and sold on a break-up basis. In such cases these lenders are very unlikely to provide funding. It is, however, often the case that it is for the benefit of unsecured creditors that the business continues to trade as a going concern. However, even if they had the wherewithal, these unsecured creditors are unlikely to be willing to provide funding on an unsecured basis if the company enters into administration, as this could be simply throwing good money after bad; moreover the secured creditor is further protected while they take the risk. The courts have, however, been willing to accept in appropriate cases that funding provided to an administrator is a potential expense of the administration and therefore been able to give the funder some form of 'partial' priority over floating charge realisations.

Despite these innovations one of the difficulties facing the UK insolvency system is not just lack of support but actually the lack of any real interest by creditors once a corporate insolvency process is initiated. Creditors are central to any insolvency process, vital in 'endorsing' the appointment of a particular insolvency practitioner and in regulating the proceedings (i.e. through the administration proposals). The role of the creditor in any corporate insolvency in scrutinising the conduct of the directors of the insolvent company and insolvency practitioners themselves remains vital if the standards of business efficacy are to be maintained. However, the use of administration can mean the creditors have very little involvement in the process, particularly where meetings can be dispensed with and/or conducted by correspondence. The creditor's role can also be extremely limited if key steps, such as the sale of the business and assets, have already taken place prior to the initial meeting, which occurs in the majority of cases prior to 10 weeks from the date upon which the company enters into administration (and the holding of the creditors' meeting). Even where a sale has not taken place, the administrator will be seeking a broad unfettered ability to sell. The consequences of this are that creditors are likely to lose interest in the administration process. This in turn leaves room for abuse from both unscrupulous company directors and in some instances insolvency practitioners, who may wish to use administration where liquidation is most appropriate and to use the procedure to avoid more difficult, unpleasant, 'section 98' meetings which would occur if the company were to be liquidated. As a result, administration may result in less scrutiny of the conduct of the directors.

Notwithstanding these concerns and the significant development of pre-pack sale practices, it should, however, be remembered that the pre-pack will often save businesses and jobs which would almost certainly have been lost if the company had first gone into liquidation. In the right circumstances a pre-pack sale may be the only credible means of saving a business as a going concern, ensuring that the workforce is kept together and customers and suppliers supported. It should be noted that the goodwill of the business can almost immediately be destroyed on the publicity of an insolvency event. Staff are likely to feel demotivated and may seek to leave the business; this is particularly problematic in the case of service companies where certain employees may be crucial to continuation of the business. Creditors, customers and suppliers may thus be 'panicked' into withdrawing support from the company. In such instances pre-pack administration, which to the outside world does no more than change the corporate ownership and allows the business to continue, provides an immediate solution to these problems. The price of this solution may be the fact that it is 'imposed' on certain stakeholders, but this should not detract from its use in the right cases and at the right time, as a legitimate and welcome corporate rescue technique.

One final problem and solution emerging from the current recession is the issue that currently the UK administration procedure is 'blind' to whether the debtor company is large or small. One of the criticisms prior to the reform process was that as a court-driven process, administration was seen as a cumbersome and costly process not readily available to small companies. The reforms have clearly allowed smaller companies to enter into administration not least by the introduction of out-of-court appointment procedures. The simple and flexible code, however, is of equal application to all sizes of companies. It is of note that the banking crisis led to the administration of certain Icelandic banks and the US investment bank Lehman Brothers. The strain that this has caused led to the Banking Act 2009 which came into force on 23 February 2009, which specifically provides for a series of new measures and provisions to deal with bank and building society administrations. New laws to deal with the insolvency of investment firm vehicles are also likely to be introduced.

8.4 FOREIGN AFFAIRS

On the introduction of the Enterprise Act the then Secretary of State Patricia Hewitt lauded the Enterprise Act as providing encouragement to entrepreneurs by giving them a second chance following business failure which would ultimately see the UK as one of the best places in the world to do business. Such were the perceived benefits of the newly reformed regime it was felt that businesses may be set up in the UK and/or new investment would be encouraged. While that is difficult to judge, as we shall see, one development post-2003 has been so-called 'forum shopping', which is a shorthand term applied for the initiation of a corporate insolvency in a given jurisdiction so as to use insolvency processes and procedures considered favourable to the relevant stakeholders.

Traditionally the question of jurisdiction has been focused on multi-jurisdictional restructuring, coupled with the debtor company often wishing to use Chapter 11 proceedings and the US court's attempts to impose extraterritorial jurisdiction. However, it is of note that at or about the same time as the UK was reforming its insolvency regime other European countries were also introducing new measures. In France the Business Safeguard Act of 2005 was introduced on 1 January 2006; in Italy and Spain new insolvency laws were introduced, and Germany saw a relaxation of its stringent insolvency tests until 1 January 2011. Each reform has been implemented to provide debtor companies with some form of breathing space and chance to restructure and return to profitability. Each jurisdiction would claim some advantage for its process and encouragement for stakeholders to commence proceedings in that jurisdiction.

In parallel to local domestic reform on the international stage cross-border insolvency work has been greatly assisted by the introduction of the EC Regulation of 29 May 2000 on insolvency proceedings (Council Regulation (EC) No.1346/2000) and UNCITRAL model law. While cross-border co-operation and recognition mean that an insolvency practitioner's reach in main proceedings is now increasingly international, it should be remembered that the exercise of powers and treatment of creditors remain subject to local laws. Indeed, European jurisdictions have developed very distinct insolvency procedures driven by local customs, practices and indeed each country's own fundamental attitude to debt. These factors may ultimately prevent further economic integration as there appears little likelihood of (or indeed appetite for) the harmonisation of European insolvency laws in the foreseeable future.

If as appears likely, each jurisdiction will continue to develop its own regime the concept of forum shopping will continue to develop. It is interesting to note that the UK has proved a popular jurisdiction and is responsible for some high profile COMI (centre of main interests) forum shopping. The German companies Deutsche Nickel Group in 2004 and Schefenacker in 2007 were interesting examples of a trend which saw the flexible UK reconstruction model preferred over the German court-driven process. One distinct disadvantage of the German system is the appointment of an administrator by the court as opposed to the company, the perceived advantage of the UK regime being the creditors' continued involvement and flexibility and speed in initiation of a process and restructuring solution. It will be interesting to see whether in the years ahead the UK continues to be perceived as a good jurisdiction in which to effect business rescue.

8.5 THE NEED FOR CERTAINTY

It is the experience of creditors in emerging world economies that has shown the fundamental importance of certainty as to how interests are secured and returns obtained in the event of insolvency. The bedrock of economic development is a strong insolvency regime, giving creditors confidence in receiving fair treatment, an understanding as to how they will get their money back, and a clear picture of priorities as between creditors.

Understanding how monies can be returned in the event of default is essential. Much of the market anxiety that arose during the initial phase of the credit crunch was due to the inability to understand and appreciate exactly what returns would be achieved on the default of corporate debts within certain market instruments, in particular collateralised debt obligations. A lack of transparency as to what would happen in the event of insolvency was of little concern in the booming worldwide economies of the late 1990s, as the continuing ability to trade (and package) debt was itself seen as a major component in economic success, allowing for an ever-expanding availability of credit. Problems multiplied, however, because of uncertainty as to where the debt burden would fall on debtor default, particularly with the increasing default rate in US sub-prime mortgages. The question of where the debt burden would rest caused the market in debt purchase to freeze up, triggered a lack of confidence in financial institutions that 'may' have had exposure and meant that credit lines to financial institutions disappeared almost overnight. The banking crisis was caused by uncertainty as to debt repayment, and ultimately led to the recession in the worldwide economy, which in turn caused significant corporate debt default.

To be regarded as a truly successful insolvency procedure, administration must result in a clear process, readily understood by both the debtor company and its creditors. The treatment of contracts, costs and expenses is just one of the current uncertainties in the present regime that clearly needs to be resolved.

8.6 BACK TO THE FUTURE

As previously discussed, calls for the reform of the administration process have led some to look at the attractions of US Chapter 11 processes. The advantages of this process are an ability to restructure the company's contractual arrangements, obtain super-priority funding, cram down debt (i.e. bind dissenting creditors of a particular class to a particular plan of reconstruction) and keep the management and owners of the business central to the process.

The difficulty, however, of Chapter 11 is that it is a highly court-intensive process. Ultimately, it has proved to be an expensive measure, ill suited to owner-managed businesses, with the need to consult and obtain sanction from a creditors' committee meaning that it is only available to large companies where the expenses can be paid from the company funds. Where companies are already in distress this has made Chapter 11 unattractive. Court-approved cram down has also proved unpopular as it disregards creditors' opinions and relies upon an evaluation and estimation of what creditors in a particular class would receive by means of a particular plan or reconstruction being proposed as opposed to liquidation. Ultimately, the cram down revolves around a court determination as what will be best for the creditors as a whole, disregarding the right of the creditors to take their own decision and be motivated by their own self-interest.

In the UK there is no cram down procedure in administration and this is an important factor as to why there are fewer company rescues as opposed to business rescues. The administration procedure allows the administrator to sell the business and assets of the company, meaning that effectively the creditors are disenfranchised from the process and will receive a distribution possibly through liquidation. It is possible in more complex cases for administration to lead to a scheme of arrangement which could see the dissenting creditors bound within the terms of a scheme of arrangement if 75 per cent of a particular class agree. This, however, is a complex, drawn-out process, extremely costly, and is not used save for the largest cases.

One significant difficulty for an administrator is the treatment of the company's contracts. There are some calls to make unenforceable any contractual provision that gives a party an ability to terminate or modify contractual arrangements with the debtor company in the event of administration. This, however, has been rejected and looks unlikely, as the UK remains strongly wedded to the concept of freedom (and certainty) of contract.

It is noteworthy, however, that the administrator is not entitled to disclaim contractual provisions and consequently the company remains bound. This makes administration unattractive, as the trading liabilities (such as rent) are ultimately liabilities that need to be incurred should the business trade. In the circumstances the administrator is likely to be extremely conservative and make wholesale redundancies on appointment in order to cut costs and ensure all other costs and expenses can be met. This in turn creates a view of administration as a method of last resort. As a result it is not just psychological factors that cause administration to be viewed as a prelude to the company's demise.

To counter the problems associated with company rescue, in the 2009 Budget, proposals put forward by Alistair Darling included the extension of the moratorium against creditor action for all companies as opposed to small companies in a company voluntary arrangement. This would have significant attractions to companies using the CVA procedure. Other proposals mooted included some form of debtor in possession finance such as 'simple' super-priority funding, or a new secured charge for companies in administration, or a limit on asset-based lending arrangements to assets or book debts pre-dating insolvency to provide additional working capital. In the report on the consultation process in November 2009, the Government indicated that it would be moving forward with further consultation regarding the CVA moratorium but would not be taking forward any plans for debtor in possession financing at the present time. Such plans, it was felt, might have a negative impact on lending institutions' views towards businesses in general. There is some anecdotal evidence that the cost of lending in the US has been increased through the use of super-priority funding as it could be that lenders are more inclined to withdraw funding levels from distressed businesses if they feel that once in an insolvency process other lenders might obtain super-priority funding.

Against this argument is the fact that the lack of funding, uncertainty as to costs and expenses during administration and the inability for an administrator to disclaim onerous contractual obligators have resulted in large escalation in the use of pre-packaged administrations. Ultimately, this is the cost of business rescue but the media, certain MPs and certain pressure groups have expressed extreme concern that pre-packs lack transparency, disenfranchise creditors and provide a potential ability for buyers to engage in 'phoenix operations'. This in part led the Insolvency Service to issue Statement of Insolvency Practice (SIP)16 in July which became effective on 1 January 2009. In each pre-pack, a report now needs to be issued to the creditors and sent to the Insolvency Service as soon as reasonably practicable explaining the rationale for the pre-pack. Although the Insolvency Service is not responsible for the regulation of the insolvency practitioners (this remaining the responsibility of their own licensing authority) it is noteworthy that the Insolvency Service has used the report to provide information to various insolvency practitioner authorising bodies. In the report on SIP16 in July 2009 it found that information provided by insolvency practitioners to creditors was deficient in over one-third of cases. In 17 insolvency cases, 29 insolvency practitioners were reported to their authorising body for misconduct of some degree; this accounted for three per cent of all reported cases. The report from the Insolvency Service encouraged insolvency practitioners to send a SIP16 statement to creditors upon completion of the sale, disclose the valuation figures obtained and show more clearly any connection between the insolvency company and the purchaser. A further report is promised in the early part of 2010.

Ultimately, a warning has been sent to the insolvency industry and the regulatory bodies that, if they cannot regulate their own conduct, then it is probable that the Government will intervene and legislate further.

Despite criticisms and calls for reform, administration since the Enterprise Act has clearly been cheaper and quicker, more readily available to a wider variety of companies and has resulted in significant examples of business rescue. It has redressed the balance between secured creditors and debtors and certainly provides owner-managers with an ability to use a corporate rescue procedure. What it has clearly not done is encourage company rescue. This failure may lead to the reform of the CVA procedure and possibly more wholesale reform of Company Act schemes of arrangement. Ultimately, however, there needs to be a change in attitude as to what administration can achieve, and this results only when both insolvency practitioners and creditors understand and agree what the process is attempting to achieve.

Such a change in attitude will be of more use than yet more reform. Uncertainty leads to instability and novelty discourages use; as a result the temptation to introduce yet further reforms should perhaps be resisted while the current processes and procedures develop to deal with the present recessionary climate.

This chapter provides a final coda to what is hoped to be a practical guide to the use of administration. As we have seen administration has become somewhat maligned but in this author's opinion, at least, there does not appear to be too much wrong with the procedure; it is a flexible and (at least in its commencement) cost-effective process, which has resulted in significant advances in business rescue. It is the misuse and abuse of the procedure by certain individuals that is wrong and it is this that needs to be monitored and regulated.

Keeping firmly in mind that financial difficulty will always cause conflict and no one will be entirely happy with the result, the following words of wisdom resonate with anyone who has to deal with insolvency:

Money can't buy friends, but it can get you a better class of enemy.

Spike Milligan

Money is better than poverty, if only for financial reasons.

Woody Allen

Table: Comparative analysis of corporate insolvency procedures

	(LPA) receivership	Administrative receivership	Administration	Company voluntary arrangement	Creditors' voluntary liquidation	Compulsory liquidation	Members' voluntary liquidation
Purpose	To recover money owed to secured creditor	To recover money owed to secured creditor	To rescue an insolvent company, or achieve a better result than winding up, or realise property for the secured or preferential creditors	To allow company to reach binding agreement with creditors	To allow an insolvent company to wind up its affairs	To compel a company to wind up its affairs	To allow a solvent company to wind up its affairs
Commenced by	A fixed charge holder	A floating charge holder	Court order or out-of-court appointment by the insolvent company and/or its directors or a qualifying floating charge holder	The directors of the company	The shareholders	Court order	The shareholders
Insolvency practitioner (IP)	Receiver (does not need to be licensed IP)	Administrative receiver	Administrator	Nominee who becomes supervisor	Liquidator (nominated by shareholders approved by creditors)	Official Receiver may become liquidator or private practice IP may be appointed by BIS or by creditors after a meeting	Liquidator

APPENDIX 1

The use of receivership vs. administration

1. Guide to Procedure 1 – Appointment of a receiver
2. Summary 1 – Advantages and disadvantages of receivership as against administration
3. Summary 2 – Prohibition on appointment of an administrative receiver and exemptions

GUIDE TO PROCEDURE 1

Appointment of a receiver

1. The borrower falls into arrears/defaults on terms/is in breach of covenant.
2. A letter of demand is sent providing the borrower a reasonable time to remedy the breach/default – which can be a short period of time – in certain circumstances as little as an hour (see *RA Cripps (Pharmaceutical) and Son Ltd* v. *Wickenden* [1973] 2 All ER 606; *Sheppard & Cooper Ltd* v. *TSB Bank Plc (No.2)* [1996] BCC 965).
3. In the absence of the borrower remedying the breach/default, the charge holder sends in writing a notice of appointment to an individual 'qualified to act'.
4. The appointment must be accepted by the individual before the end of the next business day after the notice has been received.
5. Subject to the above, the appointment is deemed to commence at the time when the instrument of appointment is received.
6. On appointment the receiver shall:

   (a) send notice of appointment to the company;
   (b) ensure that notice of appointment is sent to Companies House, although this is in fact a duty of the charge holder (Companies Act 2006, s.871);
   (c) ensure that all documents issued by the company contain a statement that a receiver has been appointed.

SUMMARY 1 – ADVANTAGES AND DISADVANTAGES OF RECEIVERSHIP AS AGAINST ADMINISTRATION

Advantages to secured creditor of receivership over administration

- The principal obligation of receiver is to the appointor; in administration the principal obligation of the administrator is to the creditors generally.
- The appointment of an administrator is in theory open to greater challenge by unsecured creditors.
- Potential capital gains tax consequences of administration.
- The expenses of administration are recoverable from floating charge realisations.

- Likely greater costs of administration, although receiver's costs can lack transparency. Control of the administration process 'in theory' rests with creditors as a whole.

Advantages to secured creditor of administration over receivership

- The administrator takes control of the management and entire assets of the borrower company.
- The company enjoys the benefit of a moratorium preventing creditor action against the company save for that agreed by the administrator or where permission of the court is sought and obtained.
- The administrator enjoys wide powers of investigation, etc., can compel officers of the company to assist, and can obtain company papers and documentation.
- Flexibility. Administration can be used to save the company, stabilise and then lead to a plan of reconstruction but may also be used solely to realise the whole/part of the security of the lender.

The greater powers of the administrator and the flexibility of the process mean that it is more open to the use of innovative means to deal with secured assets (e.g. transfer to a special purpose vehicle).

SUMMARY 2 – PROHIBITION ON APPOINTMENT OF AN ADMINISTRATIVE RECEIVER AND EXEMPTIONS

The holder of a qualifying floating charge in respect of the company's property may not appoint an administrative receiver of the company (IA 1986, s.72A(1)).

A qualifying floating charge is one that is created by debenture, which:

(a) states that IA 1986, Sched.B1, para.14 applies to the floating charge;
(b) purports to empower the holder of the floating charge to appoint an administrator of the company;
(c) purports to empower the holder of the floating charge to make an appointment which would be an appointment of an administrative receiver within the meaning given by IA 1986, s.29(2); or
(d) purports to empower the holder of a floating charge in Scotland to appoint a receiver who would on appointment be an administrative receiver (IA 1986, Sched.B1, para.14(2)).

The prohibition against the appointment of an administrative receiver applies in all cases except where:

(a) the debenture was created before 15 September 2003; or
(b) the appointment falls within one of the specific statutory exemptions provided in IA 1986, ss.72A–72GA and/or further statutory instrument.

Exemptions under IA 1986, ss.72B–72GA are as follows.

First exemption: capital market (IA 1986, s.72B)

An agreement is or forms part of a capital market arrangement (as defined by IA 1986, Sched.2A, para.1) if:

(a) a party incurs or is expected to incur a debt of at least £50m under the arrangement; and
(b) the arrangement involves the issue of a capital market investment (as defined by IA 1986, Sched.2A, paras.2 and 3, i.e. a debt instrument within art.77 of the Financial

Services and Markets Act 2000 (Regulated Activities) Order 2001, SI 2001/544 and is rated, listed or traded or designed to be rated, listed, traded).

Second exemption: public–private partnership (IA 1986, s.72C)

This is a project company (as defined by IA 1986, Sched.2A, para.7) where the project company is a public–private partnership (PPP) project and includes step-in rights (IA 1986, Sched.2A, para.9).

Step-in rights are those where the person providing the finance (including an indemnity) for a project has the right to take sole or principal contractual responsibility for carrying on all or part of the project upon the occurrence of certain agreed events or to make arrangements for the carrying out of all or part of the project.

It should be noted that there is no monetary threshold applicable to this exemption and it is interesting to see that where the Government is seeking to extract private finance to assist in public projects an exemption is retained. The Government's justification is that administrative receivership is required to protect public services developments, for example the building of new schools and hospitals which would otherwise be delayed by administration, an exception it is not willing to provide generally.

Third exemption: utilities (IA 1986, s.72D)

This exemption covers a project company, where the project is a utility project and includes step-in rights.

A utility project means a project designed wholly or mainly for the purposes of regulated business. The regulated businesses are as defined in statute (IA 1986, Sched.2A, para.10).

Urban regeneration projects (IA 1986, s.72DA)

This exemption covers a project company which is designed wholly or mainly to develop land which at the commencement of the project is wholly or partly in a designated disadvantaged area outside Northern Ireland and includes step-in rights ('urban regeneration projects' as defined by Finance Act 2001, s.92).

Fourth exemption: project finance (IA 1986, s.72E)

This exemption covers a project company where the project is a financed project which includes step-in rights and where a debt of at least of £50m is incurred, or expected to be incurred, for the purpose of carrying out the project.

This exemption is therefore intended to cover large project finance developments not otherwise covered by the PPP or utilities exemptions and was subject to much scrutiny during the reform process. The commercial property industry lobbied hard for these additional exemptions and argued that the threshold should be lowered for property finance projects, from £50m to between £5m and £10m. This call was supported by the Association of Property Bankers, the Royal Institution of Chartered Surveyors and the British Bankers Association. It was feared that the lack of administrative receivership as an available rescue mechanism and the important ability to step in and continue the project would cause great difficulty for commercial property developers. It remains to be seen whether small to mid-market commercial property developments are adversely affected as a result of the loss of administrative receivership.

The meaning of 'financed project' and 'step-in rights' was considered in *Cabvision Ltd v. Feetum* [2006] BPIR 379, a case which held that the prohibition against appointment also applies to limited liability partnerships.

Fifth exemption: financial markets (IA 1986, s.72F)

This exemption covers a company by virtue of the market charge, a system charge or a collateral security charge. (See Companies Act 1989, s.173; Financial Markets and Insolvency Regulations 1996, SI 1996/1469; Financial Markets and Insolvency (Settlement Finality) Regulations 1999, SI 1999/2979.)

Sixth exemption: registered social landlords (IA 1986, s.72G)

Registered social landlords (generally meaning a housing association) are exempt, and those who provide low cost housing who have generally taken over responsibility for such housing from the local authority (defined in Housing Act 1996, Part 1).

Protected railway companies, etc. (IA 1986, s.72GA)

Further exemptions relating to protected companies were inserted by Insolvency Act 1986 (Amendment) (Administrative Receivership and Urban Regeneration etc.) Order 2003, SI 2003/1832 namely:

(a) a company holding an appointment under Water Industry Act 1991, Part II, Chapter I;
(b) a protected railway company (see Railways Act 1993, s.59);
(c) a licence company within the meaning of Transport Act 2000, s.26.

Further possible exemptions

The Secretary of State may by delegated authority insert additional exemptions, provide that exemptions may cease to have effect or amend ss.72A–72G or Sched.2A by statutory instrument. As can be seen above, since 15 September 2003 when the prohibition came into effect two further exemptions have been added.

The procedure for appointment of an administrator

1. Guide to Procedure 2 – Application for an administration order
2. Guide to Procedure 3 – QFCH appointment out of court
3. Flowchart 1 – Initiation of administration out of court by directors where QFCH
4. Guide to Procedure 4 – Appointment of administrator by company/directors out of court

GUIDE TO PROCEDURE 2

Application for an administration order

1. File at court:

   (a) application (in Form 2.1B);

   (b) affidavit in support (or witness statement) (IR 1986, r.7.57);

   (c) written statement from proposed administrator (in Form 2.2B).

2. Interim moratorium takes effect.
3. Give not less than five days' notice of hearing to:

   (a) any person who has appointed/may appoint an administrative receiver;

   (b) any QFCH who may appoint an administrator;

   (c) such other persons as necessary (e.g. petitioning creditor, the company, any administrative receiver or supervisor of CVA in office);

   (d) the proposed administrator.

4. File affidavit of service (in Form 2.3B).
5. Hearing takes place and administration order may be made (in Form 2.4B).

GUIDE TO PROCEDURE 3

QFCH appointment out of court

1. If appropriate, the holder of a qualifying floating charge (the appointor) shall prepare and file at court a notice of intention to appoint an administrator (in Form 2.5B).
2. At the same time as filing the notice of intention, two days' notice must be provided to any prior floating charge holder, giving them two clear days' notice of the proposed appointment.
3. If the prior floating charge holder consents or fails to reply, or in the case that there is no prior floating charge holder, the appointor shall prepare a notice of appointment of an administration (Form 2.6B).
4. The appointor or representative must provide a statutory declaration (contained in Form 2.6B) which cannot be made more than five days prior to appointment.

5. File notice of appointment at court with three copies.
6. The notice of appointment shall be accompanied by:
   (a) an administrator's witness statement (in Form 2.2B);
   (b) evidence that notice has been given.
7. The court shall issue two sealed copies of the notice of appointment to the appointor who shall as soon as reasonably practicable send one to the administrator.
8. If the appointment is sought out of court hours, notice of appointment shall be in Form 2.7B.

FLOWCHART 1
Initiation of administration out of court by directors where QFCH

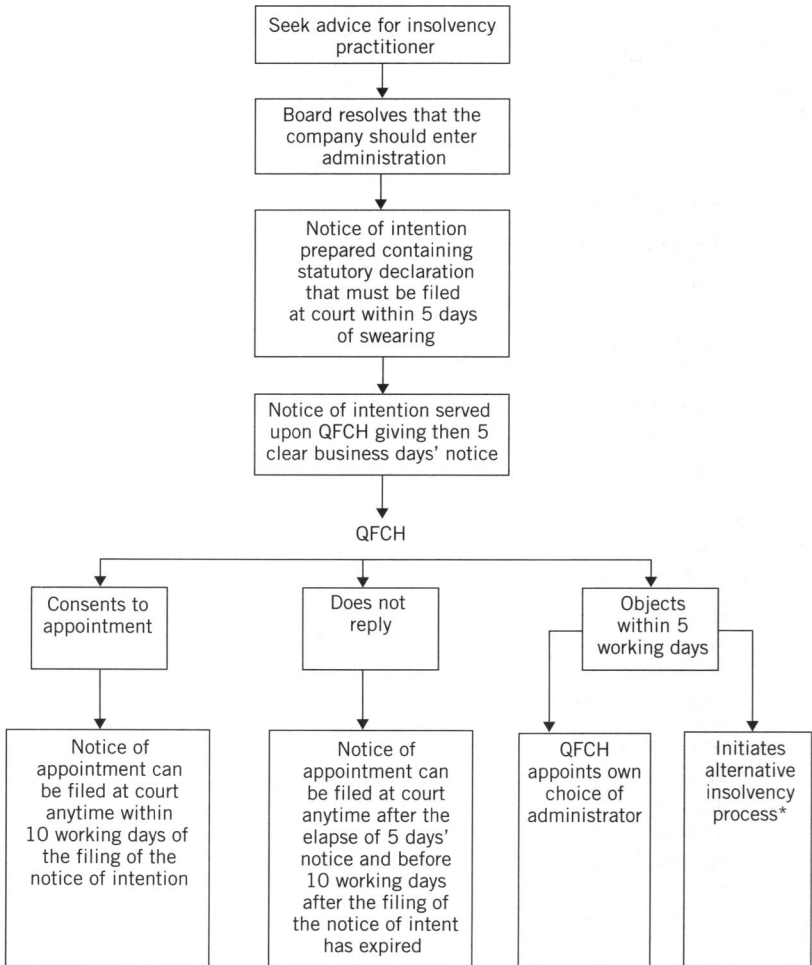

*Receivership, liquidation or in theory could apply to restrain appointment by company of an administrator.

GUIDE TO PROCEDURE 4

Appointment of administrator by company/directors out of court

1. Obtain agreement from an insolvency practitioner to act as an administrator of the company.
2. If the company is subject to a floating charge, the company/directors must prepare a notice of intention to appoint in Form 2.8B.
3. If the company has not granted a floating charge the company/directors may prepare a notice of intention or may proceed immediately to prepare a notice of appointment in Form 2.9B.
4. Attach to Form 2.8B or Form 2.9B as applicable the record of company resolution/ directors' decision regarding administration.
5. Notice of intention must then be served on QFCH giving at least five business days' notice.
6. A copy of the notice of intention is to be filed at court as soon as reasonably practicable after service upon the QFCH; this must be done within five days of making statutory declaration contained in notice.
7. The notice of intention is endorsed by the court with date and time of filing and required number of copies provided to the appointor (see notice provisions below).
8. Interim moratorium takes effect (10 days maximum).
9. The notice of intention (Form 2.8B) must also be sent to:

    (a) any High Court enforcement officer (sheriff) charged with execution;
    (b) any creditor who has distrained;
    (c) any supervisor of a CVA;
    (d) the company (if appointed by directors).

10. Upon service of the notice of intention (Form 2.8B) the QFCH:

    (a) consents to appointment, in which case the company/directors can complete statutory declaration contained in notice of appointment (Form 2.10B) and therefore move on to make the appointment; or
    (b) fails to respond to notice; company/directors can after five days complete statutory declaration contained in notice of appointment (Form 2.10B) and therefore move on to make the appointment; or
    (c) objects and/or makes appointment of their own choice of administrator or appointment of administrative receiver (if the option is available to them).

11. The notice of appointment (Form 2.9B or Form 2.10B) is filed at court with administrator's statement (in Form 2.2B) with appropriate number of copies for service which the court endorses with date and timing of filing. This must be within 10 business days of the filing of the notice of intention.
12. Administration commences.

The administration process and procedure post-appointment

1. Flowchart 2 – Process of administration from appointment to proposals to creditors
2. Flowchart 3 – Process of administration from proposals to exit
3. Guide to Procedure 5 – Administration: appointment to progress report
4. Summary 3 – Methods by which administration may come to an end

FLOWCHART 2

Process of administration from appointment to proposals to creditors

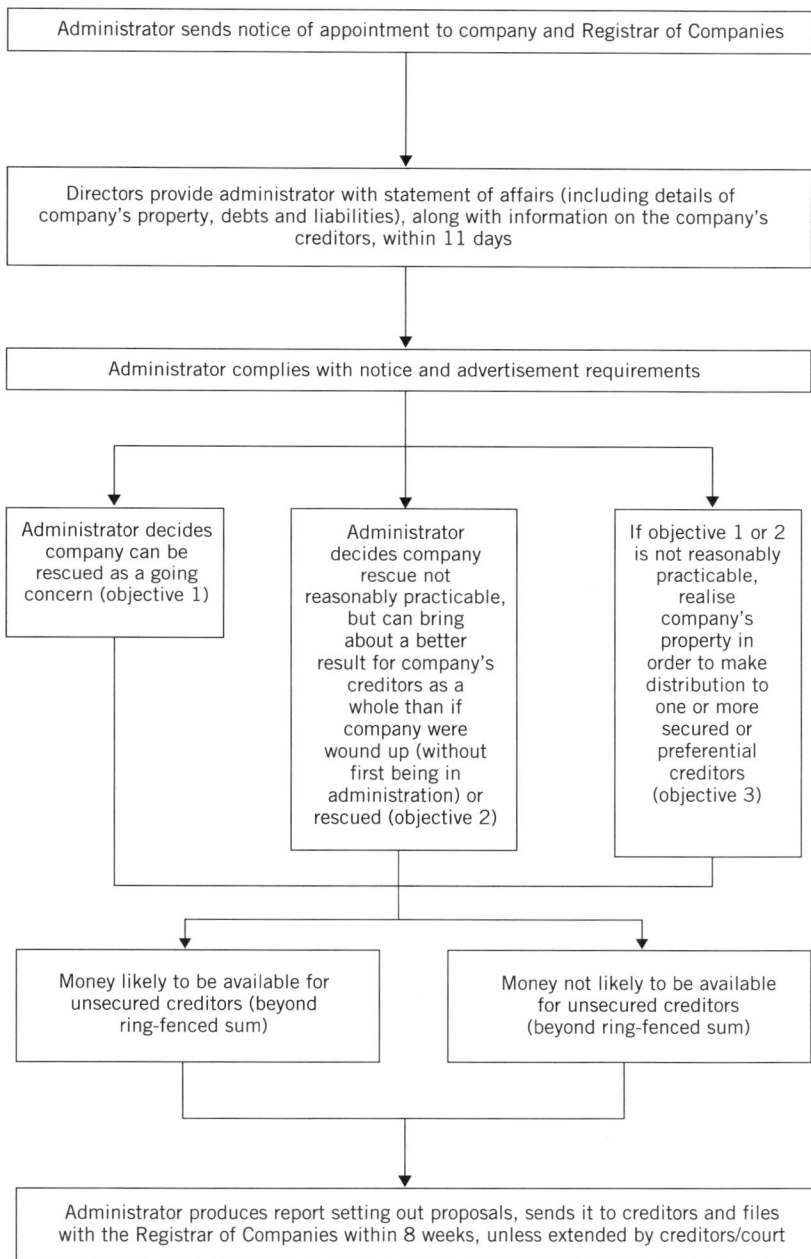

```
┌─────────────────────────────────────────────────────────────────────┐
│  Administrator sends notice of appointment to company and Registrar   │
│                          of Companies                                 │
└─────────────────────────────────────────────────────────────────────┘
                                    │
                                    ▼
┌─────────────────────────────────────────────────────────────────────┐
│  Directors provide administrator with statement of affairs (including │
│  details of company's property, debts and liabilities), along with    │
│      information on the company's creditors, within 11 days           │
└─────────────────────────────────────────────────────────────────────┘
                                    │
                                    ▼
┌─────────────────────────────────────────────────────────────────────┐
│     Administrator complies with notice and advertisement              │
│                       requirements                                    │
└─────────────────────────────────────────────────────────────────────┘
```

| Administrator decides company can be rescued as a going concern (objective 1) | Administrator decides company rescue not reasonably practicable, but can bring about a better result for company's creditors as a whole than if company were wound up (without first being in administration) or rescued (objective 2) | If objective 1 or 2 is not reasonably practicable, realise company's property in order to make distribution to one or more secured or preferential creditors (objective 3) |

| Money likely to be available for unsecured creditors (beyond ring-fenced sum) | Money not likely to be available for unsecured creditors (beyond ring-fenced sum) |

```
┌─────────────────────────────────────────────────────────────────────┐
│  Administrator produces report setting out proposals, sends it to     │
│  creditors and files with the Registrar of Companies within 8 weeks,  │
│              unless extended by creditors/court                       │
└─────────────────────────────────────────────────────────────────────┘
```

FLOWCHART 3

Process of administration from proposals to exit

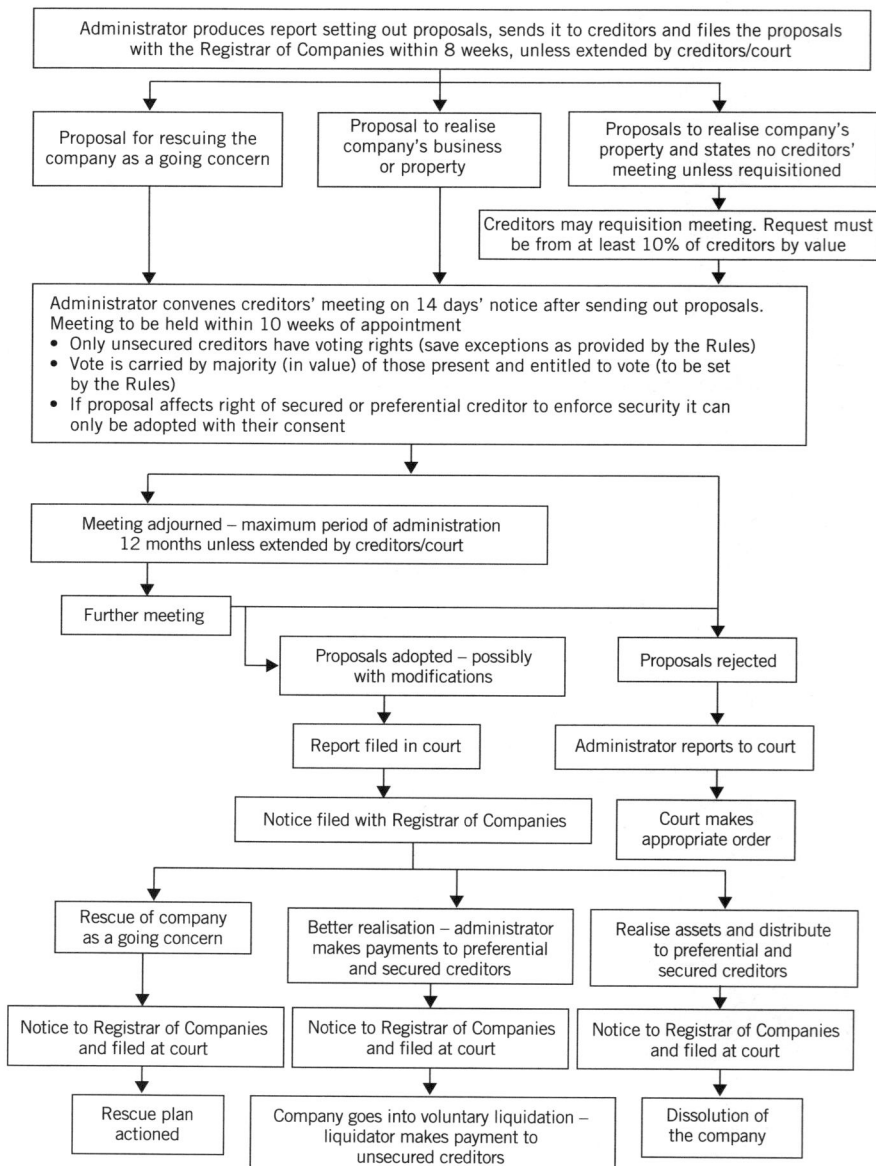

Administrator produces report setting out proposals, sends it to creditors and files the proposals with the Registrar of Companies within 8 weeks, unless extended by creditors/court

Proposal for rescuing the company as a going concern	Proposal to realise company's business or property	Proposals to realise company's property and states no creditors' meeting unless requisitioned

Creditors may requisition meeting. Request must be from at least 10% of creditors by value

Administrator convenes creditors' meeting on 14 days' notice after sending out proposals. Meeting to be held within 10 weeks of appointment
- Only unsecured creditors have voting rights (save exceptions as provided by the Rules)
- Vote is carried by majority (in value) of those present and entitled to vote (to be set by the Rules)
- If proposal affects right of secured or preferential creditor to enforce security it can only be adopted with their consent

Meeting adjourned – maximum period of administration 12 months unless extended by creditors/court

Further meeting

Proposals adopted – possibly with modifications	Proposals rejected
Report filed in court	Administrator reports to court
Notice filed with Registrar of Companies	Court makes appropriate order

Rescue of company as a going concern	Better realisation – administrator makes payments to preferential and secured creditors	Realise assets and distribute to preferential and secured creditors
Notice to Registrar of Companies and filed at court	Notice to Registrar of Companies and filed at court	Notice to Registrar of Companies and filed at court
Rescue plan actioned	Company goes into voluntary liquidation – liquidator makes payment to unsecured creditors	Dissolution of the company

GUIDE TO PROCEDURE 5

Administration: appointment to progress report

1. Administrator's appointment (Form 2.11B) advertised 'as soon as reasonably practicable'.
2. Notice of administrator's appointment served 'as soon as reasonably practicable' on:

   (a) company;
   (b) petitioning creditor;
   (c) creditors (Form 2.12B).

3. Notice of appointment filed with the registrar of companies (within seven days).
4. Administrator sends notice to 'relevant person' to complete a statement of affairs (Form 2.13B).
5. 'Relevant person' to complete and return statement of affairs (within 11 days).
6. Administrator files statement of affairs (Form 2.14B) with registrar of companies and court (Form 2.16B).
7. Administrator to prepare statement of proposals.
8. Statement of proposals to be sent by administrator to company's creditors and members (within eight weeks of appointment) (with notice of meeting).
9. File statement of proposals with registrar of companies (within eight weeks of appointment) (Form 2.17B attaching proposal).
10. Provide at least 14 days' notice of initial creditors' meeting (to be held within 10 weeks of appointment) (Form 2.20B).
11. Send notice to directors/officers – whose attendance is required (Form 2.19B).
12. If meeting is by correspondence instead of actual meeting send notice (in Form 2.25B).
13. Following meeting send notice of result to company's creditors and members, file with registrar of companies (Form 2.23B).
14. Provide progress report within six months and every subsequent period of six months (Form 2.24B).
15. Administration ends on expiry of 12 months unless extended by court order or creditor consent.

SUMMARY 3

Methods by which administration may come to an end

- Automatically by effluxion of time.
- On application to court by the administrator (which may be allied to a winding-up petition).
- On filing of notice that purpose of administration has been achieved (out-of-court appointment application only).
- Court order (e.g. appointment of administrator was for an improper purpose or on challenge to administrator's conduct).
- Public interest winding-up petition (IA 1986, s.124A; or FSMA 2000, s.367).
- Creditors' voluntary liquidation following administration by notice.
- Dissolution.

The effect of administration and distribution to creditors

1. Summary 4 – The effect of administration
2. Flowchart 4 – Priority of payments to creditors where fixed and floating charge security and surplus
3. Summary 5 – The prescribed part payment

SUMMARY 4

The effect of administration

- Any outstanding winding-up petition shall be dismissed (unless the appointment of the administrator was by the holder of a floating charge by the out-of-court route).
- Any administrative receiver shall vacate office.
- Any receiver of part of the company's property shall vacate office on the administrator's request.
- No resolution may be passed for the winding up of the company (voluntary liquidation).
- No order may be made for the winding up of the company (compulsory liquidation).
- No step may be taken to enforce security over the company's property except with the consent of the administrator or permission of the court.
- No step may be taken to repossess goods in the company's possession under any hire purchase agreement except with consent of the administrator or permission of the court.
- The landlord may not exercise any rights of forfeiture by peaceable re-entry in relation to premises occupied by the company except with consent of the administrator or permission of the court.
- No legal process (including legal proceedings, execution, distress and diligence) may be instituted or continued against the company or the company's property except with the consent of the administrator or permission of the court.
- No administrative receiver can be appointed.

(IA 1986, Sched.B1, paras.40, 41(1)–(2), 42(2)–(3), 43(2)–(3), (4), (6), (6A))

FLOWCHART 4

Priority of payments to creditors where fixed and floating charge security and surplus

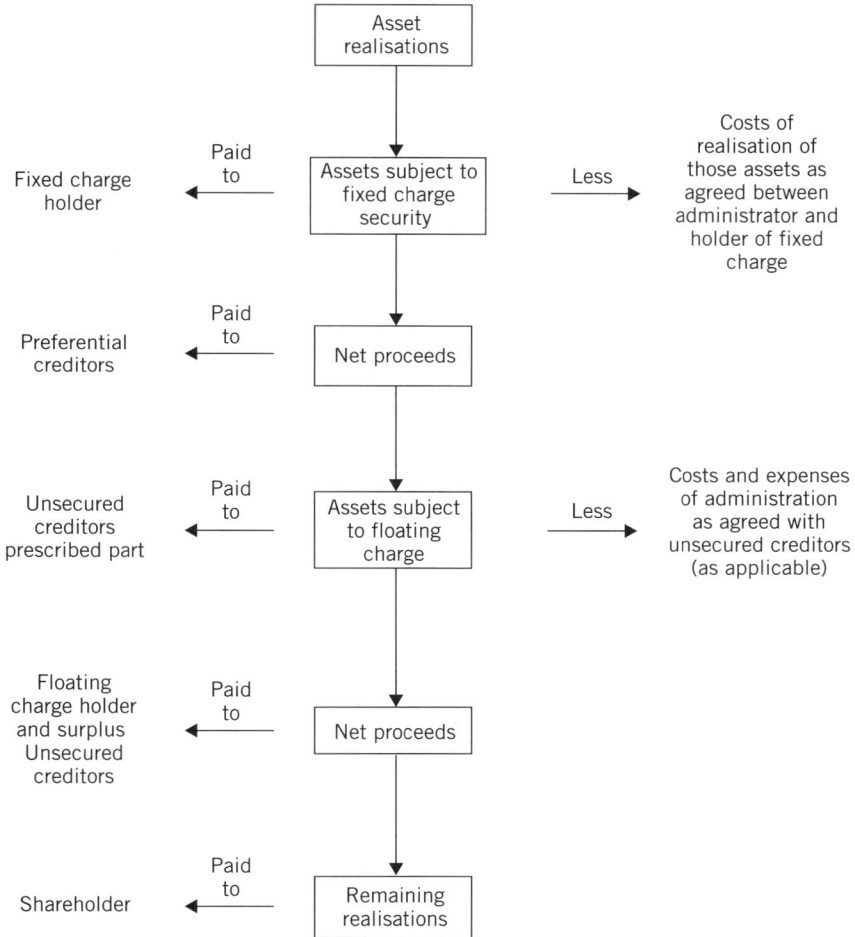

```
                          ┌─────────────────┐
                          │      Asset      │
                          │   realisations  │
                          └─────────────────┘
                                   │
                                   ▼
                                                      Costs of
                                                   realisation of
┌──────────────┐   Paid   ┌─────────────────┐      those assets as
│ Fixed charge │    to    │ Assets subject  │  Less agreed between
│    holder    │ ◄─────── │    to fixed     │ ───► administrator and
└──────────────┘          │ charge security │      holder of fixed
                          └─────────────────┘         charge
                                   │
                                   ▼
┌──────────────┐   Paid   ┌─────────────────┐
│ Preferential │    to    │                 │
│   creditors  │ ◄─────── │  Net proceeds   │
└──────────────┘          └─────────────────┘
                                   │
                                   ▼
                                                   Costs and expenses
┌──────────────┐   Paid   ┌─────────────────┐     of administration
│  Unsecured   │    to    │ Assets subject  │  Less  as agreed with
│  creditors   │ ◄─────── │   to floating   │ ───► unsecured creditors
│prescribed part│         │     charge      │      (as applicable)
└──────────────┘          └─────────────────┘
                                   │
                                   ▼
┌──────────────┐
│   Floating   │   Paid   ┌─────────────────┐
│ charge holder│    to    │                 │
│ and surplus  │ ◄─────── │  Net proceeds   │
│  Unsecured   │          └─────────────────┘
│  creditors   │                   │
└──────────────┘                   ▼
┌──────────────┐   Paid   ┌─────────────────┐
│              │    to    │    Remaining    │
│ Shareholder  │ ◄─────── │   realisations  │
└──────────────┘          └─────────────────┘
```

SUMMARY 5

The prescribed part payment

Pursuant to IA 1986, s.176A (see also Insolvency Act 1986 (Prescribed Part) Order 2003, SI 2003/2097) the administrator is obliged to make available from the floating charge realisations a payment to be made available to the unsecured creditors as follows:

Where the net property does not exceed £10,000		50% of that property
Where the net property exceeds £10,000		First £10,000 50%
		Thereafter 20%

('Net property' is the amount of property which but for s.176A would be available to the holder of the floating charge.)

The total maximum prescribed amount that can be paid is £600,000.

Where the net property does not exceed £10,000 and the costs of making distribution would be disproportionate to the benefit the administrator can determine not to make a distribution.

Where net property exceeds £10,000 but the administrator considers the costs of making the distribution would be disproportionate to the benefit the administrator can apply to court for an order disapplying the provisions of s.176A.

(See *Re Courts Plc* [2008] BCC 917 also *Re International Sections Ltd* [2009] BCC 574.)

A floating charge holder is not entitled to claim for any part of the prescribed part for any unsecured deficit on realisations of the secured assets (*Re Permacell Finesse Ltd* [2008] BCC 208 and *Re Airbase Services International Ltd* [2008] BCC 213).

Glossary

Administration A process to effect corporate rescue, initiated by court order or by a floating charge holder or the directors/company filing requisite notice with the court resulting in the appointment of an administrator

Administration order An order made by a county court or the High Court appointing an administrator to take control of the company

Administrative receiver Insolvency practitioner appointed pursuant to a floating charge in an administrative receivership

Administrative receivership A process to effect the realisation of secured assets for and on behalf of a floating charge holder

Administrator Insolvency practitioner appointed in an administration

Bankrupt Commonly used to denote an inability to pay debt but more correctly describes the legal status of an individual adjudged by court order

Bankruptcy The legally recognised status of an individual adjudged by court order

Book debt Sum owed but as yet unpaid

Company voluntary arrangement (CVA) An agreement in the form of a statutorily imposed binding arrangement by a company debtor with its creditors

Composition An arrangement between a debtor and a creditor whereby the creditor compromises or releases rights against the debtor in respect of a pre-existing debt and receives in exchange and in full satisfaction whatever payment terms are offered by the debtor

Compulsory liquidation A form of liquidation for a company or partnership which follows a court order

County court administration order An alternative to bankruptcy, where an order is made by a county court in respect of an individual debtor whose total combined debts do not exceed (at present) £5,000 and where at least one of those creditors has obtained a county court judgment, for that debtor to pay the debts by regular weekly or monthly instalments

Creditor A person/company who is owed money

Debenture Instrument evidencing a secured debt over the assets of a company. Often used to describe a fixed and floating charge type security

Debt A legally enforceable liability whereby a debtor can be compelled to render what is due at the instance of a creditor

Debtor A person/company who owes money

Directors disqualification order An order made by the court, pursuant to Company Directors Disqualification Act 1986 following an application by the Secretary of State, disqualifying an individual from being a director or concerned directly or indirectly in the control, management or promotion of a company for a period of up to 15 years

Dividend A sum distributed to a creditor during an insolvency process

179

Fixed charge Security over specific and identifiable assets, e.g. land, property and goodwill

Fixed charge holder A secured creditor possessing a form of security over specific and identifiable assets of the debtor. Default in the terms of the security by the debtor may entitle the fixed charge holder to appoint a receiver

Floating charge Security over general assets of a company that are liable to change from time to time during the ordinary course of business (e.g. stock)

Floating charge holder A secured creditor possessing a form of equitable security which is subject to change from time to time in the ordinary course of the debtor's business. If such security is possessed over the whole or substantially the whole of a corporate debtor's business, on default in the terms of the security it may give the floating charge holder the right to appoint an administrative receiver and/or administrator

Fraudulent trading A civil offence pursuant to IA 1986, s.213; also a criminal offence, committed by directors if the business of the company has been conducted with an intention to defraud creditors or for any other fraudulent purpose

Insolvency The status of a debtor when they have an inability to pay debts as they fall due (cash flow basis) or where total liabilities exceed total assets (balance sheet basis)

Insolvency practitioner A person authorised and licensed by a recognised professional body to act in relation to insolvency matters. Sometimes referred to colloquially as the 'IP'

Interim receiver An insolvency practitioner or Official Receiver appointed by the court after the presentation of a bankruptcy petition but before the making of a bankruptcy order to safeguard and protect the debtor's property where there is fear of disposition

Liquidation Insolvency process leading to the dissolution of a company after realisation and distribution of available assets to its creditors and/or members

Liquidator An insolvency practitioner or Official Receiver appointed to realise company assets and distribute proceeds to creditors on the liquidation of the company

LPA receiver Law of Property Act 1925 receiver. An individual (not necessarily an insolvency practitioner) who is appointed to realise fixed charge assets on behalf of a fixed charge holder

Member A person registered as a shareholder or subscriber at Companies House in respect of a company. Also may refer to the member of a partnership

Members' voluntary liquidation A form of liquidation where the company has an ability to pay all of its debts and a return is likely to be made to its members. Also referred to as a solvent liquidation

Moratorium A suspension of creditors' rights to take action to enforce payment of their debt

Nominee An insolvency practitioner who assists the debtor to put forward a voluntary arrangement with his/its creditors and is proposed to be the supervisor of an approved voluntary arrangement

Office holder A generic description applied to an insolvency practitioner taking an appointment during a process of insolvency

Official Receiver Official of the Insolvency Service who deals with bankruptcies and compulsory company liquidations

Preference A payment or action taken by a debtor which leads to a creditor being placed in a better position vis-à-vis other creditors in the circumstances of an insolvency, which can be set aside in certain circumstances: IA 1986, s.239 (re company debtor); IA 1986, s.340 (re individual debtor)

Preferential creditor A creditor who is accorded by statute a status giving them special rights to be paid/receive a distribution subject to the claims of secured creditors other than floating charge holders

Pre-pack administration A colloquial term for a sale by a company administrator of assets immediately upon or soon after appointment which has been arranged prior to the administrator's appointment

Prescribed part   An amount set aside from floating charge realisations to pay unsecured creditors pursuant to IA 1986, s.176A, sometimes referred to as the ring-fenced sum. Only applies to security created after 15 September 2003

Proof of debt   A statutory prescribed form completed by a creditor and submitted to an office holder for verification in evidence of a debt due from the insolvent debtor

Provisional liquidator   Insolvency practitioner appointed by the court to safeguard and preserve the company's assets pending the hearing of a winding-up petition

Proxy   A form appointing a person to represent a creditor at a creditors' meeting

Receiver   An individual (not necessarily an insolvency practitioner) who is appointed to realise fixed charge assets on behalf of a fixed charge holder, sometimes referred to as an LPA receiver. The term is also commonly misused to denote an administrative receiver

Receivership   A process to effect the realisation of secured assets for and on behalf of a fixed charge holder, commonly also to denote the realisation of fixed and floating charge assets as per administrative receivership

Ring-fenced sum   See prescribed part

Scheme of arrangement   An arrangement between a debtor and a creditor involving something other than the release or discharge of a debt, such as agreement to a moratorium, rescheduling of debt or restructuring of debt, such as a debt for equity swap

Secured creditor   A creditor possessing a mortgage, charge, lien or other instrument effecting security over the property of a debtor. Sometimes referred to as a charge holder

Solvent liquidation   A form of liquidation where the company has an ability to pay all of its debts and a return is likely to be made to its members. Also referred to as a members' voluntary liquidation

Statutory demand   A demand made by a creditor to a debtor in a prescribed manner for payment within 21 days of an undisputed debt in excess of £750

Supervisor   An insolvency practitioner appointed pursuant to the terms of an approved voluntary arrangement who will assist in the implementation of the proposals and enforce the debtor's compliance with the terms of the arrangement

Trading administration   A term attached to the position whereby after appointment the administrator continues to trade the business of the company

Transaction at an undervalue   A transaction which results in the transfer of a debtor's assets to a third party for less than their true worth, which can be set aside in certain circumstances: IA 1986, s.238 (re company debtor); IA 1986, s.339 (re individual debtor)

Trustee in bankruptcy   An insolvency practitioner or Official Receiver appointed by order of the court after the presentation of a bankruptcy petition to realise the debtor's assets and distribute proceeds to creditors

Unsecured creditor   A creditor possessing no security over any property of his debtor, sometimes referred to as an ordinary creditor. Will receive payment/distribution subject to the claims of secured creditors and preferential creditors

VAT bad debt relief   Tax relief obtained by a creditor from HMRC for a debt which remains unpaid for more than six months, and therefore commonly claimed on the insolvency of a debtor

Voluntary arrangement   An agreement in the form of a statutorily imposed arrangement binding on creditors to accept a compromise or scheme of arrangement in respect of the payment of their debt. Can be either an individual voluntary arrangement or a company voluntary arrangement

Voluntary liquidation   A form of liquidation commenced other than by court order and taking the form of either a creditors' voluntary liquidation or a members' voluntary liquidation

Winding-up order   Order made by the court following petition leading to the compulsory liquidation of a company. The term 'being wound up' is often used in substitution for 'in liquidation'

Wrongful trading   A civil offence pursuant to IA 1986, s.214 committed by directors if before the insolvent liquidation of a company it was inevitable that the company would enter into liquidation yet they failed to take every step to minimise loss to creditors

Index

administration process 5–6, 106, 177–8, 179
  administrator's proposals 110–13
    contents 112–13
    creditors' committee 118
    creditors' meeting *see* creditors' meeting
    preferential creditors, protection for 126
    publication 111–12
    purpose 111
    revision 117–18
    secured creditors, protection for 126
    statement of revised proposals 118
    substantial amendments 117–18
    time limit 110–11
  advantages of administration 12–13, 169—70
    breathing space 13–14, 16, 93
    cheap and easy process 14
    efficient transfer of business and assets 16–17
    flexibility 14, 38
    gateway 15
    melting ice cube theory 15
    moratorium 13–14, 16, 93–4
  advertisement of administrator's appointment 107–8
  attitudes to 2, 149–52, 161–2
  availability 7–9
    excluded undertakings 8–9
    insolvent company 9–10
    likelihood of achieving purpose 10–12, 42–3
  capital gains 37
  collective nature 7, 94
  commencement 2, 41
  comparative analysis 163
  costs and expenses 3, 14, 18, 19–21, 37
    expenses incurred post-administration 20–1, 130–1
    pre-administration costs 22–4
  cram down procedure 159–60
  disadvantages of administration 2–3, 169–70
    costs and expenses 19–21
    funding 17–19, 155–6
    loss of management control 22
    pre-administration costs 22–4
    tax consequences of administration 24
  effect *see* effect of administration
  ending *see* ending administration
  failure 132
  flexibility 14, 38
  flowchart 177–8
  foreign registered companies 7–8
  funding 17–19, 34, 37, 155–6
    super-priority funding 18, 19, 152, 155, 159, 160–1
  initial steps 5, 106–8
  initiation of process
    creditor 39–40
    insolvency officer holder 40
    magistrates' court/Financial Services Authority 40
    see also appointment of administrator
  length of process 132
  limited liability partnerships 8
  liquidation and 94, 95, 97
  moratorium *see* effect of administration
  nature of process 7, 94
  numbers of administrations 4–5, 149

administration process *continued*
partnerships 8
pre-pack administration *see* pre-pack
administration
pre-planning stage 33–4
progress report 118–19, 179
publicity 106–7
purposes of administration 2, 4,
10–12, 42–3, 90
receivership compared 2, 163,
169–72
statement of company's affairs
108–10
statement of concurrence 109–10
tax consequences 24
trading administrations 21, 153–4
administrative receiver
appointment 10, 52–3, 61
exemptions 170–2
prohibition 170
see also receiver
administrative receivership 2, 35
'abolition' 4
capital market arrangements 170–1
comparative analysis 163
effect of administration 95–7
interim moratorium 104
project finance 171
protected railway companies 172
public-private partnerships 171
registered social landlords 172
tax position 24
urban regeneration projects 171
utilities 171
see also receivership
administrator
agent of company, as 6, 120, 122
appointment *see* appointment of
administrator
challenge to conduct of company
126–9
charged property, power to deal with
124–5
contractual liability 6, 13, 20–1,
129–30, 154, 160
court directions 6, 123
creditors' meeting *see* creditors'
meeting
discretionary powers 6
duties and obligations 6, 7, 37
expenses incurred post-administration
130–1
fiduciary duties 6

hire purchase agreements 125–6
indemnity 6
interference with 6
investigatory powers 124
management of affairs and business
120–4
powers 6, 38, 122
charged property, dealing with
124–5
discretionary powers 6
investigations 124
property subject to hire
purchase agreement 125–6
preferential creditors, protection for
126
proposals for administration *see*
administration process
removal 17
remuneration 130, 146–7
replacement 17, 144–5
resignation 143
role 6–7, 120–4
rule in *Ex parte James* 6
secured creditors, protection for 126
statement of company's affairs
108–10
status 5–8
unfair/unnecessary harm to interests
of creditors 7, 10, 11, 38, 61, 98,
102, 124
challenge to conduct of
company 126–9
unfair prejudice 127
vacation of office
discharge from liability 145
effect 145
removal 17
replacement 17, 144–5
resignation 143
air traffic control companies 8
appointment of administrator 5, 173–5
advertisement 107–8
cessation on public interest winding-
up petition 139
challenge to appointment
alternative process 12
improper purpose 12
company/directors, by
alternative options 30–2
conflict 53–4
duties and responsibilities
27–8
initial steps 25–7

liabilities on insolvency 28–30
out-of-court appointment *see*
  out-of-court appointment of
  administrator
timing of decision process 26,
  32–4
court appointment 41, 173
  affidavit 50–2
  costs and expenses 55
  EC Regulation on insolvency
    proceedings 51–2
  Form 2.1B 45–50
  grounds for application 41–4
  hearing of application 54–6
  interim order 55
  likelihood of achieving purpose
    of administration 42–3
  notice of application 52–4
  persons applying 39–40, 44–5,
    55–6
  service 54
  standard of proof 45
  winding-up petition, as 5
  withdrawal of application 56
  witness statement 50–2
ending of administration 132
improper purpose 12
notice of appointment 10
notice of intention to appoint 9–10
out-of-court appointment *see* out-of-
  court appointment of administrator
qualifying floating charge holder, by
  1, 4, 7, 49, 50–1, 52, 56, 72
  alternative options for secured
    creditors 35–8
  initial steps 34
  meaning of 'floating charge'
    57–8
  meaning of 'qualifying floating
    charge' 58–9
  mortgagee in possession 35–6
  notice of application 53
  out-of-court appointment *see*
    out-of-court appointment of
    administrator
  receivership 36–8
  timing of decision 38–9
  winding-up order in place,
    where 55–6

balance sheet test 9, 26, 28, 31
banking crisis 157, 159
banks 8, 19, 149, 155, 157

Barrett Shoes 155
Blacks 155
Budget Cars 15
building contract disputes
  effect of administration 100
building societies 8
business rescue 1, 152, 155, 158, 160,
  161, 162

capital gains
  sale of company property 37
capital market arrangements
  administrative receivership 170–1
cash flow test 9, 26, 28
Chapter 11 proceedings 15, 22, 118, 148,
  150, 154
  Conservative Party proposals 155
  court-intensive nature 159–60
  cram down debt 159–60
  forum shopping 157–8
  funding 155
Chrysler 15
company
  alternative options 30–2
  appointment of administrator 26
  limited liability 26
  liquidation 32
  restructuring 13, 15, 31, 94, 99, 104,
    124, 133, 140, 154, 155, 158
  scheme of arrangement 14, 32, 113,
    126, 128, 133, 136, 139, 140, 160
  voluntary liquidation 32
  see also directors
company voluntary arrangement (CVA)
  13–14, 31–2, 126, 128, 133, 136, 139,
  140
  administrator's proposals 113
  company size 160
  increased use 155
  moratorium 13–14
  pre-pack administration and 155
  reforms 155, 160, 161
conditional fee arrangements 142, 151
contracts of employment
  effect of administration 129
  executive directors 28
Cork Report 2
costs and expenses of administration 3,
  14, 18, 19–21, 152
  creditors' meeting 117
  post-administration 20–1, 130–1
  pre-administration costs 22–4
  pre-pack administration 23, 24, 44

costs and expenses of administration
continued
    rates, liability for 130–1
    statement of company's affairs 110
    trading administrations 153, 154
credit crunch 19, 150, 155, 159
    see also recession
creditors
    application for administration order
      39–40, 44, 50, 173
creditors' committee 37, 115, 118, 137,
    145, 159
    administrator's remuneration 146
    replacement of administrator 144
creditors' meeting
    adjournment 114, 115
    administrators' proposals 113–14
    admission or rejection of claims
      115–16
    chair 114
    correspondence, by 117
        notice of result 117
    costs and expenses 117
    further meeting 118
    initial meeting 113–17
    modifications to proposals 114–15
    no obligation to hold 116
    notice 114
    report of decision 116
    request to hold 116–17
    resolutions 115
    timing 113–14, 116–17
    venue 114
    voting entitlement 115, 116, 117
creditors' voluntary liquidation 12, 123,
    139–41, 163
    see also voluntary liquidation
criminal proceedings
    effect of administration 100
cross-border 'forum shopping' 49, 78,
    82, 88, 157–8
Crown preference 151

Darling, Alistair 17, 160
debentures 36, 57, 58, 59, 60
debtor-friendly approach 22, 148, 150–1,
    154
Deutsche Nickel Group 158
directors
    application to court 44
    appointment of administrator *see*
      appointment of administrator
    disqualification 30

    duties and responsibilities 27–8, 103
    effect of administration 103–4
    executive directorship 27
    fraudulent trading 30
    personal liability 26, 27
    potential liabilities on insolvency
      28–30
    removal/appointment by
      administrator 6, 103
    timing of decision process 26, 32–4
    wrongful trading 28, 30
    see also company
dissolution of company 141–3
dot.com boom 148

EC Regulation on insolvency
    proceedings 49, 51–2, 113, 158
economic recession *see* recession
effect of administration 180
    building contract disputes 100
    contracts of employment 129
    criminal proceedings 100
    directors' powers 103–4
    employment tribunal claims 100
    enforcement of security 97, 98
    hire purchase agreements 98, 102
    interim moratorium 104–5
    landlord's right to forfeit 99–100,
      102–3
    legal processes
      commencement or continuation
        100
      court's permission to take legal
        proceedings 100–3
      moratorium 98–100
    moratorium 7, 13–14, 16, 38
      contractual rights and
        obligations 13
      enforcement of security 98
      insolvency proceedings 97
      interim moratorium 104–5
      introduction 93–4
      Limitation Act and 13, 94
      pre-pack administration 16–17,
        93
      purpose 7, 13, 93
      relaxation 93
      repossession of goods under
        hire purchase agreement 98,
        102
    patent, revocation of 100
    receivers 95–7
    secured creditors 95–7

tax position 24
tenant's application for new lease 100
winding-up petition 94–5
  advertisement 100
employment tribunal claims
  effect of administration 100
ending administration 132–3, 179
  administrator's remuneration 146–7
  automatic end 133–4
  cessation of appointment on public interest winding-up petition 139
  court, by, on application of creditor 138–9
  creditors' voluntary liquidation, move to 139–41
  determination on application to court by administrator 135–7
  dissolution, move to 141–3
  extension 133–4
    court order, by 135
    creditors' consent, by 134–5
    slip rule 133–4
  objective achieved, where 137–8
  replacement of administrator 144–5
  resignation of administration 143
  vacation of office, effect 145
energy companies 8
Enron 15
expenses *see* costs and expenses of administration

financial institutions 8
financial markets
  administrative receivership 172
Financial Services Authority (FSA)
  initiation of administration process 40
Focus DIY 155
Football League 16
foreign registered companies 7–8, 49
forum shopping 49, 78, 82, 88, 157–8
France 158
fraudulent trading 30
friendly societies 9
Frisby, Sandra 15

Germany 158

Her Majesty's Revenue and Customs (HMRC)
  attitude to debt recovery 151–2
  Business Payments Support Service 152
  distraint actions 33
Hewitt, Patricia 157
hire purchase agreements
  administrator's powers 125–6
  creditors' meeting 116
  effect of administration 98, 102
  repossession of goods 98

industrial and provident societies 9
insolvency officer holder
  initiation of administration process 40
insolvency practitioner 13, 81
  appointment 12, 156
  ceasing to act as 143, 144
  creditors' meeting 114, 115
  determination of insolvency 9, 33, 50
  ending administration 132
  enforceability of floating charge 59–60
  independence 17
  likelihood of achieving purpose of administration 43
  more than one 70
  pre-administration costs 23
  purposes of administration 90
  regulation 161
  remuneration 146, 150, 154
  role 33
  Rule 2.2 Report 2–3, 11, 33, 43
insolvent company 9–10, 26–7
  alternatives to administration 30–2
  balance sheet test 9, 26, 28, 31
  cash flow test 9, 26, 28
  statutory declaration as to 10
  see also company; directors
insurance companies 8
Italy 158

JJB Sports 155

landlords 102–3, 154, 155
  effect of administration 99–100, 101, 102–3
  liability for rates 130–1
  moratorium and 33, 38
  pre-pack administration 17, 99, 103
  recession and 130–1
  registered social landlords 172
  right to forfeit 13, 32, 99–100, 101, 102–3

Lehman Brothers 15, 157
limited liability partnership 8
liquidation 2, 15, 29–30, 94, 133
    administration and 94, 95, 97
    compulsory 32, 39, 49, 163
    creditors' meeting 114, 115
    expenses 20, 21, 130
    tax liability 20, 130
    voluntary *see* voluntary liquidation

magistrates' court
    initiation of administration process
    40
Mandelson, Peter 148
melting ice cube theory 15
moratorium *see* effect of administration
mortgagee in possession 35–6

**out-of-court appointment of
    administrator** 5
    administrative receiver in office,
        where 61, 74, 95
    advantages 14
    company/directors, by 14, 25, 175
        commencement of process
            73–4
        Form 2.10B 10, 85–90
        notice of appointment (Form
            2.9B) 10, 14, 63, 81–90
        notice of intention to appoint
            (Form 2.8B) 10, 14, 25,
            75–81
        restrictions on appointment
            74–5
    Form 2.2B 11, 23, 33, 52, 78, 88,
        89–90
    qualifying floating charge holder, by
        10, 34, 56, 173–4
        court appointment 72
        meaning of 'floating charge'
            57–8
        meaning of 'qualifying floating
            charge' 58–9
        notice of appointment (Form
            2.6B) 63, 67–71
        notice to holder of prior floating
            charge (Form 2.5B) 38–9,
            62–7
        out-of-hours appointment
            (Form 2.7B) 71–2
        procedure 173–4
        restrictions on appointment
        38–9, 60–2

unenforceable charge 10, 59–60
    winding-up petition and 61, 62,
        66, 67, 70, 72, 95
    recovery of pre-administration costs
        23–4
    see also appointment of administrator

partnerships 8
'phoenix trading' 139, 150, 161
Polaroid 15
pre-pack administration 23–4, 54, 138,
    153, 156–7
    advantages 11, 16, 20, 22
    best interest of creditors 11
    costs and expenses 23, 24, 44
    CVA and 155
    effect 16–17
    increased use 5, 18, 34, 103, 151, 152
    landlords 17, 99, 103
    meaning 5
    melting ice cube theory 15
    moratorium and 16–17, 93
    owner-manager/buy-out teams 22
    Statement of Insolvency Practice 16
        11, 17
    transparency issues 161
prescribed part payment 112, 116, 120,
    122, 134, 137, 142, 145, 146, 181–2
**'Productivity and Enterprise:
    Insolvency - A Second Chance' White
    Paper** 3–4
progress report 118–19, 179
project finance
    administrative receivership 171
public-private partnerships
    administrative receivership 171
publicity requirements 106–7
purposes of administration 2, 4, 10–12

railway companies, protected 8, 172
receiver
    appointment 2, 36, 169
        court, by 36
        fixed charge, under 36
        floating charge, under 36
    costs 37
    duties and obligations 36–7
    effect of administration 95–7
    remuneration 37
    see also administrative receiver
receivership 1–2, 36–8
    administration compared 2, 163,
        169–72
    see also administrative receivership

recession 2, 4, 150, 157, 162
  1990s 2, 73, 148
  administration process and 2
  banking crisis 159
  HMRC and 151–2
  landlords and 130–1
  property market 99
  see also credit crunch
registered social landlords
  administrative receivership 172
**Report of the Review Committee on
  Insolvency Law and Practice (Cork
  Report)** 2
restructuring officer 31
Review Group 3
Rule 2.2 Report 2–3, 11, 33, 43

Schefenacker 158
scheme of arrangement 14, 32, 126, 128,
  133, 136, 139, 140, 160
  administrator's proposals 113
secured creditors 10, 37, 38, 61, 116, 122,
  133
  administrative receivership 35
  appointment of administrative
    receiver 10, 95–6
  appointment of administrator 7
  effect of administration 95–7
  enforcement of security 97, 98
  methods of realising securities
    35–8
  mortgagee in possession 35–6
  protection 126
  receivership 1, 2, 36–8
Spain 158
statement of company's affairs 108–10
statement of concurrence 109–10
Stylo Plc 155
sub-prime mortgages 159
super-priority funding 18, 19, 152, 155,
  159, 160–1

trading administrations 21, 153–4
turnaround consultant 31
TWA 15

United States
  insolvency *see* Chapter 11
    proceedings
  sub-prime mortgages 159
unsecured creditors 54, 61, 117, 140
  administrator's proposals 110, 112,
    113

company voluntary arrangements 32
  distributions to 20, 112, 116, 122–3,
    130, 133, 137, 140, 142, 145
  effect of administration 17, 37, 43–4,
    101, 102
  expenses of administration 156
  no general duty to 17, 37
  pre-pack administration 23, 43–4
  prescribed part payment 112, 116,
    120, 122, 134, 137, 142, 145, 146,
    181–2
  receiver's remuneration 37
  replacement of administrator 144–5
  unequal treatment 7
urban regeneration projects
  administrative receivership 171
utilities
  administrative receivership 171

voluntary liquidation 5
  administrator's proposals 112
  appointment of administrator 61, 63,
    74, 75
  comparative analysis 163
  creditors' voluntary liquidation 12,
    123, 139–41, 163
  see also liquidation

water and sewerage undertakers 8
**White Paper 'Productivity and
  Enterprise: Insolvency - A Second
  Chance'** 3–4
winding up 29, 30, 32, 40, 116
  compulsory 133, 136, 140
  voluntary 141
winding-up petition 25, 32, 105, 107
  advertisement 100
  application for administration order
    and 43, 45, 49, 50, 51, 54, 55
  effect of administration 94–5, 100
  out-of-court application for
    appointment
    company/directors, by 74–5, 78,
      79, 82, 85, 88, 89
    qualifying floating charge
      holder, by 61, 62, 66, 67, 70,
      72, 95
  public interest 61, 95, 97, 105, 132,
    139
  Societas Europaea 95, 97, 139
wrongful trading 28, 30